Independence Public Library

D0723542

Crater Lake National Park

A History

Crater Lake National Park

A History

by Rick Harmon

2949 7952

INDEPENDENCE PUBLIC LIBRARY
175 Monmouth Street
Independence, OR 97351

Oregon State University Press
Corvallis

Substantial gifts from the following donors
helped make publication of this book possible.
The Oregon State University Press is grateful for their support.
The Chiles Foundation
The family of Gladys Lou Arthur, in her memory

Cover images: courtesy National Park Service, Crater Lake National Park
Museum and Archives Collection.

The paper in this book meets the guidelines for permanence and
durability of the Committee on Production Guidelines for Book
Longevity of the Council on Library Resources and the minimum
requirements of the American National Standard for Permanence of
Paper for Printed Library Materials Z39.48-1984.

Library of Congress Cataloging-in-Publication Data
Harmon, Rick.
  Crater Lake National Park : a history / Rick Harmon.
      p. cm.
Includes bibliographical references and index.
  ISBN 0-87071-537-2
1. Crater Lake National Park (Or.)—History. 2. Crater Lake National
Park (Or.)—Management—History. I. Title.
  F882.C8 H37 2002
  979.5'915—dc21
                                            2001006375

© 2002 Rick Harmon
All rights reserved. First edition 2002
Printed in the United States of America

Oregon State University Press
101 Waldo Hall
Corvallis OR 97331-6407
OREGON STATE 541-737-3166 •fax 541-737-3170
UNIVERSITY   http://oregonstate.edu/dept/press

Dedication

To Geneva Draper Harmon, Jack Harmon, and Viola Stewart Harmon for their love and support from the very beginning.

Contents

ॐ

Acknowledgments

I WANT TO THANK THE FOLLOWING PEOPLE for helping me in a variety of ways: Joe Anthony, Kay Atwood, Joe Bailey, Mike Balter, Judy Bell, Tom Booth, Mary Braun, Felicity Devlin, Lou Flannery, Candice Goucher, Steve Hallberg, Robert Johnston, Bill Lang, David Luft, the late Terry O'Donnell, Sue Seyl, Jim Strassmaier, and Johnyne Wascavage.

Thanks to the following institutions and organizations for the assistance of staff and resources: Crater Lake National Park, Klamath County Museum, Klamath Tribes, Mazama Club, Oregon Historical Society, Oregon State University Archives, and Southern Oregon Historical Society.

Thanks to Mac Brock, Dick Gordon, Doug Larson, Chuck Lundy, Steve Mark, John Miele, and Kent Taylor for allowing me to interview them.

Thanks to Jo Alexander, Bill Alley, Mary Benterou, Judith Hassen, Sharon Howe, Glen Kaye, Doug Larson, Steve Mark, Angie Michaelis, Valerie Neubert, and Taylor Tupper for their help in tracking down and identifying pictures.

Special thanks to Jo Alexander, Glen Kaye, Jeff LaLande, Steve Mark, and Kenn Oberrecht for their valuable advice and editorial help.

Thanks to the Friends of Crater Lake National Park, especially Glen Kaye, for hiring me to write this book, and to Nathan Douthit for putting me in touch with the Friends. Generous gifts from the Chiles Foundation and the Arthur family helped cover the costs of writing and publishing. The Arthur family's gift was made in memory of Gladys Lou Arthur, with fond recollections of summers spent in and around Crater Lake National Park from 1958 through 1970.

Thanks to the faculty advisory board and staff of Oregon State University Press for publishing the book.

Thanks to Ruby and Wolsey for brightening all my days. My everlasting love and appreciation to Jane Malarkey Harmon for her support and encouragement, in the writing of this book and in everything else I do.

The book is dedicated to my paternal grandmother, my father, and my mother.

Introduction

THIS BOOK ORIGINATED IN THE DETERMINATION of several people to commemorate the one-hundredth anniversary of Crater Lake National Park with a written history. While the backers of this idea were initially driven by the approaching centennial, they also understood that the century between 1902 and 2002 barely qualifies as elapsed time in the overall record of Mount Mazama and Crater Lake. From the broader perspective of the region's natural history, Crater Lake National Park took shape on Mount Mazama's landscape just yesterday. And short of forecasting immediate volcanic doom, we can safely predict that the park is only a temporary occupant of Mount Mazama. Its complete life history, we can be fairly sure, will eventually register as no more than an episode among epochs.

The forty-million-year period of Mount Mazama's origin, growth, and collapse in eruption represents a stretch of time that dwarfs the park's one-hundred-year history by a ratio of 400,000 to 1. Moreover, many of the most significant events in the geological evolution of Mount Mazama and Crater Lake took place over tens of thousands of years, a duration in which we now think human life could change beyond recognition or maybe disappear altogether. Such awareness of the age and pace of Nature helps balance our tendency to lift the relatively brief era of human history above everything else.

But even after acknowledging the smallness of our place in the big picture, we contend that this is *our* time, our *only* time, and we long to make sense of it. And while this may be yet another rationalization for elevating human history and human life above all other facets of the earth's history, it serves here as a partial explanation for why forty million years of the Crater Lake region's past is covered in just one-seventeenth of this book and the last two hundred years consume the rest.

THERE IS ANOTHER REASON FOR THIS IMBALANCE. Our culture—the one that came to dominate the region by 1870—has over centuries used reading, writing, and record keeping to trace its past and document its present. These habits have produced piles of material that we now bring to bear in piecing together the history of the Crater Lake region over the past two hundred years. By comparison, the amount of "evidence" left behind by the previous forty million years is scant. Thus we strive to use our reading, writing, and record-keeping habits to examine our tenure at Crater Lake, to comprehend our impact, and to prepare ourselves to be better custodians during whatever future remains.

Of the two hundred years that occupy most of this book, about seventy-five were taken up by the efforts of white-skinned newcomers to wrest the region from its native inhabitants, about twenty-five by the campaign for a national park, and another hundred by the building and operating of the national park. Some of the Indian people with traditional ties to the Crater Lake region remained in significant numbers after the whites gained control, and this book attempts to sketch their course to the present. Although the fate of these Indian neighbors has not been tightly bound to the hundred-year history of Crater Lake National Park, the peoples of the Klamath Tribes constitute the area's oldest community, with the deepest ties to the park area and its features. For this reason alone, a summation of the Indian story deserves to be told in connection with the park's history.

Although the native community's seniority overshadows, by far, that of any other human community that has affected the Crater Lake region, the impacts of some of these other communities have been greater. For example, the financial and political elites of Portland have been a pivotal force. The state's political and governmental core in Salem has also made a significant mark. People living in the Crater Lake vicinity, especially in the towns of Medford and Klamath Falls, have maintained all sorts of meaningful ties. And, of course, the National Park Service and its several generations of employees stationed locally have exerted the most profound influence.

This book attempts to show how the hundreds of Park Service and concession company employees assigned to Crater Lake over the last century have formed a succession of small communities, miniature social systems shaped by the site's remote mountain location, by the personalities and talents of individual residents, by National Park Service leadership and policies, and by the tenor of the times. It is impossible to portray the park's one-hundred-year history accurately without accounting for the everyday concerns—roads, sewage systems, housing, snow removal, and much more—of these successive Crater Lake communities. A view of the park and its workings on such a mundane level will help readers and visitors see clearly that nature hikes and "campfire talks" make up just a part of the Crater Lake National Park story.

The Park Service, during its nearly ninety-year lifetime, has evolved into a complex bureaucracy defined by a distinct set of hierarchies, rules, practices, and conventions. This book attempts to show how Crater Lake's communities have been extensions of that evolving Park Service bureaucracy. Short of understanding this basic fact of bureaucratic primacy in the national parks, one is hard-pressed to fathom much of Crater Lake's social and administrative past. (The ability to cooperate effectively with the Park Service on *contemporary* policy issues also depends on such understanding.)

Though many who have lived and worked at Crater Lake have struggled with feelings of isolation (especially during winter), the park as a whole has never been truly isolated. Because of its relationships with surrounding communities and its life-sustaining connection to the Park Service bureaucracy, people outside the park have frequently been more important to its fate than those inside. Nonetheless, themes of independence, autonomy, and self-direction run prominently throughout National Park Service history at Crater Lake and elsewhere. A somewhat ironic general pattern is evident: for most of the twentieth century, while the Park Service promoted maximum public "use" of the national parks, Park Service officials guarded their decision-making independence fiercely, in effect shouting to the outside world, "Leave us alone! We're the professionals." In contrast, by the late twentieth century, Park Service officials were both questioning the soundness of the agency's long-held maximum-visitation philosophy and beginning to acquiesce to federal laws inviting citizen participation in agency decision making.

The national park phase of this book reveals a historical path for Crater Lake that might be described as one of "unfulfilled promise" or "failed destiny." Though such phrases may be unlikely candidates for a centennial celebration theme, they nonetheless capture an important aspect of park history from the perspective of the past century. But the book also illustrates how one era's "unfulfilled promise" can become another era's "challenge and opportunity." And though "unfulfilled promise" may be an apt judgment for Crater Lake according to predominant twentieth-century Park Service values, "challenge and opportunity" is likely to be a more fitting theme in light of the agency's twenty-first-century priorities.

But after all the judgments and assessments of Crater Lake National Park in its various guises—as a vacation spot, as a site for scientific research, as a place for learning, as an extension of the Park Service bureaucracy, and so on—we are driven back to Crater Lake itself, unimaginably sprawling and unspeakably blue. And while this book encourages a view of the park and its history that extends well beyond the lake, we also recognize that for most people, the Crater Lake experience begins and ends with the lake. The lake is indisputably an awesome thing, whether seen for the first time or the hundredth, whether observed with intricate knowledge or in relative ignorance. But besides noting its obvious magnificence and beauty, we spend little time here trying to describe the indescribable. Too many words have already fallen too far short. We offer instead a simple suggestion: Behold it, and silence yourself.

Chapter I

Beginnings

Prelude

LONG BEFORE THERE WAS A NATIONAL PARK, there was a magnificent, deep-blue lake. And long before there was a lake, there was a grand, mountainous volcano. The origin of that volcano, which came eventually to hold the lake and contain the park, takes us back around forty million years, to a time when shallow seas stretched across parts of western North America, forming a coastal area along what is now Oregon's Willamette Valley.

The geological forces that eventually produced the great Mount Mazama caldera were blind. Those geological forces, still at work today, were not "aiming" at Crater Lake, any more than they are aiming now at the unforeseeable landscape of forty million years hence. Crater Lake—geologically speaking, a late development—is a gift bestowed upon our recent and probably brief human era. The gift is a product of natural processes, not Nature's design. We contemporary humans have the capacity to understand these natural processes and, at least in small areas of the earth, learn to live in harmony with them. This, we hope, becomes our single-minded intention for Crater Lake: to preserve an exquisite unintentional gift for its own natural processes, its own natural ends.

Crater Lake occupies southern Oregon's Mount Mazama remnant, vacated by a volcanic eruption still widely recognized as the earth's most violent explosion of the last ten thousand years. The lake is about six miles wide and nearly two thousand feet deep; its surface covers a twenty-square-mile area, and its elliptical shoreline stretches twenty-six miles. The lake's waters were originally formed by accumulated rain and snow. And since Crater Lake has no natural inlet or outlet, its water volume—deepest among lakes in the United States and seventh deepest in the world—is maintained primarily by rain and snow. The lake's extraordinary clarity and reflective properties are the result of its natural isolation from organic materials, sediments, and chemicals typically borne by incoming streams and rivers. Its breathtakingly blue color, in turn, is a product of its great depth and clarity. The walls of the spectacular basin in which Crater Lake lies are made up of multicolored volcanic rock formations that reveal the site's dramatic story.

Formation of the Cascade Mountains

OVER THE COURSE OF SEVERAL MILLION YEARS, beginning some forty million years ago, immense plate-like portions of the earth's outer shell shifted and converged, causing the Cascade Mountain corridor to uplift and the surrounding ocean to recede. Eventually, the slow crawl of these subterranean plates created fractures in the earth's crust, allowing pressurized lava to rise to the surface. Intermittent flows of lava over the next several million years built a high plateau extending from southern British Columbia to northern California—a base upon which further eruptions of molten material shaped the oldest Cascade volcanoes.[1]

While formation of the earliest Cascade Mountains (referred to now as the Western Cascades) was radically altering part of Oregon's prehistoric landscape between ten and thirty-five million years ago, the region to the east of what is now Crater Lake remained a low, gently rolling plain crossed by broad, winding rivers. Vast lakes still dotted the moist landscape of what is now arid central Oregon. In the mid-twentieth century, geologist Howel Williams, one of the most imaginative and vivid interpreters of the region, described how the prehistoric plant and animal life of this country "was remarkably different from that of today. . . . Avocadoes, cinnamons, figs, and persimmons flourished," and odd creatures, such as "small, graceful horses, not more than a foot high," roamed the terrain. Showers of volcanic ash and floods from rivers swollen by ash and lava flows intermittently assaulted the flora and fauna of this mostly peaceful, temperate environment.[2]

Meanwhile, ongoing volcanic action in the region created conditions for major climatic change. Around 3.5 million years ago, the great mountainous barrier of the High Cascades, just east of the older Western Cascades, began to take shape from the huge outpourings of erupted volcanoes. This new range of mountains, in combination with the progressive tilting of the Western Cascades (a process that began some five million years ago), produced a barrier to moisture-laden winds

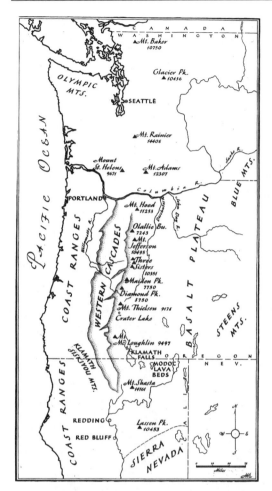

The Cascade Mountains of the Pacific Northwest began their evolution around forty million years ago. Crater Lake and the remnant of Mount Mazama lay in the southern portion of the more recently formed High Cascade peaks, which stretch from southern British Columbia to northern California. (Courtesy National Park Service, Crater Lake National Park Museum and Archives Collection.)

from the west. As a result, the eastern country began to take on a more desert-like character, and the plant and animal life on the two sides of the Cascade Range diverged.[3]

Forests on the still-forming Cascade Mountains then looked much as they do today, but many of the region's animals appeared strange and unfamiliar. Giraffe-camels and bear-dogs roamed the forests and meadows, Williams speculated, and "short-legged, semi-aquatic rhinoceroses lived along the streams and on the edge of marshes." Around two million years ago, the climate of the Cascades grew much colder. At first, snow began to persist on the region's peaks through summers; then, over millennia, as the cold deepened, accumulating snow hardened into glaciers. While the earth settled in for an era dominated by ice, the eventual fount of Crater Lake—Mount Mazama—inched toward birth.[4]

The Rise of Mount Mazama

SLIGHTLY MORE THAN FOUR HUNDRED thousand years ago, at points underlying and adjacent to contemporary Crater Lake, recently opened cracks in the earth's crust signaled the ascent of a great new volcano. The release of enormous underground pressure from these vents lifted a slow tide of magma (molten rock) toward the surface, and lava flows twenty to thirty feet thick were deposited across the landscape. (By way of similar processes, Mounts Rainier, Hood, and Shasta also rose to prominence within the High Cascades during this era.) These oldest Mazama lavas are found today in a volcanic-cone remnant, called Phantom Ship, near the southern edge of contemporary Crater Lake, and to the east, in Mount Scott, the highest point in Crater Lake National Park.[5]

In time, a vast chamber of magma and plutonic rock (solidified magma) took shape three to five miles beneath the earth's surface. This "reservoir" of molten and crystalline rock, according to geologist Williams, supplied much of the raw material for the further building of Mount Mazama. Later, cracks in the roof of the magma chamber provided routes for the gassy volcanic material to rise. Increasingly violent surges from below piled volumes of molten rock, ash, and pumice (lightweight volcanic glass) upon earlier volumes. Eventually, a period of cooling and hardening set in, at least on the surface, and intervals of relative quiet—often lasting centuries—alternated with episodes of eruption.[6]

As the peak rose to a height of several thousand feet, eruptions on its summit were joined by frequent outbursts on its flanks—eventually producing Mazama's gently sloping, asymmetrical formation consisting of several overlapping volcanoes. By perhaps fifty thousand years ago, Mount Mazama, at its maximum height of eleven or twelve thousand feet above sea level, dominated the landscape. For the next more than forty thousand years, the great mountain was visible from the Rogue River valley to the west and from the high desert to the east.

Later, as volcanic activity at the summit subsided, new vents opened farther down the mountain and on flatlands to the east. When this latest eruptive phase finally ended some twenty-eight thousand years ago, trees and other vegetation began to accumulate again on the ash-covered mountain. Another period of outer calm set in, belying the upheavals brewing below.[7]

☾☽

This imaginative rendering of Mount Mazama before its great eruption depicts a volcano that towered over the southern Oregon landscape. (Courtesy NPS, CLNP Museum and Archives Collection.)

DURING THE COURSE OF MAZAMA'S steady growth over millennia, episodes of glacial accumulation alternated with periods of volcanic eruption. Lava flows and showers of ash sometimes completely dissipated the glaciers, setting off torrential melt-waters that swept through adjoining valleys. When the glaciers held sway, vast tongues of ice scraped and sculpted their way down the mountain, carrying tons of rock and relentlessly eroding the landscape. Winding, V-shaped river valleys were transformed into straighter, U-shaped canyons. Towering piles and long ridges of displaced rocky debris marked the terrain long after the glaciers had receded.[8]

At the time of the glaciers' greatest expanse, ice stretched westward from the Mazama summit seventeen miles into the upper Rogue River drainage; the mountain's north-moving glaciers converged with those extending from Mounts Bailey and Thielsen, spreading over what is now Diamond Lake. Plateaus, canyons, and valleys immediately to the east and south were similarly choked with ice. Then, roughly ten thousand years ago, the snowfall lessened, and rising summer heat began to melt the glaciers faster than they were replenished. The twilight phase of Mount Mazama was approaching.[9]

Mazama's Great Eruption

AROUND SEVENTY-NINE HUNDRED YEARS AGO, after about twenty thousand years of relative dormancy, "a semicircular arc of vents opened on [Mount Mazama's] north flank, approximately 5,000 feet below the summit," according to the eruption sequence fashioned by Howel Williams in the mid-twentieth century. By that time, Mazama's once-mammoth glaciers had receded in most places to less than a fifth of their largest size, and forests on the volcano were sparse. Outbursts at this northern site produced a lava mass twelve hundred feet thick (known as Llao Rock, prominent on today's caldera rim). Then, about two hundred years later, the culminating eruption began. A cloud of ash rose amid thunderous explosions and flashes from the summit crater, melting the surface of the remaining glaciers and producing river-like torrents. Huge boulders collided in the swirling canyon bottoms, and clouds of ash turned daylight into dusk. The scene was surely one of cacophony and confusion, with birds screeching and beasts fleeing in terror.[10]

"Day after day, night after night, the eruptions continued," Williams wrote, with pauses usually preceding eruptions of ever-greater magnitude. Winds spread thickening clouds of dust, ash, and smoke far to the north and northeast, and any human being standing close to the mountain would soon have lost sight of his or her outstretched hand. After probably several weeks, this convulsive prelude to Mazama's

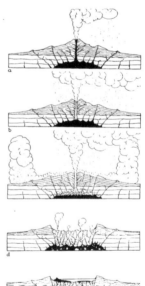

The basin in which Crater Lake eventually formed was created by the eruption of Mount Mazama, shown here diagrammatically in successive stages (from top to bottom). In the fourth stage, the volcano summit has collapsed into the magma chamber. (Courtesy NPS, CLNP Museum and Archives Collection.)

final destruction ceased, and a pall of winter-like desolation covered the land. Ejected pumice fragments formed steep banks near the base of the mountain and foot-thick piles as far as seventy miles away.[11]

The final act then came quickly. And once again a cloud lifting from the summit presaged the violence. This time, though, amid deafening crashes, the cloud spread and then surged down the flanks of the mountain with enormous speed. "At the base of each advancing cloud . . . an incandescent avalanche of fragments" raged, Williams imagined. These gas-powered waves of magma incinerated forests and most other forms of life twenty-five to thirty-five miles in all directions.[12]

While Mazama's peak was completely shrouded in smoke and ash, a frightening new sound came from the darkness on high—not the sharp detonations of the earlier destruction but a "tumultuous roar," signaling the terminal cataclysm. Probably not until days later had the wind cleared the scene well enough to reveal an astonishing transformation. "The majestic ice-clad peak that had formerly dominated the landscape, rising in lofty grandeur above all the surrounding peaks, had disappeared," in the dramatic words of Howel Williams. The great mountain dome, with much of its pressurized core evacuated by eruption or absorbed into internal fissures, had collapsed inward.[13]

The resulting caldera, not yet softened by the clear blue lake that would eventually form within, surely presented a hellish visage. Williams wrote colorfully of "jets of steam [that] hissed and roared from countless fissures . . . [and] pungent smells of sulphur and smarting fumes of acid [that] rose from the awful pit." An enormous portion of the mountain that had once risen above was now strewn, in fragments large and small, both within the caldera and outside of it. The jagged edges and plummeting walls of the newly formed basin, remnants of the volcanic cones and glacial valleys that had made up Mount Mazama in its fullness, would have to wait thousands of years to tell their story to scientists.[14]

Meanwhile, for years to come, the eruption's fallout of atmospheric ash created luminous sunrises and fiery sunsets, continuous reminders to distant eyes that something truly momentous had happened.

Human Arrival in Northwest North America

THE FIRST HUMANS TO ARRIVE in North America probably crossed the Bering Land Bridge from Asia between fourteen and eighteen thousand years ago, during the later stages of the most recent Ice Age. By 11,500 years ago, and maybe earlier, people lived in areas throughout North

America, including present-day Oregon, where numerous spear points of the sort used by humans during this era have been found. As the climate warmed and dried in North America between ten and eleven thousand years ago, life for peoples on both sides of the Cascade Mountains changed. The big-game hunting characteristic of earlier centuries gradually gave way to the foraging and gathering practices typical of later times.[15]

Archaeological discoveries in the Fort Rock and Connley caves of south-central Oregon (just fifty to sixty miles northeast of Crater Lake) have shown that a highly mobile culture based on grinding seeds, weaving textiles, and hunting small animals was well established in that area nine thousand years ago, more than a millennium before the cataclysmic eruption of Mount Mazama. When the volcano began a new phase of explosiveness approximately seventy-nine hundred years ago, these people undoubtedly observed the tumult with fear and foreboding.[16]

While the earth's ominous stirrings may have troubled the dreams of these ancient high-desert people for generations, they clung tenaciously to their cave dwellings and their precarious existence, perhaps accounting for the distant fire and thunder in their myths and religion. The changed climate had already made the lives of these people more difficult by drying up springs and reducing lakes in the region, extinguishing life for some of the plants and animals they relied upon. But with Mazama's conclusive eruption and collapse seventy-seven hundred years ago—which buried plant life and clogged lakes and marshes with a nearly six-inch mantle of ash and pumice in the Fort Rock Lake basin—existence for the Fort Rock people in their familiar valley became untenable. Those with sufficient strength for the journey moved elsewhere.[17]

Earliest Native Cultures of the Region

THE KLAMATH BASIN LIES SOUTHWEST of the Fort Rock Valley and south of Crater Lake, within an elevated plateau on the eastern slope of the Cascade Mountains. Although archaeology has not yet proved that humans lived in the Klamath Basin at the time of Mount Mazama's eruption, cultural evidence suggests that forebears of the Klamath Indians—some perhaps having migrated earlier from the Fort Rock Valley—witnessed the blast. Vivid mythic understandings of the mountain's volatile displays (including the cataclysmic finale) were passed on through generations of the Klamath people. And certainly the Klamath Basin of eight thousand years ago was rich enough in resources, and hospitable enough, to attract human habitation.[18]

If, as seems likely, ancestors of the Klamath Indians were living in the Klamath Basin eight to nine thousand years ago, they undoubtedly passed through the Mount Mazama region during the volcano's prolonged dormant phase, perhaps en route to huckleberry fields or in pursuit of trade with other native people. But when eruptions resumed around seventy-nine hundred years ago, these high-country excursions near Mazama surely ceased. The major eruption some two hundred years later devastated the immediate landscape and probably terrified any people within sight or sound of the upheaval.[19]

With the decisive eruption, thick deposits of ash degraded the lands surrounding Mount Mazama to the north and east. To the west, enormous amounts of pumice and ash clogged the upper portions of westward-draining rivers. These obstructions soon gave way, releasing water in great torrents and depositing Mazama pumice in layers downstream. In this manner, floods associated with the eruption temporarily destroyed the habitats of people, plants, fish, and other animals even at lower elevations. The Klamath Basin environment, to the south, was also seriously affected by the discharge and its aftermath, but probably not made uninhabitable.[20]

Fort Rock, a prominent rocky mass in south-central Oregon's Lake County, marks the vicinity of one of the region's oldest known native cultures. The lives of the ancient people of Fort Rock Valley were, at different times, strongly influenced by the volcanic activity of Mount Mazama. (OHS neg. OrHi 81073.)

☙

FOR ANY HUMAN OBSERVERS, the eerie aftermath of Mazama's decapitating explosion would surely have accentuated the otherworldly associations already growing around the volcano. The seething floor of the caldera, littered with partially molten debris, rocky fragments, and pools of bubbling mud, likely took decades to become stable and cool enough for something resembling a lake to form. In the meantime, a thunderous landslide within the gaping mountain signaled to the natives that the spirits inhabiting Mazama were still far from pacified.

Eventually, though, over the course of a couple hundred years, a lake did take shape in the Mazama caldera—first, as an array of small pools, then as larger pools joined by channels, and finally as a continuous, ever-deepening body of water. Three hundred years after the eruption (approximately seventy-four hundred years ago) the lake had probably risen to slightly more than half of today's depth of nearly two thousand feet. Around the same time, Wizard Island, an active volcanic cone perched underwater on a lava platform near the western edge of the lake, began to erupt and grow toward the surface. A little more than seventy-two hundred years ago, a final surge of eruptions lifted this newer volcano's summit well above the water level, even as the lake itself continued to rise by a few hundred feet.[21]

During the centuries immediately following Mount Mazama's destruction—at a time, as we have seen, when the aftereffects of the explosion remained vivid—orally transmitted recollections of the awesome events were woven into the religious, magical, and ritual understandings of nearby native people. Though Klamath people may not have regularly entered the region in search of food or other necessities, the place became increasingly endowed with mythic meanings and powerful associations, and the mountain and its features thereby assumed great ritual importance.[22]

The extraordinary happenings of the post-eruption millennium—the gradual filling of Crater Lake, the sporadic volcanic eruptions, the slow emergence of Wizard Island from the lake, the regeneration of plants and forests—were certainly noted by the Klamath people, and might well have been observed at close hand by particularly brave or powerful native visitors. In any case, Crater Lake (or *gi'was*, in the aboriginal tongue) eventually became a well-known fixture in the Klamath world. According to anthropologist Robert Winthrop, *gi'was* was recognized "as a place of power and danger, renowned as a spirit-quest site, yet also feared for the dangerous beings" who lived there.[23]

Phantom Ship, an eerie rock formation near the southern edge of Crater Lake, contains the oldest lavas in the entire caldera. As the Mount Mazama basin filled with rain and snowmelt during centuries after the great eruption, the 160-foot rise of Phantom Ship was all that remained visible of a massive ridge or volcanic cone extending from the basin floor. (Photo courtesy of Klamath County Museum.)

This primal scene, viewed northerly from the cone of Crater Lake's Wizard Island, conveys the powerful, godlike character of Llao Rock, commanding the caldera rim. (OHS neg. OrHi 45174.)

Klamath ritual life was organized around the quest for "spirit power," which usually required retreats to remote, mountainous, watered places, where the Indians believed sacred beings dwelled. It is therefore understandable that Crater Lake and much of the surrounding region included in today's Crater Lake National Park became important features in Klamath religious life. Klamath spiritual specialists—referred to at different times as medicine men, doctors, diviners, conjurers, or shamans—frequently took the lead in the rigorous, physically demanding spirit quests, as well as in other important communal acts. And like the spirit-power sites themselves, the religious figures who embarked on these quests, or who mediated and prescribed such journeys for others, were both venerated and feared.[24]

During winter, when the Klamath people settled in to their partially submerged lodges on lakeshores and in river valleys of the Klamath Basin, the telling of mythic stories and the acting out of other rituals helped bind them together. Traditional understandings of Crater Lake's origin and ritual meaning were probably prominent among the teachings of shamans and other spiritual figures during winter evening conclaves.[25]

Even though, as anthropologist Melville Jacobs has pointed out, Indian mythic traditions of the Pacific Northwest have been widely

These small huts—one covered with mat (woven tules), the other with cloth—are of a kind traditionally used by the Klamath in their summer camps. (Photo courtesy of Klamath County Museum.)

"remodeled, edited, cheapened, censored," and "Europeanized," some can still be traced reliably to versions in the native languages. Such is true of the Klamath myth of Llao (Chief of the Below-World) and Skell (Chief of the Above-World), whose primordial battles have for millennia explained the intertwined natural and spiritual qualities of Crater Lake and the surrounding country. These narrative myths have taught generations of Klamath young how Mount Mazama collapsed and gave birth to Crater Lake (the result of warfare between the masters of the above and below worlds), and how Wizard Island (the head of Llao, severed by Skell in battle and flung into the lake) came into being. In these accounts, the role and power of the Crater Lake region as a sacred landscape was explained and confirmed.[26]

Prehistoric Indians and Archaeological Traces

IN ADDITION TO THE KLAMATH, three other tribes once occupied territories that either included or adjoined the area of today's Crater Lake National Park: the Takelma and Upper Umpqua, who lived in the interior valleys of southwestern Oregon, and the Molala, who lived along the slopes of the Cascade Mountains. In fact, these tribes, may have had more reason to visit the Crater Lake area in their regular rounds of seasonal hunting and gathering than did the Klamath, who relied so heavily on the lake and marsh resources (fish, fowl, pond-lily seeds, and tule) of the Klamath Basin for their material needs.[27]

The Molala, whose permanent homes were closest to Crater Lake, were well known for their hunting prowess, and they traditionally drew upon the Cascade uplands for roots, berries, and such large game as deer, elk, and bear. The Takelma and Upper Umpqua, for their part, sought out the Mazama region's distinct types of fish, game, and plants from their spring and summer upland camps.[28]

However, unlike the Klamath, whose isolation in homelands east of the Cascades helped shield them from the worst depredations associated with the coming of Euro-Americans in the mid-nineteenth century, the Takelma, Upper Umpqua, and Molala were largely obliterated by contact with the newcomers. By the last third of the nineteenth century, most survivors among these three tribes had been transplanted from their ancestral lands to reservations in northwestern Oregon and elsewhere, making efforts to understand their cultures, including traditional links to the Crater Lake environment, far more difficult.[29]

Though only a small sample of prehistoric objects have been recovered from the area of Crater Lake National Park, these finds do substantiate an ancient Indian presence. (Only about 2 percent of the park's 183,000 acres have so far been surveyed. Most archaeological materials predating the Mazama eruption would have been buried under great quantities of volcanic debris.) Several prehistoric Crater Lake sites consist of rock-cairn features, probably associated with spirit quests. Anthropologist Kathryn Winthrop predicts that future archaeology will locate more rock-feature sites (cairns, stacks, rings, or walls) on peaks and other high locations; small campsites near water sources; hunting and gathering spots throughout the park; and burial or cremation sites—all prehistoric vestiges of the people who once lived nearby and considered the Crater Lake region part of their homeland.[30]

Traditional Life among the Four Tribes of the Crater Lake Region

SOMETIME BETWEEN TWO AND THREE thousand years ago, the climate, vegetation, and animal life of the Crater Lake region settled into forms that would last, generally speaking, until the present. During this same millennium, the Indian cultures of the region, mirroring their environments, took shape in ways that would endure until Euro-Americans began to arrive in significant numbers around the middle of the nineteenth century.[31]

Perhaps reflecting the pressures of increased population, about a thousand years ago the hunting and gathering expeditions of Indian peoples living west of Crater Lake began to reach into higher-elevation areas well beyond their permanent winter dwellings. Native hunting parties entered the Crater Lake region more frequently at this time. Among the Upper Umpqua, for example, the old and the infirm remained in lowland villages during summers while younger tribal members set up camp in the mountains, where men hunted for fattened elk and deer. Though the Klamath continued to rely on their unique lake and marsh environment for most of their food and other material needs, certain desirable foods, such as huckleberries, elk, black-tailed deer, and salmon, could be found only at higher elevations or on the western slopes of the Cascades. Huckleberry Mountain, just beyond the southwestern border of today's Crater Lake National Park, some ten miles southwest of the lake, was the Klamaths' main source for berries. And since Huckleberry Mountain was close to established hunting and salmon-fishing sites, the area also served as an important center for Klamath social life and a key point of contact with other groups, especially the Southern Molala.[32]

Klamath Indians, shown here navigating their familiar lake and marsh environment in traditional shovel-nosed dugout canoes, collect tules and cattails for basket making. (OHS neg. OrHi 35789.)

The main trail between the Klamath Basin and Huckleberry Mountain, bustling with travelers in late summer, linked a series of well-known campsites near areas rich in food and other resources. (Many of these traditional campsites lie within the current boundaries of Crater Lake National Park.) Likewise, a complex network of interior mountain trails kept the Molala Indians connected to each other and to their Klamath friends, with whom they sometimes intermarried. This era also saw the Upper Umpqua Indians develop a wide trading network, which included highland areas frequented by both the Klamath and the Molala.[33]

The more active trading of this time took the Klamath regularly into areas now occupied by Crater Lake National Park. Klamath Basin obsidian (volcanic glass) was highly prized among the Klamaths' western neighbors for the manufacture of arrows and daggers, and obsidian artifacts have been found by archaeologists in the southern Cascades and in the Rogue River area.[34]

DESPITE SEASONAL ABUNDANCES, the Indians of the Crater Lake region frequently suffered privation in the centuries before the coming of whites, especially during severe winters. As they faced hunger during

Klamath shaman donning a type of regalia sometimes worn in ceremonies and sacred initiations. (OHS neg. OrHi 87491.)

long winter nights in their shelters, the mysteries surrounding life and death became subjects of performance, narration, and contemplation. Some solace could be found in the recounting of myths and stories, which provided explanations for human tribulations of all sorts.[35]

Supernatural power, usually obtained by way of vision (or spirit) quests, gave shamans and others the ability to alter conditions, such as weather, during times of extreme need, and the skill to hunt, fish, gamble, and fight with special competence. Such spirit power was often acquired through retreat to hallowed places where, according to Indian myths, sacred beings lived. Song was usually called upon to convey power from spirit to human.[36]

At puberty, Klamath boys were sent to remote and dangerous mountain locations. There each boy fasted, built rock cairns, and swam in mountain streams, suffering physical hardship while awaiting a dream or vision through which some supernatural or spirit being would become his ally. Similarly, young Molala boys were sent into the mountains to encounter guardian spirits, which they believed would give them shamanistic powers. Among the Takelma, the guardian spirits were most often associated with animals or geographical features. In all of these cases, according to anthropologist Robert Winthrop, the spirit quest took place within a "spiritual geography," a homeland whose mountains, lakes, and rivers were inhabited by specific spirits or powers.[37]

Within this general framework of "spiritual geography," especially the Klamath considered the Crater Lake area to be a place of

A park ranger sits next to rock cairns—evidence of native religious practice—on a peak in the Crater Lake vicinity during the national park's early years. (Courtesy NPS, CLNP Museum and Archives Collection.)

extraordinary offerings and powers. Based upon their cultural understanding of how the great lake arose from the mountain's explosion, early Klamath Basin people developed a thoughtful and practical relationship with Crater Lake, one characterized by reverence for this most potent feature of a larger sacred landscape that served their material and spiritual needs. Many peaks in today's Crater Lake National Park, as well as the entire rim of the Crater Lake caldera, were used in the vision quests of those "who had reached advanced stages of their shamanistic training." Anthropologist Douglas Deur has written that the site "was considered too powerful, and potentially hazardous, to someone who had not undergone adequate training and had not first sought visions in less imposing places." Crater Lake was a place of special importance in the vision quest, but it was also a place feared because of its dangerous spirits.[38]

In addition to its role in conveying power to those prepared to receive it, Crater Lake also served the Upper Umpqua and the Klamath as a site for meditation on moral lessons. For example, it was believed that persons who had killed animals improperly were imprisoned after death at the bottom of the lake or trapped in the caldera's rocky formations. One can easily imagine native religious seekers perched on the rim of *gi'was*, contemplating the fearful exile of those who had transgressed the natural order.[39]

Chapter 2

Clash of Cultures

1820-1885

The Four Tribes and the Coming of the Euro-Americans

EURO-AMERICAN EXPLORATIONS of the northwest coast in the sixteenth, seventeenth, and eighteenth centuries had little, if any, impact on the native peoples of the Crater Lake region. But the operations of merchants and traders in the late eighteenth and early nineteenth centuries *did* affect the lives of Klamath, Molala, Takelma, and Upper Umpqua Indians, at least indirectly. This influence was exerted through coastal and northerly native intermediaries, who dealt directly with both the whites and the southern Oregon natives. The American Corps of Discovery expedition of 1804-1806, led by Meriwether Lewis and William Clark, proved to be an even more significant portent of change for native Americans of the West. Though largely benign in its direct contact with western Indians, the Lewis and Clark expedition ushered in an era of American territorial expansion and migration that would change the native cultures forever.

In 1824, George Simpson, governor of the British Hudson's Bay Company (HBC), resolved to broaden HBC enterprises in what the company referred to as the Columbia Department—the territory lying between the Russian settlements in Alaska and Spanish California, and between the Rocky Mountains and the Pacific Ocean. Dissatisfied with the commercial yield from the HBC's initial thrust into the vast "Snake River country" south of the Columbia River, Governor Simpson appointed veteran explorer and trader Peter Skene Ogden to lead an all-out effort to strip the region of its furs.[1]

During more than six grueling years (1824-1831) of trapping and reconnaissance between Idaho and the Gulf of California, Ogden and his troops made several momentous discoveries. In 1826, when they advanced into a part of southern Oregon still unmapped and virtually

Hudson's Bay Company explorer, trapper, and trader Peter Skene Ogden, whose "Snake Country Brigade" in 1826 became the first Euro-American party to establish significant direct contact with the Klamath Indians of southern Oregon. (OHS neg. OrHi 707.)

unknown, Ogden and his "Snake Country Brigade" became the first whites to establish meaningful contacts with Indians of the Crater Lake region. (HBC trapper Finan McDonald had visited the Klamath briefly just a year earlier.)[2]

By the time Ogden and his company reached the Klamath and their closely related southern neighbors, the Modoc, in 1826, the Klamath were already caught up in the new trade and commerce introduced by the Euro-Americans. Power and social influence among the Klamath and other tribes of the region rested primarily on wealth, and possession of slaves had become an important determinant of wealth. The Klamath and Modoc took most of their slaves from the Pit River Indians of northeastern California, and their raids on these neighbors to the south accelerated in the early nineteenth century, when the Klamath began to deal regularly with the Columbia River Indians at the Dalles. By that time, the great Indian trading center on the Columbia was strongly under the influence of the whites, and the Dalles market provided both an outlet for Klamath slaves and a source for horses, firearms, and other "new" commodities.[3]

Political developments in native society went hand in hand with changes brought on by commerce. Some village headmen and regional chiefs became more powerful during a transformation in which approximately seventy Klamath villages (with a probable total population of between one and two thousand) consolidated into "tribelets," essentially alliances of villages. In addition to their regular rounds of hunting, gathering, and trade, these Klamath tribelets made war on other Indian groups and sometimes on one another. New wealth from trade combined with successes in war to strengthen certain up-and-coming Klamath headmen and chiefs.[4]

◌◯◌

THE LIVES OF THE KLAMATH PEOPLE in 1830 were far more influenced by white trading partners they had never seen than by those whom, in 1826, they had actually encountered. Ogden, with a party consisting of nearly forty French-Canadian and Indian trappers, their native wives, and more than a hundred horses, was single-minded in his pursuit of furs, especially beaver. He drew upon Klamath Indians as guides, and he traded with them for food, but he wanted no more than to pass peacefully through their territory, and to prosper from it. Though he sometimes remarked upon their "starving" condition, and he wondered at the sight of numerous "new Graves," Ogden considered the Klamath, on balance, a "happy race."[5]

Ogden and his British employers were certain that Americans would soon overrun the native peoples of the Oregon Country, and that the entire region south of the Columbia River was destined for American occupation: thus the HBC strategy in the 1820s to deplete the inland Northwest of furs before the Americans arrived in overwhelming numbers. In this forecast, the company men were, of course, correct. But the Ogden party's Klamath associates would be less overwhelmed by the flood of newcomers—at first, anyway—than were the other three Indian tribes of the Crater Lake region.

The first positive identification of Molala people by Euro-Americans did not come until 1841, when members of the tribe encountered an expedition led by Lieutenant George F. Emmons of the U.S. Exploring Expedition en route from the Columbia River to California. By that time—more than a decade before full-scale war broke out between American settlers and the Indians of southwestern Oregon—these natives of the Cascade slopes had already suffered great losses from diseases introduced by the whites.[6]

Despite the protection provided by a homeland east of the Cascades, the Klamath were hardly exempt from the violence and death connected with the Euro-American conquest of the West. In May 1846, Lieutenant John C. Fremont, in the later stages of a three-year mission to explore transportation routes between Oregon and California, led a weary party of seventeen men into a camp at Denny Creek, between Upper Klamath Lake and the foot of the Cascades. (Although the party likely passed through the Wood River valley, near the southern base of Mount Mazama, they apparently never saw Crater Lake.) Toward dawn, Klamath Indians attacked the sleeping travelers, killing three. One Klamath was also killed in the assault. That single casualty, though, was not nearly enough to quench Fremont's appetite for revenge.[7]

After Fremont and scout Kit Carson reunited with their main party, the combined government force, equipped with state-of-the-art rifles, swept down on a vulnerable Klamath village. Killing men, women, and children indiscriminately, the American invaders torched nearly everything of value in the village. Fremont later expressed satisfaction with "the swiftness of his reprisal," which had made no effort to differentiate Indians responsible for the attack from those innocent of it.[8]

In the same year, 1846, several Willamette Valley residents, led by Jesse Applegate, Lindsay Applegate, and Levi Scott, scouted a wagon route to the southern Willamette Valley (intended to bypass the treacherous Snake River portion of the Oregon Trail and the difficult final leg between the Dalles of the Columbia and the Willamette River). The first overland migrants who traveled this new Southern Emigrant Route—which passed directly through the Klamath Lake area of the Klamath Indian homeland—reached the Rogue Valley in the fall of 1846. Hundreds more soon followed.[9]

In 1847, Crooked Finger, leader of the much-weakened Molala, sought recruits from neighboring Indian groups, including the Klamath, for an uprising against the tide of Rogue Valley settlers. But by the time the natives were ready to act, in the winter of 1848, the whites had been forewarned. The encampment of Indians preparing to attack was instead surprised and routed by a combined force of settlers and sympathetic local Indians. In the judgment of Theodore Stern, "The legacy of hatred left by the Fremont expedition [had] undoubtedly . . . [been] instrumental in drawing Klamath into the hostile camp in the Molala war."[10]

Despite sporadic conflict and a steady stream of new settlers into southwestern Oregon, violence remained somewhat muted until 1851, when the discovery of gold lured a new brand of men into the region. (The Rich Gulch gold strike, which set off the mid-century gold rush in southern Oregon, was located some eighty-five miles west of Crater Lake, near present-day Jacksonville.) Prospectors set upon southern Oregon from the north and south, and soon violence between Indians (collectively referred to as "the Rogues") and volunteer militias of

Kate Chantèle, a Molala Indian consultant for anthropologists in the 1920s and 1930s, displays items of traditional dress and adornment of her largely decimated people. (OHS neg. OrHi 65285.)

prospectors and settlers became fierce and regular. With the end of the Rogue River Wars of 1855-1856, and with the forced removal of the region's Indians to reservations, the Molala, Takelma, and Upper Umpqua were effectively shattered as a people.[11]

First "Discoveries" of Crater Lake by non-Indians

GOLD IN SOUTHERN OREGON BROUGHT ON aggressive strivings and passions of all sorts; it also led indirectly to the first "discovery" of Crater Lake by non-Indians. In the late spring of 1853, a troop of prospectors from California and Oregon set out from the rough-and-ready mining town of Jacksonville in search of the mythical Lost Cabin Mine. Stranded near the headwaters of the Rogue River, with their provisions nearly exhausted, seven men from the larger party rode ahead to hunt for game. Three of them—including Oregonians John Wesley Hillman and Isaac Skeeters—after trudging up a long, gradual slope, found themselves at the edge of a steep, rocky wall, where far below lay what Hillman described as "the bluest lake I ever saw."[12]

Weakened by hunger, the three men quickly abandoned the urge to climb down to the lake's surface. According to Hillman's recollections, they instead decided to name their discovery Deep Blue Lake, wrote that name and their own names on a piece of paper, stuck the paper onto a stick planted in the ground, and rejoined their party. When the prospectors returned to Jacksonville, they found little interest in their high-mountain adventure. Local Indians denied any knowledge of the scene the miners described, and nearly everyone else seemed caught up with finding gold and staying clear of hostile Indians.[13]

For the next ten years or so, Crater Lake maintained its place in Indian life while whites apparently either forgot about or ignored it. Although the Takelma, Molala, and Upper Umpqua peoples were all but eliminated by the violence and social convulsions of mid-century, the turmoil of the time may actually have stimulated the Klamath's use of the Crater Lake area for food and other raw materials, travel, and spiritual quests. And while the path of the new Southern Emigrant Route brought whites into increasing conflict with the Modoc, the Klamath adjusted to the wave of new residents more smoothly. Some even began to work for American settlers in the Rogue and Willamette valleys.[14]

In the fall of 1862, another band of prospectors—this group traveling southwesterly across the Cascades, from goldfields near the John Day River to Jacksonville—stumbled upon Crater Lake while searching for water and a camping spot. By that time, the town of Jacksonville finally

John Wesley Hillman, the Oregon prospector whose chance discovery of Crater Lake in 1853 with fellow Oregonian Isaac Skeeters and others was later endorsed as the first by non-Indians. (Courtesy National Park Service, Crater Lake National Park Museum and Archives Collection.)

had a newspaper, and the travelers were able to report their find, which they referred to simply as Blue Lake, in the November 8, 1862, *Oregon Sentinel*. In this first published description of the location, entitled "Head Waters of Rogue River, Blue Lake," the writer proclaimed the lake's great beauty, as would be expected; but then, in sizing up possible future "uses" of the area, he also remarked upon the abundance of bunchgrass and the scarcity of timber at the mountain's summit.[15]

After descending Mount Mazama, these miners of 1862, in their effort to gain enough elevation to pinpoint the Rogue's headwaters, decided to climb another peak in the area (near the southwestern corner of today's Crater Lake National Park). Close to the top, in a ten-by-six-foot clearing, they came upon a wall of loose rocks three or four feet high, "evidently the work of Indians in olden time," one of them noted. In honor of their country, at that time enmeshed in Civil War, the men christened the mountain Union Peak.[16]

Crater Lake as a Regional Tourist Attraction

AS THE DUST SETTLED IN THE WAKE of the Rogue River Wars, southern Oregon settlers prodded the U.S. government to seek treaties with the Indians of the Klamath Basin, and with other native peoples whose traditional lands lay close to the increasingly busy Southern Emigrant Route. Government officials, after concluding that nothing short of an agreement with the Klamath would bring security and stability to southern Oregon, focused their peacemaking efforts on several chiefs who had earlier cooperated with whites. Lileks, headman of the Klamath Marsh and Williamson River cluster of villages, had by 1850 emerged as the dominant Klamath chief, and the whites courted him aggressively after 1856.[17]

Residents of the region pressed for a military post in addition to a treaty, but the onset of the Civil War delayed both. The military post eventually took shape first, as construction of Fort Klamath—north of Klamath Lake, in the heart of Klamath country—was well under way by 1863. This modest military enclave in south-central Oregon, an official arm of U.S. national expansion, was given several key geopolitical assignments: suppress Indian unrest, discourage harassment of travelers passing through the Klamath Basin, improve supply routes between eastern and western Oregon, and build new roads.[18]

William Colvig, in later years a lawyer, prosecuting attorney, and judge in Klamath and Jackson counties, was a young soldier assigned to Fort Klamath between 1863 and 1865. Because he was skilled in the

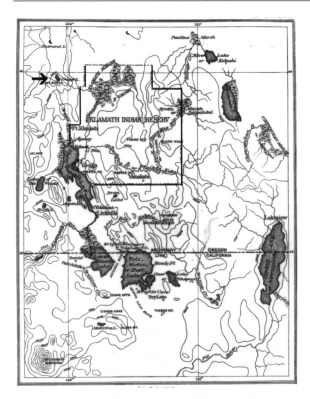

Detail of a map, drawn by anthropologist Albert S. Gatschet in the 1880s, showing the Klamath Indian Reservation in relation to Crater Lake (arrowed) and other regional landmarks. (OHS neg. OrHi 103397.)

use of Chinook jargon, the common language of cross-cultural relations in the Far West, and because he also knew a few words in the Klamath tongue, Colvig served the company commander as secretary-interpreter during his tour of duty. After first visiting Crater Lake in the fall of 1865, Colvig in time became well versed in traditional Indian stories and legends about the lake.[19]

Although his years at Fort Klamath were marked by unrest among the Indians of the Klamath Basin, young William Colvig managed to befriend Chief Lileks (known as the "Peace Chief"), whose influence eventually led representatives of the Klamath, Modoc, and Yahooskin-Paiute to sign the Klamath Lake Treaty of 1864. Through this treaty, the Indians ceded a great portion of their traditional territories east of the Cascades to the U.S. government, accepting for themselves a reservation that included Upper Klamath and Agency lakes, as well as the drainages of the Williamson and Sprague rivers. This reservation of slightly more than 1.1 million acres would not be proclaimed officially until 1870, but most of the Klamath people settled there after the Klamath agency, the government's administrative offices for the reservation, began operating at the upper end of Agency Lake in 1866.[20]

Meanwhile, during the summer of 1865, Company I of the First Oregon Volunteer Infantry, under the command of Captain Franklin B. Sprague, was ordered to construct a supply road between Fort Klamath and Jacksonville. Built to replace a cumbersome earlier route that passed over the snowy northern flank of Mount Pitt (officially renamed Mount McLoughlin in 1865), the new road would extend from Fort Klamath into Annie Creek canyon and the Union Creek region, through the southwestern portion of contemporary Crater Lake National Park. A short time after the work had begun, two of Captain Sprague's men came upon Crater Lake while hunting. They immediately reported their discovery to companions in camp, all of whom were apparently unaware of the site and its previous two "discoveries." Some eleven days later, Captain Sprague himself led a group of six men to the lake, reaching "the bluff, overlooking the lake on the west or south-west side, about 9 o'clock in the morning of a clear day, and for the first time feast[ing] our eyes on what we then pronounced the most beautiful and majestic body of water we had ever beheld."[21]

Officers, staff, and families posing at Fort Klamath in 1874. After the Modoc War, Fort Klamath gained a reputation as an attractive post with an active social life. (Courtesy NPS, CLNP Museum and Archives Collection.)

While stationed at Fort Klamath in 1865, Captain Franklin B. Sprague was among the first non-Indians to descend from the caldera rim to the shore of Crater Lake. (OHS neg. OrHi 5328.)

Lieutenant Orson A. Stearns was first among the Sprague party of 1865 to descend from the caldera rim to the lake; four other men, including Captain Sprague, soon followed. The group of five then quickly agreed upon Lake Majesty as an apt name for the breathtaking sight before them. These first non-Indian visitors to reach the shore of Crater Lake produced the second printed story about the place, this one published in the *Oregon Sentinel* on September 9, 1865. Captain Sprague also appears to have been the first observer to note Crater Lake's volcanic origins. In an account written just two weeks after the event, he remarked astutely that "the whole surroundings prove this lake to be the crater of an extinct volcano. . . . Where now is a placid sheet of water, there was a lake of fire, throwing its cinders and ashes to vast distances in every direction."[22]

After 1865, spurred on by regional newspaper stories and by word of mouth, greater numbers of people undertook visits to the great mountain lake. The era of inadvertent encounters was past: by the mid-1870s, Crater Lake had become a well-known local tourist attraction, admired both for its beauty and its commercial-recreational potential.[23]

BECAUSE IT RESULTED IN THE NAME that finally stuck, one of the most significant trips to Crater Lake during this period took place in the summer of 1869. Led by Jacksonville businessman James M. Sutton, at that time also editor of the *Oregon Sentinel*, the party included attorney James D. Fay, who had first visited the lake on a hunting trip with ten other men in 1865. While the expedition was en route, the *Oregon Sentinel* commented: "As it is reported that the party is partly composed of young ladies, you may well imagine that the desire to see and explore Lake Majesty has become intense."[24]

Setting out from Jacksonville in late July, the Sutton party traveled along a rough, dusty road that followed the northeasterly course of the Rogue River. At the point where their route met the road built a few years earlier by the Fort Klamath detachment, Sutton and his companions opened a new wagon path up Dutton Creek to the rim of the lake, where they met a party of three from Fort Klamath. Sutton later wrote that "everyone gaze[d] at [the lake] in almost tearful astonishment."[25]

Partly as a result of James Fay's earlier stay, which had ended with a vow for a return trip to the lake's intriguing island, the 1869 excursionists drove a wagon carrying the parts of a small wood and canvas boat. Upon reaching the caldera rim, the party assembled their rough-hewn boat and, taking great care to protect the little craft from the rocky cliffs, successfully lowered it some 950 feet to the water. On August 4, 1869, after five of the party, including Sutton and Fay, had spent an hour paddling to what is now called Wizard Island, they got out of their boat and congratulated themselves on becoming the volcanic

Jacksonville artist-photographer Peter Britt poses with his camera around the time of his 1874 photographic expedition to Crater Lake. (OHS neg. CN 000266.)

island's first known visitors. The group took about forty-five minutes to climb to the island's summit, where they found a well-formed crater. There they planted, among rocks piled at the crater rim, a written record of their presence, enclosed in a tin can.[26]

While the wind proved too strong and their craft too unsteady to allow extensive navigation of the lake, the men were able to take two measurements of the lake's depth. Using a rope extended from the boat, they measured 550 feet at a point about a half-mile from Wizard Island, and they speculated correctly that the lake plunged far deeper elsewhere. Before they left the place, on August 5, they christened it Crater Lake, a name that would appear in print for the first time in articles in the *Oregon Sentinel* on August 21 and August 28, 1869. Sutton included in his newspaper account of the adventure the following note: "Through the politeness of Mr. Peter Britt, I was prepared to take photographs of the lake, but owing to the smoke [from forest fires] in the atmosphere I did not succeed."[27]

THE PHOTOGRAPHIC INTENTIONS of Mr. Peter Britt of Jacksonville had to wait five more years for consummation. In August 1874, Britt himself traveled to Crater Lake in a wagon fitted out as a mobile photographic studio, stopping along the way to take pictures of Upper Rogue River falls, Mill Creek falls, and Annie Spring. The party traveled slowly because of the bulk, weight, and preciousness of their cargo: a stereoscopic camera and two large boxes, each weighing more than a hundred pounds, holding glass plates, plate frames, chemicals, trays, and other equipment needed for coating the photographic plates and developing them immediately after exposure.[28]

When, after five days of travel, the Britt party neared their destination, they left the two-horse wagon by the roadside and packed more than two hundred pounds of equipment, supplies, and camping gear the rest of the way to the caldera rim. The date was August 11, 1874, and the next forty-eight hours of cold, cloudy weather, with intermittent strong winds and rain, tested the expedition's patience and endurance. Britt needed at least a small amount of sunlight for the elaborate wet-plate photographic process he used at that time, and the group could only hope that the weather would change.[29]

Finally, on August 13, the clouds parted, the sun shone through, and Peter Britt, stationed on the south rim of Crater Lake, looking northwesterly toward Wizard Island, was able to take at least one picture of the rare sight. Over the next two days, the photographer and his

After a wait of nearly two days, a break in the cloud cover on August 13, 1874, admitted enough sunlight to allow Peter Britt to take the first photograph of Crater Lake. (Southern Oregon Historical Society #740.)

This photograph, which includes young Emil Britt, the photographer's son, in the foreground, was one of just seven that Peter Britt was able to take of Crater Lake during his party's momentous visit in 1874. (Southern Oregon Historical Society #724.)

fellow campers (who included his young son, Emil) hiked and relaxed, knowing that their main goal had been accomplished. But before the party departed Crater Lake for Fort Klamath on August 17, Britt managed to take a few more pictures of the lake. A total of seven glass-plate negatives of Crater Lake were produced during the 1874 visit.[30]

The Diller-Hayden Expedition of 1883

PETER BRITT'S PHOTOGRAPHS OF AUGUST 1874 became the strongest single influence in transforming Crater Lake from a regional curiosity to a statewide attraction, and then, in time, to an acknowledged national landmark. Despite two decades of discovery and rediscovery, and a growing regional popularity, Crater Lake did not appear on any map until after 1875. So, in a nearly literal sense, Britt's photographs of 1874 can be said to have put Crater Lake "on the map." Alan Clark Miller, a student of Peter Britt's photography, wrote that "many Oregonians gained their first knowledge of that scenic landmark through Britt stereographs, and these views became so popular that they were pirated by more famous western photographers and eventually sold, without credit line, by the stereo firm of Underwood and Underwood. Britt's picture of Crater Lake served as a model for lithographs used in commercial advertising, . . . and his famous photograph began to appear in promotional pamphlets published by the Portland Immigration Board."[31]

Through these means and others, knowledge and impressions of Crater Lake were incorporated into an expanding national awareness of American scenic wonders during the last quarter of the nineteenth century. Much of this heightened attention was a by-product of a new cultural fascination with the West in general. "By the 1860s many thoughtful Americans had embraced the wonderlands of the West as replacements for man-made marks of achievement," according to historian Alfred Runte. Magnificent landscapes, photographed or painted, thus became America's answer to Europe's superior cultural antiquity.[32]

Amid this climate of what Runte has referred to as "scenic nationalism," the notion of "national park" emerged, finding expression initially in a drive to protect Yosemite Valley in California and the giant sequoia redwoods of the Sierra Nevada. With the shameful commercialization and disfigurement of New York's Niagara Falls still fresh in the minds of opinion makers and politicians, the Yosemite Act of 1864 and the legislation establishing Yellowstone National Park in

1872 together granted a measure of protection to some of the country's great scenic landmarks. In doing so, these laws asserted a uniquely American form of cultural nationalism.[33]

By way of popular magazines and government publications, the work of American landscape painters and photographers—including Albert Bierstadt, Thomas Moran, Carleton Watkins, and William Henry Jackson—provided visual evidence of western scenic grandeur during the second half of the nineteenth century. Without the paintings of Moran and the photographs of Jackson, the designation of Yellowstone as a national park might well have taken decades longer. But as important as Moran and Jackson were in stimulating popular interest in Yellowstone, the scientific testimony of Ferdinand V. Hayden, then head of the U.S. Geological and Geographical Survey of the Territories, was the truly critical factor in convincing Congress to pass the Yellowstone legislation.[34]

☙

UNLIKE YELLOWSTONE, CRATER LAKE DID NOT YET, in 1880, have a legitimate scientific advocate. Renowned paleontologist Edward Drinker Cope stopped at Crater Lake in 1879 en route to a rendezvous with Oregon pioneer geologist Thomas Condon at the John Day fossil beds, but both he and Condon were preoccupied with central Oregon's fossil treasures at the time. Finally, in 1883, U.S. Geological Survey director John Wesley Powell, possibly moved by Britt's photographs, sent J. S. Diller and Everett Hayden to Crater Lake for an initial scientific reconnaissance.[35]

Diller and Hayden inaugurated a procession of scientists that continues to this day, for Crater Lake remains one of the richest and most remarkable geological sites in the world. The two men spent several days at Crater Lake on this first trip, concentrating on the rocky formations and lava flows that make up the caldera's rim and cliffs. After building a raft from logs rolled down the steep inner slope to the water's edge, the two scientists also paddled to Wizard Island and explored the volcano-within-a-volcano. Diller continued to think and write productively about Crater Lake during his lifetime, eventually offering an early version of the now-dominant theory that Mount Mazama's destruction resulted primarily from internal collapse rather than external explosion.[36]

The Agony of the Klamath

MEANWHILE, THE NEARBY KLAMATH INDIAN Reservation took firm root. White government officials claimed confidently that, under the treaty of 1864 and the reservation system, only a generation or two would be needed to replace the Indians' traditional native ways with the cultural practices of American settlers. As it turned out, though, the climate and generally harsh living conditions of the Klamath Basin defeated many efforts to set up workable farms and ranches, and most of the region's natives were driven back to traditional forms of hunting and gathering, supplemented by treaty rations and modest gains from farming and freighting. Population figures for both the Klamath and the Modoc reached historic lows in the 1870s, and the region's Indians sank into widespread misery and despondency. Unwittingly testifying to the natives' depressed condition, a correspondent for *Overland Monthly* magazine in 1873 blithely described the reservation Klamath as "harmless and not very degraded."[37]

Thus it soon became clear that the Klamath Lake Treaty of 1864 had provided few satisfactory or lasting solutions to the problems of Indian peoples living in the region. Although four Modoc headmen had signed the treaty, most of the Modoc people were immediately unhappy with the agreement and chose to remain on their traditional homeland rather than join the Klamath on the reservation. After violence erupted in the fall of 1872 between Captain Jack's band of Modocs and Klamath Basin settlers, the militant Indian group nearly succeeded in forming an alliance of all Klamaths and Modocs for a decisive war against the whites.[38]

Twenty-seven-year-old Captain Oliver C. Applegate, son of Lindsay Applegate and nephew of Jesse Applegate (the southern Oregon pioneers who had helped blaze the Southern Emigrant Route), set out to convince Klamath and Modoc warriors to reject Captain Jack's war campaign and remain true to the treaty of 1864. Concentrating his efforts on the influential Modoc chief Schonchin, Applegate drew upon his command of Chinook jargon and his knowledge of the Klamath language to urge Modoc and Klamath tribesmen to choose peace over war. His powers of persuasion helped limit but not prevent the conflict, and Captain Applegate was called upon to play a major role in fighting the Modoc War of 1872-1873. The war ended tragically, as Applegate knew it would, when a band of tenacious Modocs withdrew to the lava beds south of Tule Lake and were finally overcome by vastly superior numbers and arms.[39]

Captain Oliver C. Applegate (left) and Frank Riddle pose with five Modoc women in the aftermath of the Modoc War of 1872-1873. The woman standing between the two men is Riddle's wife, Winema, who helped the whites in the war. (OHS neg. OrHi 26543.)

Oliver Applegate (standing, center) poses, circa 1880, with native dignitaries, a few of whom had signed the Klamath Lake Treaty of 1864. (Courtesy Klamath Tribes.)

Following the bloody Modoc War and the hanging of Captain Jack and five others, the whites who ran the Klamath Reservation agency for the U.S. government continued to find cooperative leaders within the Indian community—men who, like the original treaty chiefs, had more varied experiences with whites, by way of education or sometimes as agency employees. The *Overland Monthly* correspondent of 1873 wrote approvingly of peace-minded head chief Allen David, who had been selected in the mid-1860s to succeed Lileks: "He is well-dressed always [and] wears an intelligent look. . . . His well-blacked boots testify that he is not indifferent to the ways of civilization."[40]

Captain Applegate's success in limiting the Modoc uprising in 1872 rested on his well-established relationships with the Klamath Reservation Indians. His long-term effort to learn about native languages and cultures, including something of the Klamaths' traditional reverence for Crater Lake, was unique among his contemporaries, and he was rewarded with genuine friendships among the Indians of the Klamath Basin. By contrast, the efforts of the Bureau of Indian Affairs to stamp out shamanism and to suppress other forms of traditional native culture in the 1870s and 1880s were more typical of the government's stance toward the reservation peoples.[41]

Despite the government's war against traditional Indian ways, aspects of the Klamaths' religious tradition proved tenacious. A witness from the 1870s remarked at how Klamath "medicine men still come [to Crater Lake], as they always came in olden time, to study spiritual wisdom and learn the secrets of life from the Great Spirit." And an anthropologist who worked among the Klamath in the 1880s observed that long after other aspects of white culture, such as dress, had been adopted by the Indians, the natives clung to their own "superstitions" and "conjurers' practices."[42]

While Indians and whites in the region regularly crossed paths without violence in the last decades of the nineteenth century, the newcomers as a whole developed little understanding of the natives. As recreational excursions to Crater Lake became more popular among whites after 1875, residents of Klamath County and the Rogue River valley regularly camped near groups of Klamath Reservation Indians at Huckleberry Mountain during the autumn berry-picking season. But most evidence suggests that stereotypes and gulfs of incomprehension, more than cultural understanding and sympathy, were deepened in such encounters.[43]

Euro-Americans who wrote or spoke about the native connection to the Crater Lake region invariably stressed Indian fear of the place, mistaking or miscasting reverence, respect, and awe for aversion. Seldon E. Kirk, influential chairman of the Klamath General Council during the mid-twentieth century, maintained that the story of the Indians' fear of Crater Lake was grossly exaggerated. He, in turn, minimized the site's supernatural character by attributing Indian avoidance of the place to mere practicality: since the area contained little food or other resources, there was little need to go there, according to Kirk. In any case, the radical reorientation of Klamath life in the second half of the nineteenth century, the population decline of the 1870s, and the spectacle of a revered landscape overrun with strangers surely combined to cast the traditional sacredness of Crater Lake in an altered light. The whites' new mastery seemed to prove that Crater Lake had lost much of its power. Religious confusion and disillusionment were the inevitable results.[44]

Chapter 3

Enter Will Steel

1885-1897

Myth and Reality

WHEN WILLIAM GLADSTONE STEEL, future instigator of Oregon's only national park, was born to his Scottish immigrant father and his native Virginian mother on September 7, 1854, in Stafford, Ohio, barely a year had passed since John Wesley Hillman and two fellow prospectors had first laid eyes on beautiful Crater Lake. Eighteen years later, when the Steel family left their farm in southeastern Kansas for Portland, Crater Lake remained virtually unknown beyond southern Oregon.[1]

Will Steel, who in time earned a substantial historical reputation for his work on behalf of Crater Lake and the forests of the Cascade Mountains, was only modestly successful in conventional terms. Once graduated from high school in Portland in 1873, he bounced from one profession to another, beginning with a three-year apprenticeship as a pattern maker for Smith Brothers Iron Works of Portland. Thereafter, the avocations of his life—mountaineering, compiling and researching geographic place names, and, above all, promoting and developing Crater Lake—consistently overshadowed his vocations.[2]

Much later in life, while fiercely guarding his claim as "Father of Crater Lake National Park," Steel harbored bitter disappointment over what he perceived as the failures of others to recognize him more lavishly and pay him more generously for his dedication to public causes. In an effort to soothe his own emotional wounds, and to create a more pleasing life story, Steel took certain liberties in representing his past. In one of his standard and most crowd-pleasing recollections—one he must have written or repeated hundreds of times—Steel described how, one day as a Kansas schoolboy in 1870, he glanced at a newspaper in which he had wrapped his lunch. There he spied a short article that told about "a wonderful lake . . . recently discovered in Oregon. . . .

William Gladstone Steel in his early twenties, not long after he began to pursue his interest in mountaineering. (OHS neg. OrHi 89161.)

This article took a great hold upon me," Steel reminisced. "So great [was my fascination] that I determined then and there to go to Oregon, to descend to the water, to climb [Wizard Island] and to take my lunch in the crater."[3]

Publication of such an article in a small-town Kansas newspaper in 1870 is perhaps not inconceivable, but the likelihood seems small. By that date only six known newspaper articles about Crater Lake had appeared in all of Oregon, and those were published in the relatively obscure Jacksonville *Oregon Sentinel*. Adding to the unlikelihood of this boyhood "recollection," Steel himself later maintained that he had been living in Oregon for nine years before he "found anybody who had ever heard of [Crater Lake]," and another three or four years passed before he met "someone who had actually been there."[4]

From our perspective, though, Will Steel's *actual* experiences—especially those connected with Crater Lake and Crater Lake National Park—need no embellishment. While credit for the preservation of Crater Lake and the establishment of Crater Lake National Park in 1902 by no means goes to Steel alone, it is difficult to imagine these achievements without him. His life provides a vivid case study of a single person's powerful impact on the decisions of government and the course of history.

Steel's First Visit to Crater Lake

WHENEVER IT WAS THAT WILL STEEL first heard of Crater Lake and determined to go there, it was not until the Oregon and California Railroad line finally reached Ashland in 1884 that the journey from Portland to Crater Lake began to appear practical to him. During the summer of 1885, the thirty-year-old Steel took brief leave from his job as superintendent of postal carriers in Portland (his brother George was then postmaster) and planned a trip to Crater Lake. Accompanied by his regular hiking and mountain-climbing partner, J. M. "Johnnie" Breck, Steel traveled by train from Portland to Ashland. There the two men arranged transfer of their bulky freight, which included a canvas-bottomed boat, from rail to stage. Steel and Breck then rode by coach across the mountains from Ashland to Linkville (renamed Klamath Falls in the early 1890s), and from Linkville to Fort Klamath.[5]

At Fort Klamath, Steel and Breck met up with two Presbyterian ministers from southern Oregon, with whom they had earlier planned the trip, and, by chance, with Captain Clarence E. Dutton and Professor Joseph LeConte. Dutton, on leave from the army for a stint with the U.S. Geological Survey, was in charge of a small military party escorting

Venerable Klamath chief Allen David, who in 1885 regaled Will Steel and others with stories about Crater Lake and its place in native traditions. (Courtesy National Park Service, Crater Lake National Park Museum and Archives Collection.)

Captain Clarence E. Dutton, whose early explorations and observations played an important role in the campaign to add Crater Lake to the select circle of national parks at the turn of the century. (Courtesy NPS, CLNP Museum and Archives Collection.)

geologist LeConte on a summer trek through the Pacific Coast mountains, a trip designed to include Crater Lake. After a night at Fort Klamath, during which Steel interviewed Klamath chief Allen David and former soldier Oliver Applegate (now an employee of the Klamath reservation) about Crater Lake native traditions, the combined wagon party set off, on August 15, 1885, for their mountain destination.[6]

Eager to see the lake as soon as possible, Steel and Breck abandoned the lumbering wagons of the main party and walked ahead the last twenty-two miles to their goal. Steel later recalled that he and Breck, gazing at the unbelievably blue waters of Crater Lake from the rim of the caldera, stood in silence for a short time before promising each other to do whatever was necessary "to save the lake from private exploitation." However memorable those first few minutes at the rim might have been for Steel and his faithful hiking partner, later conversations between Steel and Captain Dutton proved more significant for Crater Lake's future.[7]

In the March 1886 issue of *West Shore* magazine, Steel described how, during hours of conversation with Dutton in his tent near the rim, "the Captain agreed with the idea that something ought to be done—and done at once if the lake was to be saved, and that it should be made a National Park." Dutton also apparently suggested, in those first meetings with Steel, that approximately ten townships of land (about three hundred sixty square miles) surrounding Crater Lake ought to be "withdrawn from public entry" as a first priority.[8]

Steel and Breck remained in their Crater Lake camp for six days. During that time, they basked in the extraordinary setting and enjoyed some leisure; but, more important to their long-range objectives, they explored the lake and its surroundings. The canvas-bottomed canoe, brought from Portland and lowered with great difficulty from the rim to the lake on August 17, "leaked freely" as soon as they placed it in the water, Steel remembered. "It took thirty-five minutes of hard paddling—and bailing—to reach the island," which Steel promptly christened Wizard Island, "because of its weird appearance." After climbing to the small volcano's summit, the hikers ate their lunch in the hot, dusty crater, which Steel dubbed Witch's Caldron. It was also during this initial visit that Steel, inspired by his recent conversations about Indian traditions, applied the name Llao Rock (after the Indian deity who guarded the lake) to one of the rim's most prominent rocky formations.[9]

⟡

INSPIRED BY THEIR FIRSTHAND EXPERIENCE, and buttressed by the sound advice of Captain Dutton, Will Steel and Johnnie Breck returned to Portland and immediately mounted a political campaign to save Crater Lake and the surrounding area from private encroachment. Breck wrote a letter, published in the Portland *Oregonian* and reprinted in other regional newspapers, advocating national park status for Crater Lake. Steel sent out close to a thousand letters "to nearly all the large daily newspapers in the United States, asking the editors to support the idea of a Crater Lake National Park."[10]

Building on a solid base of support in Portland, Steel also developed a petition, circulated by Oregon newspaper editors and postmasters, asking that the "lake and its approaches be set apart from future settlement or other appropriation by the government, and kept and reserved as a public park for the people of the United States." The petition, which included the signatures of some of Oregon's most prominent civic leaders, was forwarded to President Grover Cleveland on December 21, 1885.[11]

Steel traveled to Washington, D.C., in January, meeting with Secretary of the Interior Lucius Q. C. Lamar and President Cleveland, and generally stoking Oregon's congressional delegation on the issue of Crater Lake. Democrat Cleveland and Republican Steel hit it off well; the Portlander found the president "a true sportsman [and] a lover of Nature's works." On February 1, 1886, President Cleveland issued an executive order withdrawing ten townships—encompassing Union

Peak to the southwest, Mount Scott to the east, and Timber Crater, Diamond Lake, and Mount Thielsen to the north, in addition to Crater Lake—from the public-lands market.[12]

Steel's campaign from afar, sealed with his personal lobbying effort in Washington, was the key factor in President Cleveland's withdrawal of the ten townships, "pending legislation looking to the creation of a public park." And it was no accident that this vital first step in the long process of safeguarding Crater Lake took place just four and a half months after Will Steel first looked upon the magnificent lake and its surroundings.

Steel's political campaign of 1885-1886 bore fruit on other fronts. In January 1886, Oregon's state legislature submitted a petition to Congress requesting national park designation for Crater Lake and a surrounding four-and-a-half-township area. The Portland Board of Trade, the Portland City Council, and various other town and county councils throughout Oregon sent similar petitions to Congress. With momentum building for protection of Crater Lake, Oregon's two U.S. senators, John H. Mitchell and Joseph N. Dolph, jumped on the bandwagon. Dolph introduced a bill in the Senate to establish a park or reserve that would include both Crater Lake and Diamond Lake. Soon after, Oregon Congressman Binger Hermann advanced a similar bill in the House.[13]

Birth of the National Park Idea

THE LATE-NINETEENTH-CENTURY MOVEMENT among prominent Oregonians and others to protect Crater Lake from private exploitation occurred against the backdrop of a broader national debate about the present and future status of public lands in the United States, especially those vast tracts still owned by the federal government throughout the West. As geographer Lary Dilsaver has pointed out, the heretofore dominant tradition in America held that the federal government ought to make most public lands available to private enterprise for "consumptive use." Federal land laws in the mid-nineteenth century treated the entire public domain essentially as agricultural land, and practically no regulation of mining and timber cutting existed on these extensive publicly owned properties. Consequently, owing to rapid industrialization and the lack of adequate controls, the country's natural resources on the public domain were depleted at an alarming rate throughout the 1850s.[14]

The doctrine of consumptive use of the nation's public lands went basically unchallenged until passage of the Yosemite Act of 1864. This legislation, which granted Yosemite Valley and the Mariposa Redwood Grove in trust to California, also provided a legal and philosophical precedent for the establishment of Yellowstone National Park eight years later. With passage of the innovative but untested Yellowstone Park Act of 1872, the United States received its first national park. Perhaps even more important, the Yellowstone law furnished a concrete example of how the federal government could create parks by withdrawing public lands from settlement and reserving them for specific public purposes.[15]

The tradition of private exploitation of public lands did not yield easily, however (and, of course, has not done so to this day). Both the Timber Culture Act of 1873 and the Timber Cutting Act of 1878, though intended as moderate conservation measures, were almost immediately used to aid and abet the fraudulent exploitation of federal forests. And though such intellectuals as John Muir, Charles S. Sargent, and Robert V. Johnson spoke out in the 1870s and 1880s against the abuse of these federal laws, calling for their reform or replacement, the depredation of forests from the cutting of timber and the grazing of cattle and sheep continued.[16]

Meanwhile, the fledgling national parks movement failed to generate another park for nearly two decades. Moreover, the government's ambivalence toward the new park idea was soon apparent in the uncertainty of Congress over how to provide for the lone national park it had authorized. The inadequacy of the enabling legislation for Yellowstone National Park quickly became obvious. Besides leaving the vast area vulnerable to private development, the law failed to provide funds sufficient for the park's management and protection. Historian Alfred Runte, in describing the tentative, nearly accidental quality of the early national parks movement, has pointed out that Yellowstone's "great size stemmed from uncertainty rather than from a deliberate attempt to protect the totality of Yellowstone's wilderness and ecological resources."[17]

Several proposals for new national parks in the 1870s and 1880s thus lost steam amid the indecision in Washington, D.C. Members of Congress were increasingly reminded that the new voices calling for protection of scenic natural areas were more than matched in volume and vehemence by the more traditional American chorus advocating maximum use of natural resources, wherever they might be found.

For Crater Lake partisans, this frustrated state of affairs became evident in 1886, when Senator Dolph's and Congressman Hermann's

Crater Lake National Park bills reached dead ends in the public-lands committees of the Senate and House. There the combined opposition of land, timber, sheep, and ranching interests proved formidable. Neither memorials and petitions from Oregon nor a widely distributed article by Clarence Dutton in *Science* magazine—in which the soldier-surveyor rhapsodized that "the beauty and majesty of the scene [at Crater Lake] are indescribable"—would move the nation's lawmakers.[18]

The Steel-Dutton Party of 1886

PARTLY TO BOOST THE ONGOING POLITICAL campaign to gain national park status for Crater Lake, and partly because of his irrepressible urge to see the place again, Will Steel conspired with Captain Clarence Dutton and Congressman Binger Hermann in the spring of 1886 to bring about a second U.S. Geological Survey expedition to the mountain lake. USGS director John Wesley Powell, persuaded by the trio's arguments, authorized a survey party for the summer of 1886, to be led by Dutton. Because the expedition was sent to conduct a thorough examination of the lake and the surrounding region, equipment and technical know-how were essential. Steel, who had by this time impressed politicians, bureaucrats, soldiers, and scientists alike with his knowledge and commitment to the Crater Lake cause, was given the critical jobs of overseeing construction of the party's boats and acquiring lake-sounding gear.[19]

Three boats were built in Portland under Steel's supervision: one for the vital task of measuring the lake's depth and two auxiliary craft (skiffs). Steel took special pride in the sounding vessel—the *Cleetwood*—a "four-oared, lap streak, cedar boat," twenty-six-feet long and nearly six-feet wide, "remarkable for the perfection of its construction and model, . . . competent to ride almost any sea," as he described it. All three boats were transported from Portland to Ashland by rail flatcar in early July of 1886.[20]

Steel left Portland for Ashland on July 1, and there he rendezvoused with Captain Dutton and his party of technical assistants, and with Captain George W. Davis, an engineer, and the ten sturdy enlisted men under his command. Dutton and Steel knew well that brawn, as well as brains, would be required for the strenuous passage from Ashland to Crater Lake, and certainly for the delicate and dangerous job of lowering the party's three boats down the steep walls of the caldera and into the water.[21]

A boat is lowered from the rim of the Mount Mazama caldera to Crater Lake during an expedition led by Will Steel in 1903. The logistics employed here were essentially those used to lower the *Cleetwood* and two auxiliary craft to the water in 1886. (OHS neg. OrHi 103402.)

The cross-country caravan, Steel recalled, consisted of "a four-mule team, . . . three double teams, horsemen, and [a] pack train," a total of thirty-five men and sixty-five horses and mules. The party left Ashland on July 7, with the *Cleetwood* "mounted upon the running gear of a wagon [pulled by the mule team] upon which a framework had been built in such a manner that the boat could be suspended in slings and bear the journey of a hundred miles over rough mountain roads without injury from shocks or strains," according to Captain Dutton's detailed recollections.[22]

Most of the seven-day journey to Crater Lake was spent in a comfortable march; the last portion, however—the ascent of Mount Mazama—required intense concentration and logistical finesse. "With great labor the wagons were hauled up the incline over snow banks and through the forest until they rested upon the brink of the cliff which looks down into the lake," Dutton wrote. Finally, on Wednesday morning, July 14, the boats were unleashed from their sturdy carriers "with scarcely a scratch to mar the paint," Steel reported proudly.[23]

The lowering of the boats to the lake—a detail directed by Captain Davis—was held over to the next morning. The two skiffs, each encased in a shield of inch-wide boards, were eased down one at a time, accompanied by four men to guide their descent. Three-quarter-inch rope, "made fast to trees, was used to hold back [each] boat, while the men urged it forward and downward over the great snow banks, talus and ledges." One of the skiffs reached the water somewhat scratched, but not significantly damaged; the other was entirely unscathed.[24]

Sounding the Lake in 1886

WILL STEEL WAS NOT A LITERARY MAN; nor did he ever pretend to be one. He lacked the background and temperament for extensive literary work, and he consistently struggled, in his writing and his life, to discipline his passions with reason. Still, those unruly passions occasionally inspired beautiful prose flourishes, and several of these can be found in *The Mountains of Oregon*, the only book ever published in Steel's name. This handsome little volume, which appeared in 1890 under the imprint of his brother David's firm, was a loosely organized collection of essays that Steel used primarily as a calling card in his political lobbying work in the 1890s. Some of the book's most vivid and colorful paragraphs describe his involvement in the 1886 U.S. Geological Survey expedition to Crater Lake.[25]

On the evening of July 15, after the two skiffs had been triumphantly lowered to the lake, the party returned to its tent encampment, pitched in a beautiful spot on the southwestern portion of the elliptical caldera rim. (The site would become Crater Lake's principal camping area for decades to come, and the future location of Crater Lake National Park's Rim Village.) Steel was mesmerized by Nature's performance that night, and he conveyed his enchantment in a vivid description of what he witnessed: "Dark and threatening clouds," accompanied by "a few large drops of rain," suddenly approached from the direction of Klamath Lake, to the southeast.

> *To the west, the sun was slowly sinking to rest, when a glowing light spread itself over the dark clouds, which became brighter and still brighter. Looking beyond, a scene of unparalleled magnificence spread before us. Through the center hung long, fleecy clouds lighted to a deep orange, while above, like a great curtain, was spread a belt of olive green. Here and there were tints of crimson, the delicacy of which no artist could approach.*

Above and parallel with the horizon stretched a long rift, in clouds rendered marvelously rich in gold and garnet, through which the blue sky beyond was visible, slightly obscured by light, fleecy clouds of silver. During all this magnificent sight the electric storm raged in the south with unabated fury, flashes of lightning and peals of thunder adding solemnity to a scene of wonderful brilliance.[26]

ON THE NEXT MORNING, THE PARTY AWOKE to the great challenge of lowering the sounding boat from the rim to the water below. Though Steel may not have been eager to risk life and limb for the two skiffs, he was prepared to do so for the sake of his pride and joy, the *Cleetwood*. He took an active part in the perilous operation from beginning to end. "A sled was made of very heavy timbers, on which [the *Cleetwood*] was placed, keel up, then lashed and braced in every conceivable manner until . . . she seemed a part of the sled itself," Steel reported. Then the

As Will Steel colorfully testified, the dramatic, magnificently varied features of the caldera walls are often experienced as if for the first time when viewed from the shore or water surface. (Courtesy NPS, CLNP Museum and Archives Collection.)

The *Cleetwood*, Will Steel's beloved sounding craft, floats on Crater Lake in 1886. Steel sits second from right, with Wizard Island and Llao Rock prominent in the background. (Courtesy NPS, CLNP Museum and Archives Collection.)

thirty-one-year-old Steel joined one of Captain Davis's young troops at the front of the nine-hundred-pound boat, guiding it down what would become the main trail to Eagle Cove, below today's Crater Lake Lodge. Rock slides and precarious footing were ever-present dangers, with potentially fatal results. "Leaving the summit at 7:30 A.M., [the effort] required the most persistent work and constant care of fifteen men eight hours to reach the lake," Steel wrote.[27]

With all three boats finally launched on July 17, and before the serious business of sounding began, several men made a quick pleasure trip to Wizard Island. On the next day, nine members of the party circuited the lake on a casual inspection tour. This initial opportunity to view the walls of the caldera from the lake's surface seems to have left Steel stupefied once more: "As we gazed in silent wonder at [Llao Rock's] rugged sides, reaching nearly half a mile above us, for the first time did we realize the immensity of such a spectacle."[28]

Though Captain Dutton was in charge of the technical aspects of sounding, Steel was deeply involved in the execution. He had been given the responsibility of gathering the sounding gear (piano wire, pipe weight, a wooden spool, and a spirit level, among a few other items), and now he looked forward to using those tools and the other equipment in the important work of measuring, surveying, and mapping the lake and surrounding area.[29]

James Sutton and his party of 1869 had made a rough measurement of 550 feet, and had predicted much greater depths. But this information appears to have been either unknown to the 1886 expedition or considered unreliable. When Steel and the sounding crew took a few casual measurements on July 17, obtaining depths of more than a thousand feet, members of the party were astonished. Now realizing the momentousness of their task—they were apparently sizing up one of the deepest lakes in the world—the men approached the formal sounding work of the next several days with an added sense of seriousness. The early, unofficial sounding measurement was enough to prompt the exhilarated Dutton to send a messenger to Fort Klamath "to telegraph to the world that [they] had found 1,210 feet of water near shore," Steel wrote.[30]

Most of the sounding work from aboard the *Cleetwood* was conducted by Captain Davis's men, "every one of whom had served an enlistment in the navy, so was an expert in all that pertained to boats," Steel assured. In addition to navigating the craft, the men used a windlass (a device that regulates the play of rope or wire around a barrel) to drop lead-weighted piano wire into the water. Each measurement thus obtained was recorded, and then a signal was flashed, via heliograph, to engineers observing from a prominent peak on the western rim (known in later years, for its role in 1886, as the Watchman). By means of the trigonometric principle of triangulation, a pattern of sounding points was plotted on the lake's surface, in a shape resembling the spokes of a wheel. The crew made a total of 168 soundings, recording depths from 93 to 1,996 feet.[31]

ᘓ

As a result of this first systematic study of Crater Lake's depths, Captain Dutton and his colleagues were able to approximate and visualize the general shape of the lake bottom. Soundings revealed three steep protrusions—one, obviously, the above-water Wizard Island—on an otherwise generally flat lake floor. Topographer Mark B. Kerr and his assistant, Eugene Ricksecker, two of Dutton's men, prepared a map from the surveying work on this trip, pegging the elliptical lake's length at 6.25 miles and its width at 4.25 miles.[32]

Other important results were obtained during the nearly month-long expedition. Dutton and his colleagues concluded that Crater Lake has no visible outlet, thus casting doubt upon theories and local folklore claiming that the lake provided headwaters for the Rogue River. Prominent rocky formations of the caldera wall and rim, scrutinized for the first time from the lake surface, were named and described in greater detail than ever before. And though Dutton was not a trained scientist, he took a near-professional interest in Mount Mazama's volcanic geology, having studied volcanoes in the Hawaiian Islands and traveled with and learned from well-known geologist Joseph LeConte. Dutton's U.S. Geological Survey report included this perceptive summary: "In a word, the basin is the heart of a great volcanic cone, truncated far down toward its base, so that only the basal portions of the volcanic pile remain." A decade later, no less an authority than J. S. Diller recognized that "Dutton was the first to discover the more novel and salient features in the geological history of the lake."[33]

The Dutton-Steel expedition of 1886 was critically important to the future of Crater Lake. For the first time, significant measurements and other data were made available to buttress arguments for protection of the region—arguments that, until then, had been based primarily on photographs and impressionistic descriptions. Clarence Dutton and Will Steel, already convinced by their visit in 1885 that Crater Lake deserved the status and protection of a national park, were even more determined to succeed in their campaign for the national park designation after their inspiring and successful experience of 1886.

For Steel, the life-altering character of the 1886 trip was captured vividly in his description of a near-mystical interlude in the group's work: "Once I left camp in the night and pulled out upon the lake's placid surface, then sat quietly in my boat and gazed at the heavens above and the heavens below. Every star above was equally bright below. A vast ball of a universe was around and about me, and I [was] suspended in the center. A great equator hung in space as a monstrous knot hole, and I looked above and below it. Unconsciously I grasped the boat's side with such energy as to ruffle the water, spoil the picture and fix myself on the earth again."[34]

Crater Lake Legislation

SENATOR JOSEPH DOLPH, WHOSE NATIONAL PARK bill for Crater Lake had stalled in committee in 1886, introduced a similar bill in late 1887, in the wake of the successful Dutton-Steel expedition. While that second bill was under consideration by the Committee on Public Lands, U.S. Geological Survey director John Wesley Powell submitted an assessment of the Crater Lake legislation to committee members. Written in terms typical of his keen understanding of the western American landscape, Powell's analysis of the Crater Lake region seems, in many ways, as apt and relevant today as it was more than a hundred years ago.

Powell, in referring to Senator Dolph's bill as "eminently wise and proper," clearly believed that Crater Lake should join Yellowstone in America's exclusive national park pantheon. Comparing the scenic magnificence of Crater Lake and its surroundings favorably to Yellowstone Canyon and Yosemite Valley, the usually stolid Powell declared that "not many natural objects in the world . . . impress the average spectator with so deep a sense of the beauty and majesty of nature."[35]

Powell also grasped the great scientific significance of the region. Demonstrating his rare appreciation for the biological interconnectedness of natural environments, Powell urged an expansion of the proposed park's boundaries in order to accommodate and preserve the area's distinct web of natural life. Referring to a "belt of yellow pine" and to the "winter range and breeding ground of . . . deer and antelope," Powell pointed out that "the eastern boundary, as defined by the [Crater Lake] bill, would exclude portions of the flat summit of the Cascade Range, which ought, by reason of continuity, unity and similarity of features, to be included within the reservation." Likewise, Powell concluded that the designated western boundary would be inadequate. Referring to grand, old-growth forests and grassy parkland areas—acreage containing raw materials that would soon be coveted by timber harvesters, cattle ranchers, and sheepherders—Powell strongly advised extension of the boundary by "some eight or ten miles" to the west. Only by such extension, he argued, could great forests of "Douglas spruce [fir]," sugar pine, and white pine, as well as the "breeding grounds and summer pasturage" of deer and "numerous beaver dams," be protected.[36]

Though Powell's analysis granted that "the northern and southern boundaries of the proposed park" were "well selected," the northern boundary specified in the Crater Lake legislation then under consideration extended some five to six miles beyond the boundary eventually designated in the park's enabling act of 1902. Powell would likely have cautioned against this truncated northern boundary (which remains in effect today), again citing biological factors.[37]

DESPITE POWELL'S CAREFUL ASSESSMENT and recommendations, the Dolph bill succumbed to congressional opposition and inaction in early 1888. At that point, after explaining to Will Steel that "there is no possibility of securing the passage [of a law creating a national park at Crater Lake] at the present session of Congress, and I fear not at any future Congress," Senator Dolph changed course: he introduced a new bill to give the land surrounding Crater Lake to Oregon in trust for a state park.[38]

Steel immediately notified Senator Dolph of his opposition to the state park idea. Arguing that "the state would never make proper provision for [the park's] maintenance" and protection, Steel warned Dolph that he would travel to Washington, D.C., to "do his utmost to defeat such a bill." Even though the federal government had not yet proved willing to maintain the only national park so far established in the United States, Steel believed that the national park designation offered the most promising long-term prospect for the protection of Crater Lake. He was undoubtedly influenced in this belief by John Muir and others who, in the 1870s and 1880s, began to argue for a broadened federal role in the protection of national scenic treasures and publicly owned natural resources.[39]

Despite Steel's dissent, Senator Dolph was able to get his state park bill through the Senate in March 1888. But eventually Steel's opposition combined with the long-standing opposition of special interests and with general congressional apathy to stop the legislation in the House Committee on Public Lands. Steel later exaggerated the impact of his resistance, writing that his initial objection had "had the effect of the senator dropping the entire matter." In fact, Dolph pursued the idea, with at least partial success, not only in 1888 but in 1890, 1892, and 1893.[40]

Mountaineer, Visionary, and Promoter

STEEL TOOK A BREAK FROM HIS POLITICAL campaign during the summer of 1888 to rejuvenate himself with a visit to Crater Lake. Rejuvenation for Will Steel did not mean relaxation, however—at least not in the conventional sense. In a scheme to improve the lake's recreational potential and its attractiveness to tourists, Steel determined to stock Crater Lake (which then, by most accounts, held no fish) with "trout minnows." Thus Steel and two companions set off from a ranch along the Rogue River, transporting around six hundred fish in a bucket of water covered with mosquito netting. When the party's wagon soon proved too bumpy for the delicate operation, Steel got out and carried the bucket some forty miles on foot, stopping now and then to place it "into a stream to cool and to freshen the water." Finally, on September 1, 1888, he released thirty-seven surviving minnows into the lake.[41]

Will Steel (third from right, sitting) and six fellow entrepreneur-outdoorsmen whose "illumination" of Mount Hood in July 1887 drew raves in Portland. J. M. "Johnnie" Breck, Steel's regular hiking and climbing companion, sits on the far right. (OHS neg. OrHi 103405.)

Considering the extent of Will Steel's preoccupation with Crater Lake after 1885, it is sometimes difficult to imagine that he had time for anything else. But he did. In fact, Crater Lake appears to have been merely the strongest among Steel's several strong interests. Known also as "Father of the Mazama Club," Steel's secondary paternity reflected his enthusiasm for mountain climbing in the remarkable mountainous regions of the Pacific Northwest, an enthusiasm he began to develop not long after arriving in Portland as a teenager in 1872. According to his friend Stanton Lapham, "the mind of Will G. Steel was stamped [from childhood] with love of open, wild and beautiful places . . . [while] his dislike of towns and crowded places was inherent."[42]

Understanding something of Steel's broader enthusiasms is important to an understanding of his enormous contributions to Crater Lake and its national park. Steel's passion for mountain climbing and other outdoor activities, shared by a cohort of fellow urban, middle-class professionals (most of them from Portland), was motivated by an urge to promote progress and development throughout the Pacific Northwest. In promoting the region, Steel and his associates often sought to promote their own business interests as well, and many of these first-generation entrepreneur-outdoorsmen came to see the region's interests as inseparable from their own.[43]

At least a few years before Will Steel fell thoroughly under the spell of distant Crater Lake, he was smitten by the allure of nearby Mount Hood. He used his cabin at Mount Hood's Government Camp as a base for mountain-related recreation, including his popular "illuminations." According to a cultural history of the Mazama movement, "Steel helped connect the mountain to the everyday life of Oregonians in the Portland area, as well as to the rest of the state and nation, through . . . displays of luminous explosives [illuminations] on Hood's slopes, meant to be visible in Portland." Steel's first attempt to orchestrate a Mount Hood illumination took place on the Fourth of July, 1885, just a month or so before his first visit to Crater Lake. This and a few later efforts were unsuccessful, in the sense that the displays were not visible from Portland; but Steel and his confederates finally dazzled the city with a spectacular show of fireworks on the Fourth of July, 1887.[44]

The Mount Hood illumination project moved Steel decisively into the camp of regional boosterism. He joined societies and organizations of all sorts, as member or executive, and he stepped to the forefront of the gung-ho contingent proclaiming Oregon as a modern, progressive state. In a further effort to tie together the strands of progressivism, regional promotion, and outdoor achievement, Steel founded the Oregon Alpine Club in Portland in September 1887, just a few months after his first successful illumination of Mount Hood. The organization, conceived and launched in the upper story of the Portland drugstore owned by Steel's frequent mountaineering companion, Johnnie Breck, provided a regular forum for Steel and his friends to plan and discuss their hikes and climbs in the Cascade Mountains. Though the group declared bankruptcy in 1892, the Oregon Alpine Club, during its five years of existence, brought together a broad range of Portland business and professional figures in a moderately successful program of recreation and low-key conservationism.[45]

NOT LONG AFTER HIS FIRST VISIT TO CRATER LAKE, Will Steel became convinced that the U.S. government's public-lands policy required a thorough overhaul. His advocacy of national park status for Crater Lake carried with it the conviction that the federal government should not merely distribute the public domain to private interests but should manage public lands in the people's long-term, collective interest. At the same time, while he counted himself among those favoring expansion and conservation of public lands, Steel generally supported development and "use" of the public domain as opposed to preservation of public lands as wilderness. His enthusiasms as a regional promoter and publicist easily attached to the natural areas he loved, and he avidly believed that public ownership could best be served by providing maximum access to these areas.[46]

"The average tourist," Steel once remarked, "is willing to pay for his scenery, but is not willing to endure hardship to enjoy it." In adopting this outlook, which shaped his approach to preserving Crater Lake and other scenic wonders, Steel anticipated the strategies and dilemmas of National Park Service planners and managers in the twentieth century. And in this outlook Steel more accurately reflected the values of his time than did his fellow preservationists and sometime political allies John Muir and John B. Waldo, whose more ecologically sophisticated ideas pointed ahead at least several decades.[47]

When Yosemite, General Grant, and Sequoia national parks were established in 1890, their enabling legislation continued to reflect patterns set earlier in the Yosemite Valley and Yellowstone acts. As historian Alfred Runte has observed, "There evolved in Congress a firm (if unwritten) policy that only 'worthless' lands might be set aside as national parks." In its eagerness to maintain private access to resource-rich lands—for lumbering, mining, grazing, and farming—Congress by default chose "monumentalism, not environmentalism," as the defining principle for the earliest national parks. Thus, as Will Steel and others continued their campaign for a national park at Crater Lake in the 1890s, they did so in the face of hardening national priorities that appeared to embrace scenic preservation only where it did not conflict with material prosperity.[48]

The Cascade Forest Reserve

IN AN EFFORT TO COUNTER THE CONTINUING opposition to proposals for a national park at Crater Lake, Will Steel launched another mail campaign in 1890. He quickly brought together several of his essays, intended originally as separate pamphlets, and published them in the form of a book, *The Mountains of Oregon*. Steel sent copies of the finished volume to President Benjamin Harrison and his cabinet, to members of Congress, and to newspaper editors throughout the country. Though he received plaudits for his work, concrete results were few. Congressman Hermann introduced a new Crater Lake national park bill in early 1892, but that legislation, like its predecessor in 1886, failed to survive committee debates.[49]

Though Congress had opened the door to California's three new national parks in 1890, it closed the door again—and even more firmly when the nation sank into serious economic depression in 1893. While initiative to create a national park at Crater Lake lay mostly dormant during the 1890s, the decade did witness tremendous progress in the institutionalization of federally reserved forestlands in Oregon.

In 1890, following up on nearly two decades of warnings about widespread abuse and exploitation of the nation's forests and watersheds, an American Association for the Advancement of Science committee recommended to President Harrison that forested lands belonging to the United States be withdrawn from sale and kept in reserve, pending formation of "a permanent system of forest administration." In response, and with the Harrison administration's support, Congress passed the Forest Reserve Act of 1891, which repealed the much-abused Timber Culture Act of 1873 and the Timber Cutting Act of 1878. All told, President Harrison's administration (1889-1893) set aside more than thirteen million acres of the public domain as forest reserves, most in California, Oregon, and Wyoming.[50]

Realizing that the township withdrawal of 1886 remained vulnerable to overrule by future presidents, Will Steel saw in the new Forest Reserve Act a potential bulwark against private encroachment on Crater Lake. Oregon supreme court justice John B. Waldo had first suggested to Steel, in 1886, the idea of incorporating Crater Lake into a vast federal reserve extending the entire length of Oregon's Cascade Mountain range. Though Steel remained preoccupied with his national park quest for several years after 1886, by the early 1890s he was prepared to entertain some sort of "backdoor" protection for Crater Lake.[51]

☙

JOHN BRECKENRIDGE WALDO was undoubtedly the most avid explorer of wilderness areas in late-nineteenth-century Oregon. Each summer, from 1880 until his death in 1907, he and friends explored largely untouched areas of the High Cascades. In 1888 he undertook his first and only journey all the way to California's Mount Shasta, an excursion that included his second stop at Crater Lake, made with the specific goal of reaching Wizard Island.[52]

Having failed in his bid for reelection to the state supreme court in 1886, Waldo ran successfully for a seat in the Oregon legislature in the fall of 1888, just after returning from his explorations of the southern Cascades. He then promptly introduced House Joint Memorial

Number 8, an appeal to the federal government for the establishment of a forest reserve extending twelve miles on both sides of the Cascades, into the 1889 legislative session. But the memorial eventually succumbed to the vigorous opposition of grazing interests.[53]

By 1891, when the Forest Reserve Act was signed into law, Waldo had retired from his one term in the state legislature. Steel, frustrated with the stalled national park campaign and recalling his friend's earlier interest in a national forest reserve in the Cascades, contacted Waldo with the idea that the Forest Reserve Act might be useful to their mutual aims. Waldo welcomed Steel's continued interest in the cause, and the letters between the two men reawakened an acquaintance and began a collaboration that did much not only to safeguard Crater Lake but also to lay a foundation for the modern national forest system in Oregon.[54]

The next year, with Waldo providing volunteer legal services, Steel and the Oregon Alpine Club circulated a petition calling for "a forest reserve along the entire crest of the Cascades." Having picked up widespread support in Oregon, including a memorial sent to President Cleveland from the state legislature, and with an endorsement from the Cleveland administration's own Interior Department, Steel's petition and proposal were forwarded to the president, who proclaimed the Cascade Range Forest Reserve—the nation's largest such reserve—on September 28, 1893. On balance, this proclamation was probably as important to the future of Crater Lake as Cleveland's withdrawal of the ten townships surrounding the lake had been in 1886, during his first administration.[55]

THE BATTLE WAS HARDLY WON, however, since Congress provided no means for the protection of the new Cascade reserve, or for any of the sixteen other forest reserves. Private trespass, plunder of timber and wildlife, and fire (sometimes caused by herders who intentionally burned forest to create better range for their stock) continued to plague these "reserved" forests. Interior Secretary Hoke Smith sounded a clear alarm in his annual report for 1894. Referring to the seventeen million acres of public land then reserved, Smith charged that most of these acres "are no more protected by the Government than are the unreserved lands of the United States . . . owing to the limited force of special [General Land Office] agents."[56]

While little opposition to the Cascade Range Forest Reserve was expressed at the time of the proclamation, protests escalated over the

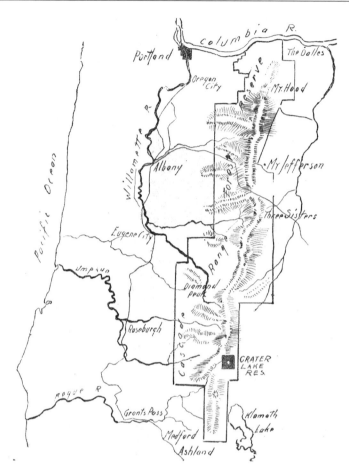

This map of western Oregon includes the outlined area of the Cascade Range Forest Reserve, which stretched nearly the entire length of the state. The reserve's boundaries embraced ten townships around Crater Lake (shaded rectangular area, at lower right), withdrawn from the market by the Cleveland administration in 1886. (Courtesy NPS, CLNP Museum and Archives Collection.)

next several years. Secretary Smith's 1894 report, citing instances of wanton destruction of public property on the forest reserves, decried "the spirit of lawlessness prevailing among those depredating upon these lands," in Oregon and elsewhere. After a federal edict in April 1894 outlawed the "driving, feeding, grazing, pasturing, or herding of livestock" on the reserves, an organized political movement against the Cascade reserve coalesced in Oregon, led by sheep owners and Klamath County settlers.[57]

Opponents mounted a vigorous propaganda campaign, aimed both at popular opinion and the state's political leadership. Their efforts were rewarded in 1895 when the Oregon legislature passed a memorial requesting that a portion of the reserve be reopened for "sale, purchase, settlement, and homestead." Reserve opponents achieved an even greater success later that year when the state's congressional delegation, which at that time consisted of John Mitchell and George W. McBride in the U.S. Senate and William R. Ellis and Binger Hermann in the House, adopted their goal to reduce the size of the reserve. Senator Mitchell took the lead, arguing, in a letter to the General Land Office, that the boundaries of the Cascade Range Forest Reserve encompassed "entirely too extensive a region" and had been a "grave mistake."[58]

Between 1895 and 1900, Steel, Waldo, and Judge Charles B. Bellinger led a staunch defense of the Cascade reserve, an extraordinary political effort that eventually defeated their own state's congressional delegation by appealing directly to the executive branch. Much of this lobbying effort was officially channeled through the Mazama Club, the mountaineering group Steel had organized in 1894 to replace the defunct Oregon Alpine Club. Representing the Mazama Club's executive council, and urged on by Waldo, Bellinger, and others, Steel set up camp in Washington, D.C., for several months during the spring of 1896 to orchestrate the political effort to save the reserve.[59]

Waldo kept in close contact with Steel during these months, advising, exhorting, and cautioning his ally as complex political maneuverings, as well as Steel's poverty, buffeted him through a range of moods and tempers. At the same time, Waldo kept up a separate lobbying campaign, representing both himself and Judge Bellinger, for example, in a remarkable appeal to President Cleveland in April 1896. Describing some of the diverse natural features of the Cascade reserve with a precision and care that came from his extensive firsthand experience, Waldo dismissed the potential for agriculture in the high-altitude, volcanic terrain of the Cascade Range, and he accused homesteaders of settling in the Cascades "not for homes, but for the timber." He saved his most colorful vitriol to describe the terrific destruction done to the Cascade forests by herds of sheep, concluding sardonically that "a wise government will know that to raise men is much more important than to raise sheep, or men of the nature of sheep."[60]

WHILE THE DEFENDERS OF THE CASCADE Range Forest Reserve were ultimately successful, the conduct of their defense revealed conspicuous

Congressman Binger Hermann, once Will Steel's ally in the long campaign to bring national park status to Crater Lake, later became his avowed enemy. (OHS neg. CN 010269.)

rifts among the partisans. And because Will Steel stood consistently in the front lines of the battle, most of these rifts touched him in one way or another. Details of the intricate political calculations brought to bear in the reserve campaign—as revealed in struggles between friend and foe, but also in disagreements among friends—pertain more to the history of Oregon's national forests than to the history of Crater Lake National Park. However, some attention to Steel's role in these disputes provides important insight into the personality of a man whose imprint on Crater Lake and its national park was profound.

When Steel traveled to Washington in 1896, his primary *acknowledged* purpose was to represent the coalition resisting organized efforts to reduce the size and diminish the protections of the Cascade Range Forest Reserve. Steel's less-acknowledged goal was to land a job for himself. As he saw it, he had already worked more than a decade in the public interest, spending his own meager resources and receiving little or nothing in return. He had no expectation of lavish public compensation, but he thought it only fair that, for all his work, he would be "provided for," as he put it in a letter to Congressman Hermann in 1897. He was self-conscious about his lack of success as a businessman and his reliance on brothers and friends for support, and he rationalized, with some justification, that his hardship was the direct result of his extensive, uncompensated work in the public interest.[61]

When Steel went to Washington, D.C., in the spring of 1896, he and his allies had already concluded correctly that Oregon's congressional delegation was working against them. At the same time, Steel had his sights set on the job of superintendent of the Cascade reserve and knew that Oregon's two senior members of Congress, Senator Mitchell and Congressman Hermann, were well placed to assist him in his bid.

Because of his mixed motives, Steel's language, rhetoric, and tone changed according to his correspondent during this time. In general, he was more firm in defending the Cascade reserve in his letters to John Waldo and other reserve partisans than in his correspondence with members of the Oregon congressional delegation and other officers of the federal government. Some among Steel's Cascade reserve allies in Oregon, whose interests he was ostensibly representing, eventually came to question his judgment, especially after he briefly became a member of Senator Mitchell's staff in 1896.[62]

Portland attorney T. Brook White, then serving as Mazama Club historian, scolded Steel in a letter written in April: "It is unfortunate that your financial necessities have obliged you ever to do a stroke of work for the man [Senator Mitchell] who of all others it is most essential that you should be free of obligation to, in order to meet him on even terms." Four days later, White wrote to Steel again. Perceiving that Steel had wavered in the fight, and sensing that his ultimate loyalties might even be at stake under the influence of the wily Mitchell, White resorted to flattery: "Credit will be yours of having gone down to Washington and commenced single handed a fight against the united delegation from your own state."[63]

Steel also tried to avoid alienating Congressman Hermann, at least for as long as the job of reserve superintendent remained unfilled. However, as soon as Hermann, in his new position as commissioner of the General Land Office, appointed Captain Salmon B. Ormsby to the post, Steel unleashed his fury. Writing to Commissioner Hermann in July 1897, Steel bristled: "After your many statements in the presence of third parties, that the State of Oregon and posterity owed me a debt of gratitude for my lifelong service in the interest of our mountains and forests, I must say that I am both surprised and pained, to learn . . . that [your] friendship was not genuine. . . . I believe your sense of honor will compel you to realize that you have done wrong, have made a mistake, and I certainly hope it will be strong enough to move you to such action as will demonstrate it."[64]

The 1896 Mazama Club Convention at Crater Lake

Excursion

. . . TO . . . .

Crater Lake

UNDER THE AUSPICES OF THE

MAZAMAS

DURING WEEK OF

AUGUST 16, 1896.

❧ ❧ ❧

ASSISTED BY THE

Crater Lake Clubs of Ashland
Medford and Klamath
Falls, Or.

(OHS neg. OrHi 103399.)

As Will Steel pursued a delicate course between potentially conflicting personal and political ends during the first half of 1896, Crater Lake continued to loom large in his mind. Determined not to allow the fate of his first priority, Crater Lake, to become too strongly identified with the huge, less distinctive Cascade reserve, Steel took steps to place the cause of Crater Lake back at center stage. As founder and past president of the Mazama Club, he instigated a convention and mountain-climbing tour at Crater Lake in August 1896. Steel's earlier fruitful dealings with the U.S. Geological Survey helped him enlist an impressive company of government scientists for the gathering: C. Hart Merriam, chief of the U.S. Biological Survey; J. S. Diller, geologist of the U.S. Geological Survey; Frederick V. Coville, chief botanist of the U.S. Department of Agriculture; and Barton W. Evermann, ichthyologist of the U.S. Fish Commission.[65]

In addition to some fifty or sixty Mazama Club members and the scientists, several hundred other interested persons, including representatives of local "Crater Lake clubs," traveled to the event by wagon or on foot from Ashland, Medford, Klamath Falls, the Klamath Indian Reservation, and the Fort Klamath army post. Guided nature walks and campfire lectures on the flora, fauna, and geology of the region transformed the occasion into a kind of mountain chautauqua. Mazama Club president C. H. Sholes described the scene with graphic gusto:

> *Every day for three weeks was full of interest and charm, unmarred by a single incident or disappointment. The long days' marches through the broiling sun; pitching the nightly camp, followed by happy hours around the evening camp fire, now enlivened by songs, recitations and stories. . . . This inimitable aggregation of scientist, student, artist, explorer,*

En route to their Crater Lake destination during the summer of 1896, several dozen Mazama Club members climbed Mount McLoughlin (still known by some as Mount Pitt), the graceful peak lying south of the park and northeast of Medford. Here club members show the colors and pose triumphantly at the summit. (Mazamas 015-1993-P2.)

health-seeker and mirth-provoker, of wild jollity, exuberance and irrepressible good nature, all mingled day after day and kept in unceasing turn without one crank, are themes for the Historian's pen, and are only briefly mentioned here to revive for a moment some of the exquisite memories of the never-to-be-forgotten Mazama excursion to Crater Lake.[66]

The excursion concluded with special observances at the rim of Crater Lake on August 21, 1896. For the occasion, Fay Fuller, first historian of the Mazamas, was given charge of a ceremonial bottle of water, obtained from Crater Lake during the group's executive council meeting on Wizard Island. Stanton Lapham described Fuller's honorary role: "Enthusiastic lover of wild places, and the first white woman to climb to the top of Mount Rainier, she was honored on this occasion with the christening of Mount Mazama. She crashed the bottle of crystal water, from the bluest depths in the world, against a rock from the mountain side, declaring, 'I dedicate thee Mount Mazama.'" Later, when darkness fell, campers reassembled at the rim to watch a spectacular display of fireworks unleashed from the Wizard Island crater.[67]

Two conventioneers take time out from scheduled events for a picture at Crater Lake's Cathedral Rock. (Mazamas 015-1999-P3.)

Steel's multifaceted convention was an unqualified success: by engaging the interest and support of several prominent scientists with ties to the federal government, he managed to get the Crater Lake national park campaign firmly back on track. The country was emerging from the depression of 1893, and Congress was at last reawakening to the national park idea, as it would demonstrate tangibly in 1899 with the establishment of Mount Rainier National Park.

Riding on the momentum of the well-publicized event, the Mazama Club in 1897 launched a periodical, entitled *Mazama*, which avidly promoted national park status for Crater Lake. The second issue of the new journal, with articles by scientists Diller, Coville, Merriam, and Evermann (all of whom also came forward in support of the eventual legislation creating Crater Lake National Park), was given over entirely to the subject of Crater Lake. This historic publication, which also included an article on Crater Lake's early history and a report on the Mazama convention of 1896, served as a guidebook for Crater Lake excursionists for years to come.[68]

THE TIRELESS WILL STEEL DID DOUBLE duty at Crater Lake during the summer of 1896. In addition to staging the Mazama event, he served as guide for the Crater Lake portion of the National Forest Commission's investigation of forested reserve lands in the West. In fact, by well-conceived plan, Steel brought luminaries from the two parties together at Crater Lake in late August. This was no small physical and logistical feat: Steel took leave of his Mazama comrades during the convention, walked some eighty-five miles in two days to Medford, caught the northbound train to Portland, met and conferred with the Forest Commission members, accompanied them by train to Ashland, and then outfitted the party and escorted them over Dead Indian Road to the lake.[69]

Forest Commission members, including such big names as John Muir, Charles S. Sargent, and Alexander Agassiz, were mixed in their views of the national park campaign for Crater Lake. Emerging wilderness superstar John Muir, for one, remained lukewarm to the idea. But another key commission member, Gifford Pinchot, appears to have become a confirmed Crater Lake national park advocate as a result of his brief visit in 1896. While Muir noted later that the area's forests had been "horribly blackened and devastated by devilish fires," Pinchot proclaimed Crater Lake "a wonder of the world . . . which can best be protected as a national park."[70]

The Forest Commission eventually finished its task and reported to Congress and President William McKinley on the condition of federal forests in May 1897. While the resulting Organic Act (or Sundry Civil Appropriations Act) of 1897 reaffirmed the president's power to create reserves and confirmed all forest reserves established before 1897, the new legislation also reflected persistent divisions within the country on the disposition of public lands, especially forested lands. Congress would remain squeezed between a well-organized eastern lobby that advocated liberal forest reserves and the new science of forestry, on one side, and a militant faction in the West that opposed all public-land withdrawals and forest-protection measures.[71]

Distortion of the Crater Lake Past

IN THE COURSE OF WILL STEEL'S CRUSADE to sanctify Crater Lake as a monument to Pacific Northwest progress and enlightenment, a fundamental part of Crater Lake's past was lost, at least temporarily. This loss was by no means Steel's fault alone. But Steel, who contributed more than anyone else to the earliest public perceptions of Crater Lake, contributed both to the truths and the untruths that came to dominate those public perceptions.

A native man and woman, dressed in the garb of white settlers, pose for a photograph on the grounds of the Klamath Reservation agency. The Bureau of Indian Affairs, in its determination to quash traditional Indian spirituality, reinforced distortions of the historical link between Crater Lake and regional native cultures. (Courtesy NPS, CLNP Museum and Archives Collection.)

By the time Steel finally reached Crater Lake in 1885, the Indian peoples who had once lived in the lands surrounding the great mountain lake had been either obliterated or subdued. The Klamath Indians alone, of the four tribes whose traditional homelands lay closest to Crater Lake, continued to live in the area in significant numbers, playing a role in regional events and bearing witness to their traditional culture. During the late nineteenth and early twentieth centuries, as the new culture of the whites sealed its domination over the old cultures of the natives, the real historical relationship of the Klamath Indians to Crater Lake and its environs was gradually distorted. And as a result, the truth about the historical relationship between the Indians and the great mountain lake—an essential component of the region's past— was temporarily lost.

Will Steel knew from his own investigations that the historical link between the Klamath people and Crater Lake was rich and complex, and yet he contributed to a grossly simplified portrayal of it. En route to Crater Lake for the first time in 1885, Steel interviewed Allen David, chief of the Klamath, at Fort Klamath. Among the Crater Lake traditions that David shared with Steel was one that clearly conveyed the intricate mixture of power, awe, and reverence that the place held traditionally for the Klamath people. Moreover, a few of Steel's friends and contemporaries wrote knowingly and sympathetically of Klamath ties to Crater Lake. In 1876, for example, historian Frances Fuller Victor paid homage to the Klamaths' conduct of "solemn spiritual rites" on the "sacred ground" of the Crater Lake area.[72]

Nonetheless, Steel joined most of his contemporaries in perpetuating the crude idea that Klamath natives simply feared Crater Lake, an attitude supposedly rooted in superstitions about vengeful monsters inhabiting the place. This grotesquely oversimplified notion stemmed, in part, from the Indians' own earlier efforts to divert the newcomers' interest in Crater Lake by pretending ignorance or fear of it. By 1880, however, the Indians knew that their attempts to dissuade whites from visiting the sacred mountain lake had failed, and they began to share the real story of their peoples' deep traditional ties to the site.[73]

The failure of Steel and most of his contemporaries to embrace the more complicated version of traditional Klamath ties to Crater Lake, and to include the fuller story faithfully in their own evolving account of the Crater Lake past, is difficult to explain. One suspects a combination of the period's endemic racism, often expressed in the tendency to gloss over cultural complexities of nonwhite peoples; intellectual laziness, often manifested in oversimplifications used in political campaigns; and perhaps an apprehension that the long and difficult path to national park status could become even more treacherous if an indigenous people's religious practices were fully acknowledged.

The caricature of the Klamath relationship to Crater Lake, born in the late nineteenth century and perpetuated well into the twentieth, is exemplified in a notable incident from 1896. According to the standard account of the Mazama convention of that year, some two hundred Klamath Indians joined the final festivities at the caldera rim. The Indians, so the story goes, had maintained their dread of Crater Lake until this occasion, when whites showed them they had nothing to fear from the place. Following that demystifying lesson, Steel and many others often insisted, the Indians visited Crater Lake freely and without fear. This momentous occasion, routinely interpreted as a childlike overcoming of fear through the mediation of knowing adults, appears to us now a kind of mass religious disillusionment rooted in the desecration of a sacred place.[74]

A scene from that summer of 1896, frequently narrated for its comic effect in Crater Lake historical annals, takes on new meaning in this context: "Mr. Steel relates that an old Indian of the tribe—a gray-haired patriarch—his face seamed by many seasons, in moccasins, scanty garb and blanket, moved slowly and alone to the great brink of the Lake. Unmoving as stone, he stood on the rim for a time, his deep eyes fastened on the Lake and cliffs. He seemed a strange figure from ages long past, poised high above the mysterious Lake of legend and story. Suddenly he turned, buried his face in his hands and hurried from the scene, to be discovered afterward hiding behind one of the tents, his hands still covering his eyes."[75]

Chapter 4

Birth and Early Years of Oregon's National Park

1897-1916

Traveling to Crater Lake, circa 1900

WILL STEEL RELISHED HIS ARDUOUS mountain treks to Crater Lake. He even welcomed the occasional extra challenges posed by weather, natural encumbrances, or the need to transport something or someone other than himself. But he also knew that most potential Crater Lake visitors did not share his fondness for rugged cross-country travel.

Steel had observed that once people saw Crater Lake, they could usually be counted on to join the national park campaign. But as the new century approached, and as the time seemed ripe again to press the cause in Washington, D.C., Steel and other Crater Lake enthusiasts realized that access to the great mountain lake was still maddeningly difficult for most tourists. Between 1895 and 1905, while heightened publicity about Crater Lake sparked the interest of greater numbers of potential visitors (and potential supporters of the proposed national park), the various routes to the place remained so demanding that only the most experienced and hardened travelers dared undertake the journey.[1]

In the special 1897 *Mazama* issue on Crater Lake, Mazama Club secretary Earl Morse Wilbur dealt gingerly with the subject of access. This special issue of the journal had been planned partly as a tool of political persuasion, and Wilbur realized that his introductory essay would likely play a key role in the publication's overall impact. The Portland clergyman wrote with infectious enthusiasm about the beauty and uniqueness of the area, focusing on the landmarks and vistas that have continued to captivate visitors over decades. In describing the

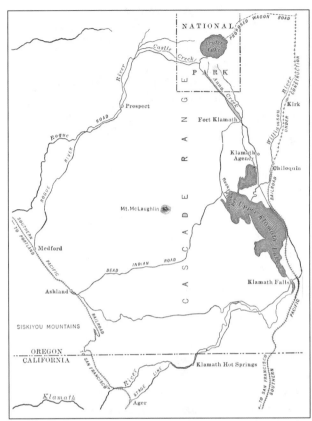

Map showing three principal turn-of-the-century routes to Crater Lake: from the southwest, along Rogue River Road; from the south, along Dead Indian Road; and from the southeast, along the Fort Klamath stage line. (Courtesy National Park Service, Crater Lake National Park Museum and Archives Collection.)

few possible routes of travel to Crater Lake, Wilbur hoped to convey the remoteness of the place and the need for improved access to it without, at the same time, discouraging anyone from attempting the trip. Consequently, he emphasized the "attractions for the tourist," as he put it, that each approach offered. The hearty adventurers who actually traveled any of the three main routes at that time tended to be more impressed by the strenuousness and tedium of their horseback, shank's mare, or wagon journey than by the "attractions."[2]

The three principal routes to Crater Lake that took shape in the second half of the nineteenth century played important roles in the region's overall history. The shortest of the three (some eighty miles) led from the Southern Pacific Railroad terminus in Medford up the Rogue River valley. This route, which required at least three days of travel, was eased by comfortable accommodations along the way, in the village of Trail the first night and in Prospect the second. The climb toward Mount Mazama was gradual for most of this river-bearing course; but the last day's journey, which took travelers of all three routes

In August 1903 Will Steel led a wagon party, which included poet Joaquin Miller, along Rogue River Road to Crater Lake. The caravan's embarkation from Medford is documented here. (OHS neg. OrHi 102403.)

across the Cascade divide some three miles south of Crater Lake, was made more difficult by steeper grades (the final three miles rising about a thousand feet) and pumice sand on the road's surface.[3]

Attractions cited by Wilbur along this route included historic Table Rock; the Lower Falls of the Rogue River, as well as Mill Creek and Barr Creek falls; magnificent sugar pine forests; a natural bridge of basalt lava stretching across the Rogue River just a few miles below the mouth of Union Creek; spectacularly deep canyons with intricately sculpted walls and raging rapids; and handsome forests of noble and Shasta fir.[4]

A second route to Crater Lake, along Dead Indian Road, covered slightly less than a hundred miles and was even more gradual in its elevation. Beginning at the railroad station in Ashland, this approach required at least four days of travel. And since lodging was either scarce or unavailable along the way, finding good camping grounds was vital. Wilbur suggested camps at Hunt's Ranch (approximately twenty-two miles from Ashland), Pelican Bay (forty-seven miles along the way), and in the vicinity of Fort Klamath (seventy-two miles distant). Citing the rockiness of the road, as well as a fifteen-mile stretch plagued by deep sand, Wilbur advised against automobile touring. From the Fort Klamath area, the final stretch followed Annie Creek and Annie Creek Canyon until it joined the Rogue River route about three miles from the rim of the lake.[5]

Some of the most enticing attractions for Dead Indian Road travelers required brief side trips. For example, while lovely Lake of the Woods lay directly along the route, at least two extra days were needed for an ascent of Mount McLoughlin, with its magnificent views of Crater Lake, Mount Shasta, Diamond Peak, the Three Sisters, and other peaks and lakes of the region. Likewise, Pelican Bay, famous for its fishing and duck hunting, was near enough to the route for travelers to enjoy

Three members of Will Steel's party of 1903 pose atop the remarkable natural basalt bridge spanning the Rogue River, one of the most picturesque spots along the southwesterly route to Crater Lake. (OHS neg. OrHi 103401.)

easily, but a close inspection of abandoned Fort Klamath required a detour of a couple miles. An additional detour of five miles from Fort Klamath led to the Klamath Reservation agency, near the Williamson River, where "the trout fishing is said to be the finest on the Pacific Coast," Wilbur claimed.[6]

The third main route left the railroad at Ager, California, and proceeded through Klamath Falls to Fort Klamath, where it joined Dead Indian Road. This longest approach (about one hundred sixteen miles) was also the easiest to travel. It was even navigable by automobile, Wilbur advised. A daily stage ran from Ager along the Klamath River and through the Cascade Range to Klamath Falls, where tourists could "obtain conveyances and camping outfits for the rest of the way." The journey between Klamath Falls and Crater Lake required at least two days.[7]

The delights of this third route included Klamath Hot Springs, increasingly well known for its mud and sulfur baths, and several points of special geological interest, such as "the older tilted lavas of the Cascade Range, . . . well exposed . . . at many points along the Klamath River road between Ager and Klamath Hot Springs," according to geologist J. S. Diller. Wilbur recommended "a side trip of two or three days from Klamath Falls to the Lava Beds, interesting on their own account, and made famous by the tragedy of the Modoc War."[8]

A wagon party, which included Interior Secretary James R. Garfield (son of the assassinated president), here traverses the Fort Klamath stage route, via Klamath Falls, in 1907. This southeasterly course was the longest but easiest to travel of the three main approaches to Crater Lake. (OHS neg. OrHi 87265.)

Late-nineteenth-century travelers of all types took a keen interest in recently abandoned Fort Klamath. Jacksonville resident Fletcher Linn, en route to Crater Lake with two male and three female companions in 1889, noted in his diary that "the 'Stars and Stripes' was still floating over the deserted spot, [which] seemed to offer all the protection necessary." And seven years later, George W. Kirkman, reporting for *Harper's Weekly*, seemed to find grisly satisfaction in his tour of the old fort: "We paid a visit to the gaunt skeleton of the scaffold from which 'Captain Jack' and other Modocs were hanged at the close of the fierce Lava Beds war of '72, and also inspected their graves near the old post guard-house."[9]

ONCE ARRIVED IN THE VICINITY OF CRATER LAKE—whether approaching from the southwest (Rogue River Road), south (Dead Indian Road), or southeast (Fort Klamath stage line)—travelers had to make the final steep climb up Dutton Creek. Then, according to Wilbur, the exhausted wayfarer finally emerged "upon a plateau, bordered with evergreen trees, and carpeted with various-hued flowers." After walking "across the plateau a few hundred yards, one finds oneself unexpectedly at the edge of a precipice," with the great lake below. At this momentous point, having arrived on the scene "just after sunrise," the Linn party of August 1889 was disappointed to find their "view of the lake . . . greatly obstructed by smoke." Because of this well-known and potentially devastating possibility, Wilbur, in his 1897 article, recommended that tours of Crater Lake be undertaken in July rather than in August or September, because later in the season "the atmosphere is often thick with smoke from forest fires."[10]

The dearth of hotel or other permanent accommodations plagued the turn-of-the-century pilgrim to Crater Lake, not just en route, of course, but at the rim of the caldera as well. Thus, upon arrival, camping needs could not be ignored amid the enchantments of the lake and other impressive sights. One such need, in those days, was finding pasture for the beasts of burden who handled much of the heavy transport for visiting parties. "Good camping grounds with plenty of pasture" were available on Castle Creek, Diller noted, but those camps were nearly three miles from the popular camping sites at the rim, where camping was easy but pasture and water were difficult to find.[11]

Despite these shortages of water and pasture—problems that would vex Crater Lake rim tourists for years to come—increasing numbers of visitors attempted to circle the lake on hiking and camping trips of

This tent encampment at the rim of Crater Lake was set up in August 1902. The party was led by Will Steel (kneeling, in mid-foreground) and included his brother James and Oregon's governor, Theodore T. Geer. (Courtesy NPS, CLNP Museum and Archives Collection.)

typically four to five days. A pack train was advised for these treks, "as the distance around the crest of the rim is over twenty miles and over much of the route traveling is difficult," Diller cautioned. Some five or six optimal camping spots, starting from the most popular above Eagle Cove, were soon well established along the way. Though the availability of water and pasture varied greatly (some of the best natural areas for grass, wood, and water had already been seriously degraded by sheep), the bounty of breathtaking views and other attractions was seemingly endless.[12]

Wilbur's recommendations for the rim circuit emphasized modest ascents: of Mount Scott ("not at all difficult [to climb] and affords a fine view"); of Llao Rock; of Red Cone (featuring a summit crater "about seventy feet deep"); of Glacier Peak; and of the Watchman. More ambitious climbers, he suggested, could take a two- or three-day side trip to Mount Thielsen, "which is steep and difficult enough to climb to challenge the skill of the mountaineer." Other rim hikers preferred less elevated locations, such as one near Grayback Ridge, where "fine firs and flowers" proliferated, Diller wrote: "The great cliffs are inspiring, and the rustling of numerous little cascades gives a life to this enclosed camp that is not to be found elsewhere about the lake."[13]

The Triumph of 1902

THE MUCH-PUBLICIZED MAZAMA CONVENTION at Crater Lake in 1896, and the scientific interest in the Crater Lake region that flourished in the event's aftermath, helped give new life to the national park campaign. The election of Oregon's Thomas H. Tongue to Congress in 1897 turned out to be equally important. The separate streams of popular, scientific, and political momentum converged during Republican Tongue's first term, when he introduced new legislation to establish a national park at Crater Lake. The four scientists who published articles in the "Crater Lake issue" of *Mazama* that same year—J. S. Diller, Frederick V. Coville, C. Hart Merriam, and Barton W. Evermann— were among those who signed on officially in support of Congressman Tongue's bill.[14]

Diller's *Mazama* article, as well as two others he wrote that year— one published in *National Geographic Magazine* and the other in the *American Journal of Science*—built upon the earlier reports and speculations of Captain Clarence Dutton and his colleagues. Comparing the geological profile of Mount Mazama and Crater Lake with

U.S. Geological Survey scientist J. S. Diller, premier geological interpreter of Mount Mazama and Crater Lake during the first quarter of the twentieth century. Diller's contribution to the Crater Lake National Park enabling act of 1902 exceeded even that of Will Steel. (Courtesy NPS, CLNP Museum and Archives Collection.)

characteristics of other notable volcanoes worldwide, Diller theorized a general framework of geological transformation that has been largely corroborated by subsequent science. His concluding paragraph in the *National Geographic* article was calculated to grab the attention of members of Congress and other political leaders: "Aside from its attractive scenic features, Crater Lake affords one of the most interesting and instructive fields for the study of volcanic geology to be found anywhere in the world. Considered in all its aspects, it ranks with the Grand Canyon of the Colorado, the Yosemite Valley, and the Falls of Niagara, and should be set aside as a National Park for the pleasure and instruction of the people."[15]

While the geological distinctiveness and sheer magnificence of the lake were bound to be central to any proposal for a Crater Lake national park, Steel and others reasoned that further evidence of the area's broader scientific significance could prove valuable to the cause. Thus Coville's "The August Vegetation of Mount Mazama, Oregon" and Merriam's "The Mammals of Mount Mazama, Oregon," both published in the special *Mazama* issue, were partly intended to push the focus of the national park drive beyond the central feature of Crater Lake, and to lend greater legitimacy to boundaries that, according to any of the various national park proposals, would encompass well over a hundred thousand acres and extend at least several miles beyond Crater Lake in each direction.[16]

Evermann's contribution to the special issue of *Mazama* dealt not just with of the presence of fish in Crater Lake (he found none, thus temporarily suggesting that Will Steel's planting of minnows in 1888

After J. S. Diller's initial visit to Crater Lake in 1883, he returned several times, building on his understanding and interpretation of Mount Mazama's geological character. This photograph, taken on one of Diller's later trips, points westerly along the south rim from Sun Notch. (Courtesy NPS, CLNP Museum and Archives Collection.)

Congressman Thomas Tongue of Oregon introduced the legislation, signed by President Theodore Roosevelt in May 1902, that authorized formation of Crater Lake National Park. Tongue posed at a scenic rim location during a triumphant visit with Will Steel and others in August 1902. (Courtesy NPS, CLNP Museum and Archives Collection.)

had been unsuccessful) but with broader questions of water quality and forms of life in and around the lake. His discoveries of small crustaceans, larval insects, and a mollusk species in the lake, and of salamanders along the shore, were important finds in themselves, as well as further indications that Crater Lake *could* sustain fish life.[17]

Nonetheless, despite impressive scientific and political support, Congressman Tongue's Crater Lake national park bill, like its predecessors, failed to come to a vote before the full House. In the next session of Congress (1899-1900), Oregon's George W. McBride sponsored a Crater Lake bill in the Senate, and Congressman Tongue advanced his legislation again in the House. Although both bills eventually fell short, Tongue's legislation did receive unanimous approval from the Public Lands Committee.[18]

By 1899, Steel felt encouraged that the Crater Lake national park campaign was back on track in Congress. He could also conclude, with some pride, that his role in the successful defense of the Cascade Range Forest Reserve had helped preserve an effective forest buffer for Crater Lake at a time when political momentum for the new national park had stalled. Steel and John Waldo joined forces to fend off one last radical attempt by sheep owners to reduce the size of the Cascade reserve in 1899. Both men emerged from the skirmish as firm opponents of continued General Land Office (GLO) jurisdiction over the forest reserves. While Waldo clearly believed that the GLO was unwilling and unable to protect the Cascade forests from damage done by sheep grazing, mining, and timber harvesting, Steel was motivated at least as much by his animosity toward former Oregon congressman Binger Hermann, now head of the GLO.[19]

IN LATE 1901, CONGRESSMAN TONGUE introduced the bill that would, in less than a year, formally establish Crater Lake National Park. Sensing an opportunity for victory, Steel fired up his publicity machine once more, calling on the state's newspapers and postmasters to circulate a Crater Lake petition addressed to the U.S. Senate and House of Representatives, and beseeching his allies to send letters of support and the names of other Crater Lake sympathizers to Tongue. Steel's circulating petition was also available for signing at Portland's Woodard, Clarke & Co., a retail outlet for photographic materials. In order to attract potential petition signers, a local newspaper reported, Steel "placed a number of photographs and charts of the wonderful lake" in the store's show window.[20]

The establishment of Mount Rainier National Park in 1899 had signaled to preservationists that additional national park designations might be possible. Nonetheless, national park supporters realized that, in advancing any new park proposals, they would have to claim that the areas in question were commercially "worthless." Accordingly, Steel's petition to Congress included a version of the disclaimer that would become commonplace in national park political campaigns and legislation well into the twentieth century: "Adjoining the lake and guarding its approaches," he assured, "the mountains are rugged, of great altitude and of no value for agriculture or mining."[21]

The forces urging national park designation for Crater Lake converged for a final push in March 1902. Steel submitted his petition— signed by more than four thousand Oregonians, including many leading figures in the state's political and business circles—to Congressman Tongue, who used it "to the best possible advantage," in Steel's estimation. The House Committee on Public Lands recommended passage of the bill unanimously, and the committee's report to the full House carried with it an impressive file of supporting letters from political and scientific luminaries. (J. S. Diller's final U.S. Geological Survey report, *The Geology and Petrography of Crater Lake National Park*, which included his impressive contour map of the lake, appeared in 1902 to aid the legislation down the home stretch.) However, Speaker David B. Henderson, who controlled the House agenda, balked at bringing Tongue's bill to the floor, contending that too many national park and battlefield proposals were already competing for the attention of Congress.[22]

Steel and Tongue, at this stage, decided to appeal directly to fellow Republican and avid outdoorsman Theodore Roosevelt, who had just become president in 1901 after the assassination of William McKinley. Steel's simultaneous pleadings with Gifford Pinchot, a rising star in the new Roosevelt administration and a Crater Lake enthusiast since his visit there in 1896, may have been even more critical to the bill's success, since it was only after Pinchot had spoken to Roosevelt about the Crater Lake legislation that the president decided to act. In any case, the popular Roosevelt eventually prevailed upon the House speaker to allow the bill to come before the full House.[23]

Tongue's Crater Lake bill was debated vigorously in the House. The Oregon congressman tried to appease his skeptical colleagues by claiming (predictably) that the proposed national park possessed "great beauty and great scientific value" but "no valuable land." The skeptics— dubious about the whole concept of national parks—were eventually rewarded with an amendment that would, under certain circumstances, allow mining within the park area, just in case the park's "worthless" acres turned out to have some mineral value.[24]

After surviving debate in the House, modified by only a few minor amendments, the Crater Lake legislation sailed through the Senate without further debate or amendment, and was signed by the president—as Gifford Pinchot predicted it would be—on May 22, 1902. Will Steel's strenuous seventeen-year campaign to bring a national park to Crater Lake was over, but he was not finished fighting, as anyone who knew him well would have happily predicted.[25]

William F. Arant, Crater Lake's First Superintendent

ON THE SURFACE, WILL STEEL WAS supremely qualified to be the first superintendent of Crater Lake National Park. One struggles to imagine anyone who could have been *more* qualified. And yet he was passed over for the job, in June 1902, in favor of William F. Arant of Klamath Falls.

Since the job of superintendent in the early national parks was essentially a political-patronage position controlled by state political establishments, some have said that Steel's rebuff in 1902 was the result of his lack of "political connections." Nothing could be further from the truth. If anything, after his long campaign on behalf of Crater Lake and his intense involvement in the Cascade Range Forest Reserve fight, Steel was *too* well connected politically. He was familiar with Oregon political figures of all stripes, and he had clashed with many of them on one issue or another. When it came time to choose a superintendent for the new national park in southern Oregon, the state's political kingpins opted for someone far more likely than Will Steel to settle quietly into the job and avoid further agitation, at least for a while.[26]

As it turned out, Crater Lake National Park's first superintendent was both politically predictable and professionally conscientious. Klamath County farmer, cattle rancher, and active local Republican William Arant received an annual salary of $900, a $100 horse allowance, and a budget of $2,000 for maintaining the park and extending its roads. He tackled his new assignment immediately in the late spring of 1902.[27]

After setting up headquarters about six miles south of Crater Lake, at Bridge Creek spring, Arant began looking in on campers and inspecting locations throughout the park during the summer season. His first major improvement as superintendent, designed to increase visitation, was a five-mile roadway from the base of Mount Mazama to the rim of the caldera. Following Dutton Creek in its final vault to the rim, Arant's new road generally traced the course of the wagon trail blazed by the Sutton party in 1869, a route that had become practically impassable by 1902. By 1905, Arant had also opened an alternative roadway to the rim, one that traversed Castle Crest after passing through Munson Valley.[28]

Road building and improvement, which in those early years often included bridge construction, remained a top priority for Arant throughout his decade-long tenure as superintendent. In addition to the all-important routes to the crater rim, Arant soon discovered that the park's main roads from the southern and western boundaries required steady attention. Widening, straightening, and repairing park roads called for never-ending but predictable labors; a less obvious but more bothersome road-related problem stemmed from the extraordinarily dusty conditions created by increased travel in the park. The area's volcanic, pumice-based soils, which generate an extremely fine dust, presented severe road-maintenance challenges for decades to come.[29]

Crater Lake National Park's first superintendent, William F. Arant, reestablished park headquarters and set up a campground in the key Annie Spring area of the south-central park in 1906. This view of Camp Arant, as the site was called during Arant's tenure, shows the mess and commons structure on the left and visitors' tents on the right. (Courtesy NPS, CLNP Museum and Archives Collection.)

Superintendent Arant inspects the abandoned camp and outfit of photographer B. B. Bakowski, who was lost and presumed dead during a photo expedition to Crater Lake National Park in January 1911. (Courtesy NPS, CLNP Museum and Archives Collection.)

During his second summer at the helm, Arant moved park headquarters to a new location at the head of Annie Creek. A park office and residence were built there in 1906, and the place soon took on the name Camp Arant. (The site would continue to play a strategic role throughout Crater Lake National Park's history.) As autumn rolled around each year and snow began to pile up, Arant moved the park office down to his ranch near Klamath Falls. Typically, by that time, the park's annual budget allocation had been consumed for weeks or even months. Though he did not raise a great ruckus about these shortfalls, Arant's annual reports to the Interior Department did regularly include firm statements about the additional funds needed to make essential improvements in the park.[30]

The great volume of snow at Crater Lake and other High Cascade regions was no secret to turn-of-the-century Oregonians. But until the park's formal opening established an official government presence there in 1902, few people understood the enormous problems involved in maintaining buildings and other features amid so much snow and severe weather. Superintendent Arant soon came to appreciate how this inescapable annual reality complicated his job. Some winters were worse than others, of course, and the winter of 1908-1909 took an especially heavy toll on some of the park's early structures. Then, following the loss and apparent death of photographer B. B. Bakowski in January 1911, Arant decided to ban all travel in the park between December 1 and June 1, without his written permission.[31]

Protecting the park and its features presented daunting challenges from the start. While Arant consistently reassured his superiors that most visitors were not inclined to damage the grounds or facilities intentionally, there were exceptions. The superintendent and the park ranger (the first appointed in 1907) made frequent patrols, even during winter, but enforcement of rules and regulations in such a large area was impossible for just one or two men. Cattle trespass was an occasional problem; forest fires and vandalism (of both the natural and the built environment) were more serious, perennial problems.[32]

In addition to protecting the park from visitors (one to two thousand for the first few years and around five thousand annually by the end of the first decade), Arant felt the burden of protecting visitors from the park, so to speak. He greatly feared the potential for injuries or even accidental deaths at heavily visited Victor Rock, on the southern rim

Several female visitors congregate at the spectacular Victor Rock location on the caldera rim, future site of Sinnott Memorial Overlook. Superintendent Arant feared disaster at this irresistible but treacherous spot. (OHS neg. OrHi 102385.)

of the caldera (current site of Crater Lake's Sinnott Memorial Overlook). And the park's principal trails—especially the steep, frequently traveled Rim Camp Trail leading from the caldera rim down to Eagle Cove, on the lake—required continuous maintenance to prevent dangerous hazards.[33]

For those visitors who made the effort to reach the lake, superintendent Arant sought to offer the option of recreational fishing. After mature trout (likely products of Steel's planting of minnows in 1888) were finally discovered in the lake in 1901, Crater Lake was opened to limited fishing in 1905. Angling was also allowed in park streams at that time, but fish were then known to exist only in lower Annie Creek. Determined to promote fishing in the lake, Arant authorized the planting of fifty thousand fry in 1910. Brown crayfish were also stocked for the lake's trout to feed on.[34]

Wildlife, as a whole, fared poorly during Crater Lake's early decades as a national park. The government's predator-control program, which targeted cougar, lynx, timber wolf, and coyote, was partly to blame, but hunters also took their toll. When animals came down from the park's high altitudes in winter, they were easily killed in lands adjacent to the park, or even poached on park property. In an effort to give greater protection to game animals, Arant proposed extending the park's boundaries to include lower-elevation areas the animals visited during late fall and winter. In 1912 the superintendent augmented his boundary-extension idea by proposing a game preserve adjacent to the northwest corner of the park. Neither proposal made any headway.[35]

Attracting Tourists to Crater Lake National Park

EVEN THOUGH WILL STEEL, to his lasting indignation, was passed over as Crater Lake National Park's first superintendent, he was determined to have a role in the park's future operations and growth. Consequently, after 1902, he gradually began to shift the focus of his life southward from Portland to southern Oregon.

In 1903 Steel organized the Crater Lake Improvement Association, which dedicated itself to the development of Crater Lake National Park as a popular summer resort. Then, in a 1907 issue of his pamphlet series, *Steel Points*, Steel revealed a more detailed plan for his own continuing involvement in Crater Lake affairs. He emphasized, above all, that "permanent camps," hospitable and inviting to the tourist trade, must be provided immediately in strategic locations throughout the park. Steel's impatience with superintendent Arant's measured approach

Will Steel, passed over in 1902 as Crater Lake National Park's first superintendent, nonetheless dedicated himself to the cause of developing and promoting the new park. (Courtesy NPS, CLNP Museum and Archives Collection.)

to growth and development was becoming increasingly obvious to anyone who listened to or read his exhortations about Crater Lake during this period.[36]

As early as 1903, Steel had informally led twenty-seven people, including poet Joaquin Miller and Senator Charles W. Fulton, on a tour of Crater Lake. Then, in 1907, after lobbying Interior Department officials, he received authorization to lead parties from Klamath Falls to tent camps within the park. The Crater Lake Company was incorporated and began operating in July 1907, and a tent city, called Camp Crater, was soon set up at the caldera rim. Here as many as fifty people could obtain meals and accommodations, and Steel himself organized boat tours of the lake from this key location. A company advertisement advised cheerfully, "We furnish everything from a good cook to a fishing rod, tents, beds and board." Far more elaborate plans were also contemplated: a hotel on "the lake's brim" and "an elevator down . . . to the water's edge." Steel began to predict openly that once his full program of development had been achieved—a plan that included comfortable hotel accommodations, boats on the lake, and other amenities—Crater Lake "would divide honors with Yellowstone and Yosemite for tourist trade."[37]

The Crater Lake Company, strengthened by the addition of Alfred L. Parkhurst as president and general manager in 1909, upgraded the Camp Crater location by installing new floored tents heated by oil stoves. The company also provided modest visitor accommodations at Camp Arant, constructed a primitive water system for use at the rim, and built the foundation for a new stone and wood-frame lodge (the future Crater Lake Lodge) at the site of the Mazama convention of 1896. Leonard "Woody" Woodford, who helped operate a stage service into Crater Lake in 1910, recalled another Parkhurst improvement of the time: "Mr. Parkhurst kept two Loco-mobiles as extra cars at the lake. These were supplied with double chain drives and equipped for heavy pulling up grades. . . . [They] met the tourist cars at the beginning of the final grade and transported them on the last lap of the journey to the rim." These various customer-convenience measures proved only partially successful. Though a company advertisement from 1907 optimistically urged stays "for the entire summer or a week or ten days," most visitors chose to camp for only a night or two.[38]

In 1912 the Crater Lake Company, facing financial and contractual worries, secured a new twenty-year lease from the government authorizing two commercial concessions in the park: one for maintaining Camps Crater and Arant and running gas-powered launches and rowboats on the lake; the other for transporting tourists through the park in automobiles. The lease granted the company a *de facto* concessions monopoly, which Steel had long pleaded was necessary for financial survival. The government soon retracted, though, by authorizing two competing concessions, one for transportation and one for photographic services.[39]

☙

THE GROWTH OF AUTOMOBILE TOURING in the United States promised increased visitation to vacation sites of all sorts, but especially to relatively remote attractions such as Crater Lake. At the same time, the advent of the automobile demanded more complex planning and safety measures. Regulations for auto traffic in the park, first issued for the 1911 season, required tourists to obtain written permits from the superintendent and specified a variety of safety precautions, several of which addressed the peculiar problems posed by mixing automobiles with horses and wagons on roadways.[40]

Automobile transportation would not bring great numbers of new tourists to Crater Lake, however, until a more useable road system took shape within the park. When the new auto regulations were issued in 1911, a new road system had been surveyed but not yet built. Congress appropriated more than $600,000 in 1912 to allow the U.S. Army Corps of Engineers to realign much of the existing road network throughout the park, and to begin construction of a road encircling the lake—a feature that Arant accurately predicted would become "one of the grandest scenic roads in the world."[41]

Steel's Coup

THOUGH WILL STEEL HAD SUPPORTED William Arant in 1909 when the superintendent came under attack by Klamath County rivals who coveted the head job at Crater Lake, by 1912 he had grown tired of his auxiliary role and resolved to have Arant's job for himself. Steel had never gotten over losing out to Arant in 1902, and he believed that most of the significant accomplishments at Crater Lake since 1902 (not to mention those before 1902) stemmed from his initiative rather than Arant's. It was Steel who, in 1909, traveled to Washington, D.C., and secured money for preliminary work on a new road system in the park. And it was Steel who then returned to Washington in 1912 to team with Oregon's Senator Jonathan Bourne to obtain the funding that allowed the Army Corps of Engineers' road building to go forward in 1913. Steel felt increasingly that he ought to have the title and the pay of park superintendent as long as he was doing much of the important work.[42]

Moreover, Steel had become frustrated with the pace of development at Crater Lake. He believed that only through much-improved access— both *to* the park and *within* it—would Crater Lake be able to realize its potential as a publicly owned tourist attraction. After a full decade as a national park, Crater Lake was still far too difficult for most tourists to reach, Steel thought; and for those who did manage to get there, travel and accommodations within the park were not inviting enough to encourage stays of more than a day or two. Steel's growing frustration had been signaled to a key audience in 1911 when, in remarks made at the National Parks Conference in Yellowstone, he described how his dreams for Crater Lake had so far been thwarted. If Arant himself had not been attending the conference, Steel might well have announced his conviction that the park needed a new superintendent, and that he was just the man for the job.[43]

Steel finally decided to force the issue in 1912. With letters to Senator Bourne, Secretary of the Interior Walter L. Fisher, and Assistant Secretary Carmi A. Thompson, he launched a coup against Arant. There was no mistaking the intent of Steel's letters: he pointed out Arant's shortcomings as superintendent, highlighted Crater Lake National Park's need for "proper development" and "management on a very much higher plane," and cited his own strong political support in Oregon.[44]

After Democrat Woodrow Wilson was elected to replace Republican William Howard Taft as president in November 1912, Steel shifted his persuasive attentions to Arant. Employing mild flattery, invoking their mutual concern for the park's best interests, and appealing to the incumbent superintendent's sense of political pragmatism, Steel told Arant that his ouster had become inevitable with the election of a Democratic president. If he resigned before the new administration took over, the lame-duck Republicans could appoint Steel as his replacement. Even though Steel, like Arant, was a Republican, Steel argued that the Democrats would accept him as the new superintendent and would refrain from appointing a Democrat disagreeable to them both.[45]

Steel preferred to dislodge Arant gently, but he was never able to obtain Arant's acquiescence. When Arant resisted, Steel brought forth the heavy armament of his superior political support. He wrote boldly of his intentions to Oregon Democratic senator George E. Chamberlain in 1913: "You know, as well as I, that practically the entire population of the state recognizes my claim and wishes me well in this matter." Confident now of Democratic party support, Steel knew Arant's days were numbered. The new Democratic interior secretary, Franklin K. Lane, soon requested Arant's resignation and simultaneously appointed Steel superintendent of Crater Lake National Park, effective July 1, 1913.

But the sordid episode had yet to play out fully. Protesting that as a civil service employee he could not be dismissed from his job without cause, Arant refused to yield the superintendent's office and residence to Steel. Only after U.S. Marshall Leslie Scott forcibly removed Arant (whom Steel called "defiant and insolent") and his wife from the government premises was Steel able to move in and take up his duties.[46]

In retrospect, Arant's discharge from the job of superintendent appears unjust, and Steel certainly played a devious role in the affair. In one of the more revealing subplots, inspector Edward W. Dixon was sent by Interior Secretary Fisher to Crater Lake in the fall of 1912 to investigate the complaints against Arant. Dixon's comprehensive report, published in 1913, largely vindicated Arant and his management of the park. But in an appointment system that was still essentially political, politics—in both Oregon and Washington, D.C.—prevailed.[47]

Steel's Term as Superintendent

IN ONE OF HIS FIRST ACTS AS SUPERINTENDENT, Steel took steps to enlarge and reorganize the park's headquarters at Annie Spring, and to change the name from Camp Arant to Annie Spring Camp. From this expanded headquarters, Steel oversaw steady growth in park visitation during

A group of visitors prepares to embark on a National Park Service motorized tour of Crater Lake's Rim Drive, circa 1918. (OHS neg. OrHi 103404.)

the next few years, including a 60 percent increase, from 7,096 to 11,371, between 1914 and 1915. Much of the increase was attributable to a wave of new vacationers, many from California, driving automobiles to Crater Lake. By 1912, half of the park's visitors were entering by automobile, and that percentage continued to rise over the next decades.[48]

The additional auto traffic benefited tremendously from the park's evolving new road system, which Steel had done so much to bring about even before he became superintendent. An article about a private automobile trip to Crater Lake during the summer of 1914 describes a three-day trip beginning in Salem, with stops in Roseburg, Medford, and Prospect. The tour as a whole was judged "comfortable," but the correspondent found the final fifty miles to "Rim Camp" (the alternative name for Camp Crater) bumpy and difficult, even after all the improvements.[49]

The Crater Lake Company, in which Steel retained his financial interest, continued to provide government-contracted transportation services in the park. And in 1914 the company sealed a deal with the Southern Pacific Railroad to offer automobile side trips to Crater Lake from Medford and Chiloquin for tourists traveling by rail between Portland and California.[50]

Steel kept up his predecessor's effort to extend the park's boundaries to the north and west, targeting Diamond Lake and Mount Thielsen as attractions that could enhance Crater Lake's recreational potential.

This Southern Pacific Railroad promotional brochure touted a Crater Lake automobile excursion for passengers traveling by rail between Portland and California. (OHS neg. OrHi 103403.)

While a larger park area promised to aid the difficult task of game protection, such a boundary extension would likely *increase* the burden of fire control. Whether the park expanded or not, however, Steel urged enlargement of the ranger force, for the sake of game protection, fire control, and all other aspects of park management.[51]

PERHAPS MOST SIGNIFICANT FOR the long-term identity of the park, the lodge begun in 1909 during superintendent Arant's tenure was finally opened in 1915 during Steel's three-year term. As construction resumed each summer after 1909, repairs on the previous seasons' work—made necessary by harsh winter weather conditions at the rim—had to be tackled before the season's new work could begin. And since the construction season at the site was so short (approximately July 1 to September 15), progress was slow. At the June 28, 1915, opening ceremonies, held in honor of Oregon's Governor James Withycombe, park officials and Crater Lake Company representatives introduced a building that was still unfinished.[52]

Though damage sustained by the lodge during its construction had given fair warning of the extreme assaults of weather in that location, Crater Lake Company president A. L. Parkhurst, contractor Frank

Keyes, and architect R. H. Hockenberry went ahead with plans for a simple wood-frame structure similar to that found in homes and other low-elevation buildings of the time. Cloud Cap Inn on Mount Hood stood as an example of the kind of heavy-timber-and-log construction necessary to withstand the heavy snowfalls at such high elevations, but the Crater Lake Lodge team proceeded with an ill-conceived design that was, moreover, never fully funded. In fact, missteps made in the original plan and construction of the lodge would indirectly contribute to the shortness of Steel's tenure as superintendent. Still, many of the earliest guests immediately fell in love with the structure, and the lodge quickly established its public reputation as a reasonably comfortable and stunningly situated visitor accommodation.[53]

∞

FINANCIAL ADVERSITY, PERSONAL AND PROFESSIONAL, was probably the most consistent thread running through Steel's life, and his years as superintendent of Crater Lake National Park were no exception. Contrary both to the assurances he gave others and to his own expectations, Interior Department appropriations for the park remained inadequate during his tenure. Adding to that burden, Crater Lake was one of only a few national parks whose founding legislation did not allow revenue obtained from leases and permits to be used in park administration. But Steel showed himself capable of stretching a penny, and his years as superintendent saw significant, if unglamorous, achievements in road and trail construction and repair, as well as in telephone, water, and maintenance systems.[54]

Considering some of Steel's grandiose plans for developing the park, we can perhaps be thankful that his funds were limited. He had long fantasized about multiple hotels on the rim of the caldera, methods of swift, easy transport from rim to lake, and steamboats plying the lake's waters. A well-publicized visit to Crater Lake from erstwhile presidential candidate William Jennings Bryan in 1915 gave Steel a chance to gain celebrity endorsement for one of his pet ideas. The rotund Bryan, after an exhausting trip by foot to the lake and back, reportedly recommended a tunnel for motorized traffic between the lake and rim, and he promised Steel his political support for the ill-conceived notion. Steel snapped up Bryan's "suggestion," and the next year formally requested $1,000 to carry out surveys for such a lake tunnel.[55]

Overall, Steel's achievements during his three and a half years as superintendent appear modest next to his earlier accomplishments on

Most of the original construction of Crater Lake Lodge took place during summers between 1909 and 1915. The lodge's wood-frame and stone fabrication was never well suited to its harsh mountain location. (Southern Oregon Historical Society #8827.)

behalf of Crater Lake. Steel obviously overestimated his ability to garner government support for the park from his new position, and most of the progress during his term as superintendent would likely have taken place under William Arant's leadership.

Steel's Dominion Challenged

Considering how long he had waited to occupy the job of superintendent, and how hard he had fought to get it, Will Steel's surrender of the park's top post in 1916, at age sixty-two, seems at first perplexing. But at a time when the country's loose confederation of national parks and monuments was tightening into a more centralized system, Steel knew that his authority at Crater Lake would soon be challenged and, most likely, diminished. And he understood himself well enough to know how difficult he would find any such abridgement of his authority and independence.[56]

A significant shadow of likely future encroachments appeared in 1914, when landscape engineer Mark Daniels visited Crater Lake to begin planning a "village landscape" near the caldera, fashioned after his earlier plan for Yosemite National Park. Daniels was then operating as general superintendent of national parks, a position created within the Interior Department that year to accelerate and coordinate development in America's national parks. Although little came of the Daniels plan, Steel undoubtedly felt the pinch of a burgeoning new authority.[57]

The pinch soon became unmistakable. In 1915 Interior Secretary Franklin K. Lane hired Chicago businessman and outdoorsman Stephen T. Mather as the department's assistant in charge of national parks and monuments. Mather, in turn, hired Horace M. Albright to be his own top aide. Mather and Albright traveled west that summer, visiting several national parks, including Crater Lake, en route to a conference at Yellowstone's Mammoth Hot Springs. Albright later recalled that "the beauty of [Crater Lake] was breathtaking, but [he and Mather] were appalled at the condition of the concession facilities and the paucity of park development." Mather's own assessment, as characterized by his biographer, was at least as severe: "In 1915 [Crater Lake National Park] was drawing next to nobody, and Mather could see why: its roads looked like animal trails, and its concession services were a joke." Though Steel, too, believed the park was vastly underdeveloped, he was offended by the harsh judgments and uninvited ideas of those he considered outsiders, including Mather and Albright.[58]

The Interior Department's two new executives were on the scene to stay, however, and their entrance into government service in 1915 would permanently change the course of scenic preservation in the United States. At a time when an emboldened U.S. Forest Service and Bureau of Reclamation were strongly advancing the notion of "utilitarian conservation"—emphasizing water engineering for land reclamation, industrial forestry, and public-domain leasing—Mather and Albright were able to stake out, defend, and even expand a more conservation-oriented fiefdom within the Interior Department. The formal establishment of the National Park Service in August 1916 provided a firm institutional platform for Mather and Albright to trumpet their concept of scenic preservation as an instrument of economic growth.[59]

Mather, feeling the strength of his prominent new position, immediately challenged Steel's leadership in a setting that was bound to humiliate him. Addressing the Portland Chamber of Commerce in early September 1916, Mather cited Crater Lake's urgent need "to improve its accessibility and service to tourists." He contrasted Oregon's tepid support for the state's only national park with the much more generous capital outlays in Washington (for Mount Rainier National Park) and California (for Yosemite National Park). Mather concluded his talk with a political threat: if Oregon business interests failed to make capital available for development at Crater Lake, he would go to California in search of the $500,000 needed for improvements.[60]

Some ten weeks after Mather's Portland speech, Will Steel resigned as superintendent. But with the help of his Oregon political friends, he found a way to remain connected to his beloved Crater Lake. Legislation ceding legal jurisdiction over the park to the U.S. government in 1915 also created the job of park commissioner (with a salary of $1,500 per year). This quasi-judicial position required the incumbent to live in the park and officiate proceedings on violations of park rules and regulations. So, coincident with his resignation as superintendent, Steel was appointed park commissioner by U.S. District Court Judge Charles E. Wolverton, on November 21, 1916. "Judge Steel," as he came to be called, remained on the Crater Lake bench for the rest of his days.[61]

Native Acquiescence to Reservation Life

NEITHER THE KLAMATH NOR ANY OTHER Oregon native people were considered or consulted in the establishment of Crater Lake National Park. As far as the government was concerned, the designated park area belonged to the citizens of the United States. The Klamath Indians, a subject people after their signing of the 1864 treaty, had their own separate reservation and agency, U.S. officials rationalized. The

These tidy buildings on the grounds of the Klamath Reservation agency served as "models" in the government's broad-based "civilizing" strategy for transforming the reservation's native inhabitants into self-sufficient farmers. (OHS neg. OrHi 51085.)

particulars of the area's traditional Indian cultures, and the centuries-old ties between Indian people and the Crater Lake region, simply did not enter into the equation.

By 1880, the Klamath had seen clearly that Crater Lake—a place of enormous significance in their spiritual traditions—was coveted by the whites. More and more non-Indian people were finding their way to the great mountain lake, some were returning often, and some seemed bent on encouraging ever more people to go there. Then, in the 1902 national park enabling legislation, as if to emphasize their radically different intentions for the place, the whites referred to Crater Lake and the new park area as a "pleasure ground." Inevitably, in the shadow of these developments, the sacred ground of Crater Lake began to appear lost to the Klamath. Alternative forms of native religious expression in the late nineteenth century—new brands of shamanism, the Ghost Dance, and a Methodist mission—acted as compensations for the dispossession and alienation of Crater Lake.[62]

🜨

AT THE TURN OF THE CENTURY, as whites wrangled over forest reserves and national parks on lands that Indians had once traversed freely, the Klamath, Modoc, and Yahooskin-Paiute peoples reconciled themselves to life on the Klamath Reservation. The reconciliation was rarely smooth. The reservation boundaries, set out in general terms in the Klamath Lake Treaty of 1864 but not established by survey until 1871 (and then again in 1888), remained in dispute for decades. Allotment of land for individual family enterprise—the specified goal of the acculturation process, which was supposed to require only a generation of reservation life—did not begin until 1895, and then was almost immediately beset by controversies. Many Klamath sought their allotments on portions of the reservation that had earlier been promised to a military road company, resulting in boundary litigation that lasted for more than a decade.[63]

Despite the controversies and turmoil, allotment did achieve some success on the Klamath Reservation in the early twentieth century. In detailing his observations made en route to Crater Lake in 1901, clergyman Alexander Blackburn allowed that the Klamath Indians "are fairly civilized, many of them having good farms and some of the finest cattle I ever saw." He qualified his general approval, though, by judging that "thrift in caring for and beautifying their homes seems to be the last thing for them to learn." The cultural gulf between whites and Indians, evident in Blackburn's assessment, was revealed more garishly

Reservation employees found their task of inculcating "appropriate aspirations" challenging, to say the least. As suggested in this photograph of a native campsite near the Klamath Reservation agency, many Indians blended vestiges of traditional culture with aspects of the new ways imposed by the whites. (OHS neg. OrHi 23618.)

in a racist remark by *Harper's Weekly* correspondent George Kirkman, who traveled to Crater Lake via Fort Klamath in 1896. Apparently striving for humor, Kirkman quipped about how at Fort Klamath he had been compelled to pull away his fascinated companion "from a miscegenative study of two dusky papooses, whose parents, odd to remark, combined the races of the negro, Mexican, and Indian."[64]

Preoccupied with legal efforts to regain full control of their reservation lands from the government and its contractors, and surely discouraged by their continuing difficulty in understanding and being understood by the whites, the Klamath pressed no claim to Crater Lake in the early twentieth century. As whites began to speak more often of a Crater Lake National Park, and as their efforts to alter the landscape quickened, the Klamath Reservation Indians maintained a frail link to the area in their seasonal travels to and from traditional huckleberry grounds just beyond the southwestern border of the incomprehensible new "park."[65]

Chapter 5

The National Park Service and Crater Lake

1916-1940

The Mather-Albright Team

BETWEEN 1916 AND 1929, the thirteen years following the superintendencies of William Arant and Will Steel, three men occupied Crater Lake National Park's head job. Two of the three, Alex Sparrow and Charles Goff Thomson, were energetic and reasonably effective in their roles. But the unofficial "*chief* superintendent" of the park during these years was National Park Service director Stephen T. Mather.

Just as Mather was plunging into the monumental task of defining, promoting, and building the new National Park Service, two major obstacles complicated his mission: the United States entered World War I on April 6, 1917; and the hard-driving NPS director was briefly incapacitated by illness. Acting largely through Horace Albright during his recovery, Mather barely broke stride. Drawing on his genius for marketing, which had helped enrich both the Thorkildsen-Mather Borax Company and himself by 1910, Mather now resolved to sell the National Park Service and its attractions to the American public.[1]

For all the complexity and political delicacy of Mather's promotional task, the National Park Service in 1920 was far more compact and uniform than the unwieldy, multifaceted NPS system of fifty years later. In 1920 the Park Service director was still able to exert a forceful, personal influence on individual parks in the emerging system, and Mather, over the rest of his tenure, exercised just such an influence on Crater Lake National Park.[2]

In 1915, while serving as Interior Secretary Franklin K. Lane's assistant in charge of national parks, Mather first announced formation of the National Park-to-Park Highway Association, a lobbying group intended to promote construction of a permanent highway circuit linking national parks in the West. His urging of Portland business leaders in 1916 to invest more liberally in improvements at Crater Lake was, accordingly, part of a larger strategy to spur development in all national parks featured in the proposed park-to-park highway chain, and especially in those parks he judged most backward.[3]

Mather believed that, in addition to improvements, a well-conceived publicity campaign would bring waves of new tourists into the national parks, and the testimonies of these new visitors would, in turn, generate more first-time guests. Mather chose veteran journalist Robert Sterling Yard as the architect of a new national park publicity blitz under his personal direction. In 1915 Yard assembled and published *The National Parks Portfolio*, which profiled the growing variety of attractions in the national park system. This book, as well as his later *Book of the National Parks* (1919), was distributed widely to newspaper and magazine editors throughout the country. Yard also wrote scores of articles and pamphlets on the national parks, and through relentless promotional efforts generated hundreds more.[4]

In his grand campaign to solidify the role of national parks in American life, Mather took an aggressive, hands-on approach to managing the Park Service. He knew that unfavorable publicity about any part of the park system, especially a key part, could undermine the larger campaign, and he was determined to minimize opportunities

Portrait of pioneer National Park Service director Stephen T. Mather surrounded by a simplified map of his proposed western park-to-park highway chain, one of several bold initiatives put forward during his landmark term of service. (Courtesy National Park Service, Crater Lake National Park Museum and Archives Collection.)

Early development at Crater Lake National Park was closely monitored by Park Service director Stephen Mather and his assistant, Horace Albright. This photograph shows construction of a bridge at the Annie Spring park headquarters, circa 1918. (Southern Oregon Historical Society #15668.)

for failure. When he and Albright personally inspected Crater Lake in 1915, they judged the park's huge potential to be largely untapped. Mather's public remarks about Crater Lake's deficiencies shortly thereafter contributed to Will Steel's decision to resign, an outcome Mather welcomed. However, with Crater Lake identified as one of the "crown jewels" in the national park treasury, and an important link in his park-to-park highway proposal, Mather suspected that the southern Oregon park, even with a new superintendent, would soon demand his further attention.[5]

In his effort to build a more unified national park system, Mather played an active role in selecting park superintendents. The job of superintendent thus became more a product of Mather's personal patronage and less an outcome of local political patronage. Although the first two Crater Lake superintendents after Will Steel were Oregonians, they were Mather's choices for Mather's reasons. Rogue River valley farmer and road engineer Alex Sparrow, who served from 1917 to 1923, was chosen because he had already spent four seasons at Crater Lake working on the U.S. Army Corps of Engineers' road construction project. By hiring Sparrow, Mather obtained an experienced hand for the Park Service and, at the same time, deprived the Army Engineers (whose presence in the park he was eager to eliminate) of Sparrow's services.[6]

Boundary Extension and Park Service Prodding

MATHER MADE HIS STRONGEST PITCH to re-create Crater Lake National Park in his own image by proposing an ambitious boundary-extension scheme designed to push Oregon's mountain park into the upper tier of the "very big national parks," as he put it. Through legislation advanced by Oregon's Senator Charles McNary, Mather's initiative sought to extend the park's boundaries some ten miles northward, to include Diamond Lake and Mounts Thielsen and Bailey, and three-quarters of a mile westward—incorporating nearly ninety thousand additional acres in all. The NPS director argued that the increased park area would offer greater camping and recreation opportunities, encourage visitors to spend more time at Crater Lake, and help protect the park's wildlife and other natural resources.[7]

This ten-year effort by Mather and superintendents Sparrow and Thomson echoed John Wesley Powell's environmental arguments about the Crater Lake region nearly thirty years before. The two superintendents knew from firsthand experience, for example, that Powell had been right in judging the original park area too small to serve as an effective game refuge. As Sparrow put it plainly, "Many of the deer get quite tame [in the park], and it seems like murder to kill them when they stray across the boundary." The proposed larger park area, in contrast, conformed more faithfully to the region's natural distribution of plants and animals, and would therefore protect species that might otherwise be threatened over time. The additional acreage was, in Mather's words, "intended by nature" to be part of the national park system.[8]

But the various versions of boundary-extension legislation backed by Mather and advanced in Congress between 1918 and the mid-1920s were defeated by the combined opposition of the U.S. Forest Service, whose national forest jurisdiction virtually surrounded Crater Lake National Park, and local interests. The politically potent Forest Service objected in 1920, for example, that the Crater Lake boundary extension would squander acreage better devoted to grazing, logging, water storage, and possibly power generation. Buttressed by local opinion that generally supported the Forest Service's more permissive stance toward hunting, recreation, and private use of federal lands, such objections were enough to defeat the Crater Lake bill in the House Committee on Public Lands.[9]

Frustrated boundary-extension efforts were by no means unique to Crater Lake. Historian Alfred Runte, in sizing up the national park picture as a whole, has written: "Each attempt to round out the parks as effective biological units proved far from successful. Traditional opponents of scenic preservation, led by resource interests and utilitarian-minded government agencies, still maintained that protection should be on a minimum scale only."[10]

☙

MATHER EMPHASIZED THAT BOUNDARY extension in itself would not, in any case, solve the park's fundamental problems. In planning his attack on Crater Lake's basic deficits, he realized that timing was essential. As he pointedly remarked in his annual report for 1918: "The development of the enterprises authorized to provide accommodations and entertainment of visitors to the extent desired by me is hardly likely to take place [at Crater Lake National Park] during the war period." Nonetheless, Mather was not willing to wait indefinitely to see park amenities and services—particularly those offered by the park's private concession—measure up to Park Service publicity. After an NPS promotional campaign had given special play to Crater Lake during the previous year, the director was able to make only a modest claim in his 1918 report: "The park held its own so far as patronage was concerned."[11]

While visitation to the park grew steadily over the next few years, accommodations and services offered by the Crater Lake Company— lodge, campgrounds, general store, in-park transportation, fishing, lake tours, and so on—struggled to keep pace with the additional guests. Increasing numbers of group visitations placed special strains on facilities. Mather was also troubled by friction between *his* superintendent, Alex Sparrow, and Crater Lake Company president A. L. Parkhurst, longtime friend and associate of Will Steel. For all these reasons, and in light of the occasionally scathing criticisms he heard from Crater Lake visitors, Mather remained skeptical about the park's readiness for growth and high-level achievement.[12]

Tensions came to a head during the summer of 1920 when Mather led House Appropriations Committee members and Southern Pacific Railroad vice president E. O. McCormick on a tour of Crater Lake National Park. Incensed at the shoddy accommodations and generally poor treatment his party received, Mather threatened to terminate Parkhurst's concession contract. Mather's ire, in turn, encouraged superintendent Sparrow to vent his own long-standing frustrations with Parkhurst and the Crater Lake Company. Mather soon signaled his intention to clean house at Crater Lake. His annual report for 1920 noted ominously: "Year after year I visited the park, found the usual indifferent service and unfinished accommodations. I pleaded for improvement, got more promises, but never any fulfillment of agreements or understandings."[13]

Mather launched his Crater Lake reformation by first inducing Oregon Governor Ben W. Olcott to appoint a commission to examine concession operations at the park. When the nine-member group of primarily Portland and southern Oregon businessmen set to work in the fall of 1920, their initial task was to investigate twenty-six charges of contractual failure leveled against Parkhurst and the Crater Lake Company by the U.S. Interior Department (namely, Stephen Mather). Though the committee's report turned out to be as critical of Mather and the Park Service as it was of Parkhurst and the Crater Lake Company, committee members acceded to Mather's bottom-line insistence that the park's concession be refinanced and reorganized.[14]

In the aftermath of the tremendous fuss he had raised, and perhaps somewhat embarrassed by the Oregon committee's partial vindication of Parkhurst, Mather nearly bubbled over in his praise for the newly organized Crater Lake National Park Company, headed by Portland businessmen Eric V. Hauser and Richard W. Price. Though the new company had by then operated for only one season, Mather's annual report for 1921 predicted optimistically that the Oregon business community had finally turned a corner in its willingness to support private concessions at Crater Lake. Service to visitors did, in fact, improve in the lodge and elsewhere, and the new company was rewarded with a new twenty-year contract in 1922.[15]

The Strains of Growth

AS STEPHEN MATHER AND HORACE ALBRIGHT struggled to carve out a permanent federal niche for the National Park Service, they had little opportunity or inclination to worry about the problems that might come with success. They sought political and bureaucratic survival for the Park Service through the aggressive marketing of tourism in the national parks, at a time when contradictions between tourism and the preservation of natural areas were barely foreseeable. The Organic Act of 1916, which authorized the National Park Service as a branch of the Interior Department, articulated and formalized (in the guise of a mission) an approach to scenic preservation that Mather, Albright, and Interior Secretary Franklin Lane had already conceived and begun to carry out a year earlier.[16]

This map of the park area was published in a 1917 National Park Service booklet about Crater Lake. Note that the north-northeastern portion of Rim Drive, covering about half of the caldera's circumference, was still under construction at the time.

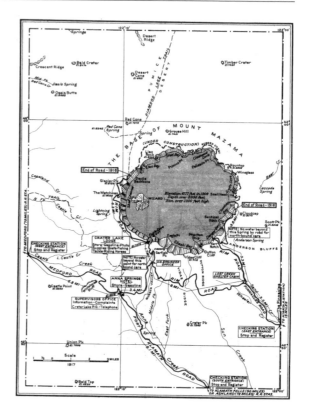

Mather and Albright were convinced that the Park Service would need vigorous popular support in order to fulfill the Organic Act's demanding dual requirement for both preservation and public recreation in the national parks. Consequently, during the Mather-Albright era (1917-1933), the agency tended to measure its popularity *and* its success by the numbers of people entering the parks. Visitor counts, according to this analysis, would increase as the parks became more hospitable and accommodating to the desires of tourists. By such logic, practiced and legitimized in the early decades of the National Park Service, Mather and Albright devised a formula for institutional strength and survival that emphasized park development and public approval. Park Service historian Richard West Sellars has aptly described this approach as "a kind of perpetual motion . . . where tourism and development [were calculated to] sustain and energize each other through their interdependence."[17]

As success and popularity (measured by increased visitation) were achieved at Crater Lake and throughout the national park system, strains became evident. Between 1921 and 1931, annual visitation at

Crater Lake National Park jumped from 28,617 to 170,284, an increase of nearly 600 percent. The park staff and operating budget also grew, but never enough to keep pace with demands. Superintendent Charles Goff Thomson, shortly after taking office at Crater Lake in 1923, described his job as "the best in the world," predicting he would die with his Park Service boots on. Four years later, Thomson despaired about Crater Lake's facilities and infrastructure, judging the park "among the most backward" in the system.[18]

ۙʘ

BACKWARD OR NOT, CRATER LAKE National Park offered seasonal laboring jobs that were often highly attractive to local men. Wages were decent and money could be saved easily, since there were "no expenses and no place to spend anything," as Albert Hackert recalled of his employment in the 1920s. Nonetheless, park employees, from superintendent to seasonal clerks, were often vexed by the contrast between Park Service executives' unrelenting concern for the comfort and care of tourists, who stayed in the park a night or two, and their apparent indifference to the basic housing and sanitation needs of Park Service employees who lived in the park day after day. At least one Park Service official agreed. NPS superintendent of construction E. E. Etherton, after inspecting park facilities at Crater Lake in 1935, reported: "Hundreds of meals are served each day . . . where there is no refrigeration for food, and the meals are prepared in an antiquated kitchen. The dormitories are equipped with unsanitary wood troughs to wash in. . . . The temporary employees residence area, commonly known as 'Scabtown'—not an entirely inappropriate name for the area—is a disgrace to the park and the Government."[19]

Superintendent Thomson, in his report for 1926, also complained about the park's inadequate ranger force, which he argued was far too small to handle its diverse responsibilities: enforcing regulations, protecting wildlife, patrolling roads and campgrounds, stocking the lake with fish, assisting visitors, preventing and fighting fires, controlling insects, supervising park entrances, compiling statistics, and overseeing communications—all spread over "249 square miles of mountainous territory." The death from exposure of chief ranger W. C. Godfrey (recalled by a young Park Service employee from that era as a rugged, "latter-day Daniel Boone") in 1930 was at least partly attributable to the park's chronic shortage of rangers.[20]

The high premium put on attracting and satisfying tourists also frequently dictated decisions about plant and animal life in the park.

Horace Albright, in his role as acting Park Service director, ruled against a permit request for some seven thousand sheep to graze in Crater Lake National Park in 1917, explaining that the mere presence of sheep was "very obnoxious to tourists." In addition to their unpleasant appearance, Albright noted, the beasts destroyed wildflowers and other vegetation that tourists enjoyed.[21]

While Albright's decision in this instance helped resuscitate plant species that had been obliterated by sheep grazing in earlier years, most decisions made in the interests of tourism were not as favorable to nature. The policy of exterminating predators in the park was rooted in the Park Service's perception that tourists yearned to see the deer and other small mammals that were the predators' natural prey. The feeding and taming of the park's bear population was likewise motivated by the perceived demands of visitors. And throughout the 1920s, with an eye to tourists' presumed delight in recreational fishing, Crater Lake—naturally devoid of fish—was stocked with twenty to thirty thousand rainbow and German brown trout minnows annually, along with freshwater shrimp for the fish to feed on. Finally, the enormous effort devoted to insect control was rooted in tourists' aversion to seeing dead, dying, or burned trees, not in principles of forest ecology or wildlife biology.[22]

A Surge of Development and Construction

AT A TIME WHEN SUCCESS IN THE NATIONAL PARKS was gauged almost solely in terms of public use and satisfaction, additional construction and development was the Park Service's preferred response to just about any perceived problem, including overuse and overcrowding. Some ways of altering park landscapes to accommodate visitors were relatively unobtrusive, but other improvements entailed far more radical interventions. For example, three new or rebuilt trails from the vicinity of Crater Lake Lodge—one from the caldera rim to the lake, one to Garfield Peak, and one to the Watchman—provided huge returns in visitor enjoyment with minimal environmental disturbance. In contrast, the much-anticipated road around the rim (completed, in its initial phase, in 1919) required significant landscape upheaval to produce a tremendous windfall in publicity and a substantial yield in tourist satisfaction.[23]

With the unstoppable onrush of the automobile age in the 1920s, the National Park Service unreservedly yielded to drivers' demands for more and better roads. Especially for remote, high-elevation parks

The Crater Wall Trail, constructed in 1928, led from Rim Village to the lake shore. Built to improve upon an earlier trail that led from behind Crater Lake Lodge to Eagle Cove, this zigzag-style trail was closed in 1959, in part because of danger posed by loose rocks and debris. (SOHS, #16840.)

This easterly view of nationally acclaimed Rim Drive, circa 1920, shows Wizard Island looming off the western shore of the Crater Lake caldera. (SOHS, #15290.)

such as Crater Lake, roads that were wide enough, smooth enough, and free enough from snow to invite automobile traffic began to seem less like mere conveniences and more like necessary lifelines. Paving, regrading, and realigning established roadways became imperative by the mid-1920s, when the private automobile emerged as the public's principal means of entering the park. Similarly, upgrading and maintaining the critical roads approaching the park demanded consistent cooperation with state and county governments. As soon as park roads were well founded and in good repair, snow removal accounted for the greatest portion of their ongoing maintenance.[24]

Even as National Park Service strategists tried, by proposing boundary extensions, to augment the number of tourist attractions within Crater Lake National Park, they also conceded to the inevitable: the lake and its immediate rim area would always be the most popular park locations. In keeping with this recognition, "improvements" were made to the natural lake and rim setting to satisfy tourist preferences. The thirty-five-mile Rim Drive was completed, and water storage for the lodge and the rim campground were expanded. Then, in 1921, the Scenic America Company, operating under National Park Service guidelines for construction compatible with the landscape, erected a small stone structure (the Kiser Studio) west of the lodge and just south of Victor Rock for the display and sale of photographs, postcards, and paintings of park scenes.[25]

AFTER THEIR STRONG START DURING the 1921 season, the new owners of the Crater Lake National Park Company enjoyed several consecutive years of increasing visitation, favorable publicity, and cozy relations with the Park Service. However, instead of taking advantage of this sunny juncture to upgrade and complete the original Crater Lake Lodge, concessionaires Price and Hauser channeled their enthusiasm, and much of their capital, into an ill-conceived lodge annex. Some of the austere annex rooms finally opened in 1924, but cost overruns soon put a halt to the planned eighty-room addition. Nevertheless, a general spirit of progress and optimism continued to reign at the rim, especially after the Park Service in 1924 built the Community House for hosting rim campers and lodge guests.[26]

Now that the park had concessionaires who demonstrated at least some capacity to raise and spend money on improvements, Mather renewed his determination to push Crater Lake National Park toward greatness. In 1926 he asked Thomas C. Vint of the National Park

An ill-conceived annex, shown here encased in scaffolding, was added to the original and still-unfinished Crater Lake Lodge in 1922-1924. (Courtesy NPS, CLNP Museum and Archives Collection.)

Service Landscape Division to create a long-term development plan for the park. Astute and prescient in much of its detail, the Vint plan's key feature was its accurate identification of what would become the three main areas of human activity in the park for the rest of the century: the rim of the caldera (especially the historic area of the southwest rim, soon to be known as Rim Village); the new park headquarters in Munson Valley; and the former park headquarters at Annie Spring (future site of Mazama Village).[27]

Vint's plan had a profound effect on Rim Village. Beginning in the 1920s, the Park Service had assumed firm control of construction and other forms of development in the popular Rim Village area. But cultivation of a true "village" ambience at the rim ultimately depended on providing more pleasant options for foot traffic. For years, automobile parking along the rim had been unrestricted and indiscriminate (one passengerless car even plunged over the edge and into the lake in 1922), and the rough comings and goings of auto traffic had produced unsightly conditions exactly where a natural appearance was most desirable. Responding to this problem, the NPS Landscape Division launched a long-term effort in 1927 to restore natural vegetation and stabilize soil conditions in the heavily used Rim Village area. In conjunction with this "naturalizing" of the terrain, an asphalt trail for walking, called the Rim Trail Promenade, was laid out and constructed. Thus a general scheme for automobile and foot traffic, with parking separated by some distance, was set for decades to come.[28]

VINT'S DEVELOPMENT PLAN REINFORCED changes taking place at another key park location. As park headquarters gradually shifted after 1923 from the Annie Spring area to the Munson Valley/Government Camp location, buildings formerly occupied by the Army Corps of Engineers road crew were taken over by park administrators. While these hand-me-down structures were not adequate for permanent park headquarters, the site itself was considered ideal, shielded from wind by Garfield Peak and adjacent forest. The Munson Valley portion of Vint's master plan, which included a new administration building, a utility and maintenance area, staff residences, and a revegetation program, began to take shape in 1927.[29]

Between 1927 and 1930, the new park headquarters site took on an aura of permanence with the construction of four small cottages, a mess hall, a comfort station (restrooms), a meat house, a warehouse, and two utility buildings. The key roadway from Munson Valley to the rim was also established in its current location during this time. While structures were grouped according to administrative, maintenance, and

Unrestricted automobile traffic near the most heavily used areas of the caldera rim decimated the natural landscape by the mid-1920s. (Photo courtesy of Klamath County Museum.)

residential function, maximum effort was made, through the use of locally quarried stone and native timber, to blend even the most utilitarian buildings with the surrounding vegetation and terrain.[30]

In 1928, toward the end of Stephen Mather's tenure as NPS director, he sought again to accelerate growth at Crater Lake, this time by dispatching NPS engineer Ward P. Webber to the park for a two-year stint. Webber oversaw substantial improvements in the appearance of roads and roadside landscapes. He also gave additional attention to the Rim Village area, supervising completion of the Rim Trail Promenade and reconstruction of the weathered and well-trodden Crater Wall Trail. In Mather's final annual report as director, he praised these improvements for "diminishing the dust evil" and for "enabling many thousands to enjoy the lake who were heretofore denied that pleasure by physical incapacity." The pioneer Park Service director retired in January 1929, just before the stock-market crash; he died in 1930, having presided over the heyday of Crater Lake's physical formation as a national park.[31]

Lasting Architectural Achievement

BETWEEN 1929 AND 1933, HERBERT HOOVER was president of the United States, Horace Albright was director of the National Park Service, and Elbert C. Solinsky was superintendent of Crater Lake National Park. While these men are not generally regarded as a conspicuous threesome, their simultaneous tenures represent an era of sorts at Crater Lake. Albright, firmly in charge of the Park Service following his mentor's retirement, chose Solinsky, former assistant superintendent at Yosemite National Park, to preside over Crater Lake's closely monitored growth. His appointment letter to Solinsky signaled clearly that ultimate authority at Crater Lake would remain in Washington, D.C. "It will be necessary for you to exercise at all times the utmost tact and good judgment and every official act must be in harmony with National Park Service policies," the new Park Service director admonished.[32]

The Hoover presidency, though inevitably associated with the Great Depression and the federal government's initially slow response to the hard times, was not as tightfisted with public monies as reputation would have it. Through the strong advocacy of Interior Secretary Ray Lyman Wilbur, the Hoover administration spawned a construction boom throughout the national park system, including Crater Lake, in the early 1930s. At Crater Lake's Rim Village, a cafeteria, store, and housekeeping cabins took shape in 1929, and the celebrated Sinnott

This view of the Rim Village landscape, with Crater Lake Lodge in the distance, reflects progress made in the late twenties and early thirties in beautifying and naturalizing this much-traveled park area. (Courtesy NPS, CLNP Museum and Archives Collection.)

Memorial Overlook was completed at the breathtaking Victor Rock location in 1931. An impressive stone parapet wall along the Rim Trail Promenade, intended to complement and protect the area's new plantings and landscaping, was also nearly completed that year. "A new conception of neatness, orderliness and care is dominating the entire park," the Medford *Mail Tribune* reported approvingly in 1930.[33]

The Sinnott Memorial both reflected and projected Crater Lake's blooming reputation in the prewar decades. Named in honor of Nicholas J. Sinnott—an Oregon congressman who, as chairman of the House Committee on Public Lands after 1919, had been an effective advocate for Crater Lake National Park and for national parks in general—the impressive stone structure was built into a steep rock outcrop (Victor Rock) fifty feet below the caldera rim, overlooking the lake. Patterned after the Yavapai Observation Station in Grand Canyon National Park, the Sinnott Memorial project presented extraordinary construction and engineering challenges that tested the ingenuity of an ambitious group of planners and builders.[34]

One of the most creative minds brought to bear on the Sinnott Memorial construction was that of Merel S. Sager, an NPS landscape architect assigned to Crater Lake in 1930 to supervise architectural, landscape, and planning work. Sager's master plan for the park provided a blueprint for the busy 1931 construction season, when substantial public-works emergency funds first became available, and throughout the 1930s. Park improvements over the next two years included both the mundane (utility systems, parking areas, and road projects) and the

Construction of the Sinnott Memorial Overlook at the spectacular Victor Rock site on the south rim of the caldera required both courage and ingenuity from the project's builders, engineers, and architects. (Courtesy NPS, CLNP Museum and Archives Collection.)

spectacular (the Watchman Lookout and Trailside Museum). Built on one of the most prominent peaks of the caldera rim, the Watchman Lookout joined the Sinnott Memorial as a monument to the skill and the audacity of the Park Service landscape architecture program of the 1930s.

In the Munson Valley park headquarters area, several significant structures were added during the 1932-1933 building seasons: the Naturalist's Residence, the Superintendent's Residence, employee residences, the Rangers' Dormitory, and utility buildings. All displayed Sager's trademark determination to minimize the gulf between the natural and the built environments. Architectural historian Ethan Carr, in assessing the overall achievement of Sager-supervised construction in Munson Valley in the early 1930s, has written: "The ensemble was the most comprehensive single building program of its type yet attempted by the [NPS] landscape division, and one of the most beautiful."[35]

Additional new roads and parking areas, auxiliary buildings, strolling paths, and plantings rounded out this substantial development program, carried out by a combination of National Park Service and contract labor. The diverse corps of contract artisans and laborers in 1930 included stonemason B. J. "Joe" Mancini and two University of Oregon football tackles, George Christianson and Austin Coburn. Crew boss Emmett Blanchfield recalled that when the two hefty linemen returned to Eugene to begin football practice in the late summer, the Park Service "had to hire a couple of mules to take their place." Mancini, whose master rockwork was located throughout the park, is remembered best for his carved-rock fountain facsimile of Crater Lake, still situated in Rim Village.[36]

In contrast to the Park Service's creative and vigorous building program of the 1930s, the privately owned and operated Crater Lake Lodge barely limped into its third decade, with both renovation and maintenance seriously neglected. While the Park Service made cosmetic improvements to walkways and landscapes near the lodge, the structure itself appeared increasingly out of place to many observers. As for those who ventured into the lodge for overnight stays, ever-larger proportions left disappointed. In contrast, the growing crowds at the park's three main campgrounds—the rim, Annie Spring, and Lost Creek—were overwhelmingly satisfied with their experiences during this period.[37]

The New Deal at Crater Lake

HERBERT HOOVER, SCORNED FOR HIS BELIEF in the soundness of the American economy in the face of a persistent depression, yielded the U.S. presidency to Franklin D. Roosevelt and his promise of a New Deal in 1933. In that same year, Horace Albright, feeling that most of his and Stephen Mather's goals had been realized, left the Park Service to become vice president and later president of the United States Potash Company. With a new director, Arno B. Cammerer, just recently in place, Roosevelt's brash new interior secretary, Harold L. Ickes, decided to clean house in Park Service ranks. Crater Lake's Elbert Solinsky, fired by Ickes in 1934 for "misappropriation of funds and irregularities in park accounts," was one conspicuous casualty of what now appears to have been, at least in part, a political purge.[38]

Solinsky was succeeded by the amiable David H. Canfield, who had been the park's chief ranger since 1931. Although the depressed economy of the early 1930s reduced visitation and caused budget cutbacks throughout the national park system, growth in park infrastructures and facilities continued as the national parks became major beneficiaries of Roosevelt administration public-works programs. If it had not been for the funding and personnel made available by New Deal agencies—the Emergency Conservation Work program and the Public Works Administration, in particular—much of the long-range planning of the 1920s would likely have come to naught. In addition to fulfilling long-range plans, however, there was a good deal

Manufacture of rustic sign lettering from redwood slabs was one of several projects supervised by NPS landscape architect Francis Lange in the 1930s. (Courtesy NPS, CLNP Museum and Archives Collection.)

Civilian Conservation Corps camp at Crater Lake National Park's Annie Spring site, current location of the park's Mazama Campground. (Courtesy NPS, CLNP Museum and Archives Collection.)

of deferred maintenance to take care of at Crater Lake. Park Service superintendent of construction E. E. Etherton minced no words in bemoaning the park's deficiencies in 1935: "It is difficult to conceive how an organization could have allowed such squandering of money on physical improvements, supposed to be permanent, yet permit them to continue in their present [unfinished, dilapidated] state so long."[39]

The work of Francis Lange, the park's resident landscape architect from 1933 to 1940, provided some of most visible returns on the government's expenditures at Crater Lake during the Roosevelt administration. In the Rim Village area, Lange continued the landscape design innovations of Merel Sager—for example, replacing painted metal directional and informational signs with more aesthetically pleasing wooden signs of his own design. He also led several other landscape architects in overseeing a second phase of work on Rim Drive, supervised the transplanting of more than a thousand trees and the transfer of enormous quantities of topsoil and peat moss from Munson Valley to Rim Village, and designed a stone comfort station for the Rim Village plaza.[40]

☺

THE EMERGENCY CONSERVATION WORK program sponsored two Civilian Conservation Corps (CCC) camps at Crater Lake National Park: one, Camp Annie Spring (1933-1941), was located near the old park headquarters; the other, Camp Wineglass (1934-1938), was set up just north of the Lost Creek campground. Throughout the 1930s and into the early 1940s, at least one CCC camp and hundreds of enrollees worked at Crater Lake National Park every year. The young men, active between mid-June and the end of September, took part in construction, furniture making, arts and crafts, landscaping, general cleanup, and insect-control throughout the park. CCC labor made an especially strong contribution at the rim campground, where the men did landscaping, completed footpaths and roads, and built picnic tables, benches, and fireplaces for individual campsites. Although tensions sometimes flared between the "low-status" emergency government workers and the "higher-status" Park Service personnel, superintendent Canfield reported enthusiastically after the 1936 season that the CCC landscaping effort at Rim Village had "transformed a former dusty and unattractive area into a scene of native beauty."[41]

CCC crews also tackled major landscaping work in the park headquarters area, transplanting more than a thousand trees and several thousand shrubs, part of the ongoing naturalization program in all areas

The Emergency Conservation Work program, which supported two CCC camps at Crater Lake National Park during much of the 1930s, contributed mightily to the park's development and maintenance. Here a well-organized CCC crew does road-landscaping work in 1935. (OHS neg. OrHi 80314.)

Beginning in the winter of 1935-1936, snowplows kept park roads navigable for year-round activities. Here workers marvel at the snow buildup at a park roadside location. (Courtesy NPS, CLNP Museum and Archives Collection.)

of the park where the built environment imposed upon the natural setting. In 1936 CCC workers transferred substantial quantities of topsoil and peat from the southern end of Munson Valley to supplement or replace pumice-based soils in the Government Camp area of the northern valley. Other additions to the headquarters region included flagstone walkways, rustic signs, stone bridges, and drinking fountains.[42]

The "CCC boys," as they were often called, played an important role in the construction of the new Administration Building at park headquarters during the 1934 and 1935 seasons. As part of this project, CCC crews constructed a plaza in front of the new building, styled to accommodate fifty cars and set off by an elliptical planting island designed and furnished by landscape architect Lange. Superintendent Canfield was thrilled with the new administrative facilities: "The novelty of having adequate space to carry on park business [has] not yet disappeared, ... crowded conditions of previous years and rat-infested quarters in a decrepit log building still being too fresh in memory. Park visitors continue to be impressed with the dignified architecture of the building."[43]

∽

THE POPULAR CANFIELD MOVED ON to become superintendent of Rocky Mountain National Park in 1937 and was succeeded by the man who would occupy the head job at Crater Lake longer than anyone else: Ernest P. Leavitt. In 1938, with much of the construction and landscaping in the Munson Valley headquarters district either finished or nearly so, superintendent Leavitt adopted Park Headquarters as the official name, dropping Government Camp in order to avoid confusion with the Mount Hood town by the same name. This decision was in keeping with Leavitt's overall emphasis on improving and promoting relations with the park's neighbors (except, notably, the Indians of the Klamath Reservation). The superintendent even seemed to enjoy the political gamesmanship of civic competition between Medford and Klamath Falls for the privilege of hosting the park's winter headquarters.[44]

Meanwhile, the park was absorbing the impact of increased winter activities within its boundaries. Aided by the addition of powerful new snowplow equipment, year-round operations first went into effect during the winter of 1935-36. Roads to Crater Lake from Medford and Klamath Falls were kept open, except in the most severe winter conditions, and visitation consequently rose to an all-time high of 180,382 the next year, some 50,000 of those entering the park during

THIS EIGHT-PAGE COLOR SECTION features three types of color media used to promote Crater Lake National Park in the era before color photography became widely available. Notes on each type follow the illustrations.

Figure 1. (Courtesy National Park Service, Crater Lake National Park Museum and Archives Collection)

Figure 2. (Courtesy NPS, CLNP Museum and Archives Collection)

Figure 3. (Courtesy NPS, CLNP Museum and Archives Collection)

GEOLOGIST HOWEL WILLIAMS drew upon reproductions of three lovely oil paintings by Paul Rockwood (1895-1972) to illustrate his popular account of Mount Mazama's geological history, *Crater Lake: The Story of Its Origin*. The paintings were intended to depict Mount Mazama in three distinct phases: at the time of its maximum height and glaciation (fig. 1), just before its cataclysmic eruption (fig. 2), and just after the destruction of its summit (fig. 3).

Artist Rockwood executed the "first" of the sequence (fig. 1) in 1963, on a commission from the Crater Lake Natural History Association. The other two paintings (figs. 2 and 3) had been completed in 1939, while Rockwood worked for the National Park Service under the auspices of the WPA. The native Californian moved to Hawaii in 1950, where he worked on assignments for Hawaii Volcanoes National Park until 1954.

Figure 4. (Lantern slide 10 courtesy OSU Archives)

Figure 5. (Lantern slide 24 courtesy OSU Archives)

Figure 6. (Lantern slide 17 courtesy OSU Archives)

Figure 7.
(Lantern slide 28
courtesy OSU
Archives)

Figure 8. (Courtesy NPS, CLNP Museum and Archives Collection)

Figure 9. (Courtesy NPS, CLNP Museum and Archives Collection)

Figure 10. (Lantern slide 29 courtesy OSU Archives)

Figure 11. (Courtesy
NPS, CLNP Museum
and Archives
Collection)

Figure 12. (Lantern slide 15 courtesy OSU Archives)

THE PRECEDING NINE PICTURES, as well as the illustration on the book's cover, were taken from two collections of "lantern-slide" images of Crater Lake National Park, all likely produced in the decades between 1910 and 1940. The manufacture of lantern slides began around the middle of the nineteenth century, when a process was devised for exposing negative photographic images on glass, and then printing the negatives as positive images on separate glass surfaces. Educators and entertainers of all sorts were able to project the resulting positive images from the transparent glass "slides" (typically 3.25-3.5 by 4 inches) onto screens or walls for small or large audiences.

Detailed hand-coloring of the slides with special tints added to their popularity with the public in the first half of the twentieth century. The lantern-slide images shown here were used to interpret and publicize Crater Lake National Park in venues both inside and outside the park, primarily in the 1920s and 1930s. Figures 4-12 show various richly (and sometimes imaginatively) colored views of the lake and park environment. Figure 11 includes Will Steel and three California Boy Scouts on a tour of the park in 1929. The daring soul visible in the cover image stands on a precarious ledge extending from the lower portion of Garfield Peak.

Figure 13. (OHS neg. OrHi 101940)

PHOTOGRAPHER FRED KISER, one of Will Steel's longstanding hiking and mountain-climbing partners, first accompanied the indefatigable Crater Lake promoter on an excursion to the new park in 1903. On this and later trips, Kiser produced some outstanding early images of Crater Lake National Park on glass-plate negatives, from which an impressive collection of hand-colored prints were then made.

Figure 13, photographed from the Watchman Peak, captures a charming late-spring or early-summer scene in a northeasterly view of the lake and caldera rim. The colorist for this print, Fred Luetters, used a form of transparent oils.

In 1907 an assemblage of Fred Kiser's colored photographs of Crater Lake toured the nation, and in 1915 the photographer installed an exhibition of his Crater Lake work in the Oregon Building of the Panama-Pacific Exposition in San Francisco. In 1921 Kiser's Scenic America Company received permission from the National Park Service to construct a small stone studio at Crater Lake's Rim Village. From that spot, and in other commercial venues, Kiser and the Scenic America Company marketed an array of the photographer's hand-colored prints, individually and in albums.

the usually barren off-season between November and late June. For those park personnel who, unlike the superintendent, remained on the job at Crater Lake throughout the fall and winter, living conditions were harsh. During the first winter the park stayed open to the public, storekeeper Doug Roach recalled hauling in wood on a toboggan pulled behind his skis. A woodstove provided the only heat for him and his wife, Sadie, in a cabin that was virtually buried in snow.[45]

Stresses and Successes

TOWARD THE END OF HIS TENURE as National Park Service director, Horace Albright revived the effort to enlarge Crater Lake National Park. Envisioned initially by John Wesley Powell in the 1880s, touted by Will Steel and others in the following decades, and first proposed in serious fashion by Stephen Mather in 1918, the enlarged park idea was broached again in 1932 by Crater Lake's superintendent, Elbert Solinsky, at director Albright's urging. The boundary-extension formula of that year, which proposed enlargement of the park to the north and west, was the most ambitious yet, but it never advanced much beyond the stage of vague discussion. This latest of the Crater Lake expansion proposals was effectively killed by the U.S. Forest Service—an even more powerful force in Oregon in 1932 than it had been in 1920—in conjunction with recreational and commercial interests favoring the status quo.[46]

Albright and Solinsky had to settle for only a modest incursion into Forest Service territory. On the strength of arguments that the park needed a more attractive southern entrance and a more accessible water supply, Albright managed in 1932 to secure 973 acres of Crater (now Winema) National Forest land for attachment to Crater Lake's southeastern boundary. Referred to in later years as the "southern panhandle," the extension incorporated a three-mile stretch of Annie Creek and a section of the state highway between Fort Klamath and the old park boundary. Though some Park Service officials complained that Forest Service resistance had resulted in an addition too small to be of great significance, the park's greater access to Annie Creek has since paid multiple dividends, especially during times of drought.[47]

Boundary-extension ideas surfaced a few more times during the 1930s, revealing the Park Service's growing concern that, without alternative recreational attractions for park visitors, the wear and tear on Crater Lake and its rim region would eventually degrade the park's central features. Park Service director Arno Cammerer, supported by

Independence Public Library

superintendents Canfield and Leavitt, gathered political muscle behind two last-ditch efforts to expand the park to the north. But once again, the local opposition of citizens and governments joined with the resistance of the Forest Service to defeat the idea. After World War II, incorporation of the Diamond Lake-Mount Thielsen-Mount Bailey region into Crater Lake National Park was never again seriously entertained.[48]

THOSE WHO OPPOSED EFFORTS TO EXPAND Crater Lake National Park into national forest areas might well have cited the numerous internal complaints of park officials about the inability of Park Service staff to meet the daily demands presented by the existing park area. In 1935 superintendent Canfield lamented shortages in personnel, especially among the ranger force, which then bore primary responsibility for both protecting the park and serving its visitors. Attributing these deficiencies to a combination of system-wide Depression hardship and the aftereffects of the Solinsky scandal, Canfield maintained that Crater Lake was losing ground to other national parks in the effectiveness of its basic operations. Moreover, the superintendent feared that Crater Lake's adversities promised only to deepen when the park inaugurated its new year-round policy. Several accidental deaths in the mid-1930s (including a young girl who fell over the rim) highlighted the personnel shortage and served as a warning that problems at Crater Lake, if left unattended, could lead to a major public-relations catastrophe.[49]

But despite such notable stresses, by the mid-1930s Crater Lake stood indisputably in the top tier of America's national parks, virtually pushed and prodded into that position by such diverse characters as Will Steel, Stephen Mather, Horace Albright, and scientist-educator John C. Merriam. One measure of the Oregon park's status during the 1930s was its selection—along with nine other national park superstars, including Yellowstone, Yosemite, Glacier, and Grand Canyon—for a U.S. commemorative postage stamp series. A photograph of the lake

by Park Service employee George A. Grant, taken from the southwestern rim of the caldera and featuring Glacier Peak, Devil's Backbone, Llao Rock, and Wizard Island, provided the original image for Crater Lake's briskly selling, blue six-cent stamp, issued in 1934.[50]

THE TRANSFER OF A YOUNG AND ENTERPRISING chief ranger, J. Carlisle Crouch, to Crater Lake in 1935 added zest to several facets of park operations. In 1938, with the backing of superintendent Leavitt, Crouch launched a park ranger training school to promote and develop professionalism and effectiveness within the Crater Lake ranger force, particularly in the realm of fire control and prevention. In conjunction with the training school, Crouch prepared the *Crater Lake Ranger Manual* to help guide rangers in their day-to-day fieldwork.[51]

Whereas Crouch's manual echoed conventional notions about the rangers' critical role in protecting the park's natural resources, *actual* ranger responsibilities were viewed primarily as adjuncts to visitor fulfillment. Thus the well-being of the park's plant and animal species, landscapes, rock formations, streams, and even the lake was not so much a primary objective as a necessary subsidiary concern in the never-ending quest to maintain and increase park visitation. For example, the use of brick salt to attract deer and other wildlife to areas of the park frequented by visitors clearly showed more consideration for tourist preferences than for the welfare of wildlife. Likewise, the planting of fish in Crater Lake and in park streams during this era was part of a calculated effort to cultivate recreational fishing, not an attempt to preserve any particular fish species or to enhance the ecological health of the lake or streams. When superintendent Solinsky remarked to the Medford *Mail Tribune* in 1930 that "it is the aim of the National Park

Crater Lake National Park rangers release minnows into the lake in September 1932. Such artificial stocking of Crater Lake was in keeping with Park Service policies throughout most of the twentieth century to promote recreational fishing in the national parks. (Courtesy NPS, CLNP Museum and Archives Collection.)

While Will Steel and his wife, Lydia, look on, park employees feed a female brown bear and her cubs, thereby encouraging the animals to rely on unnatural food sources. (Courtesy NPS, CLNP Museum and Archives Collection.)

Service to see that no fishless condition shall ever exist [at Crater Lake]," he was obviously speaking to recreational anglers, not to biologists or ecologists.[52]

The taming and feeding of bears, a well-established sideshow at Crater Lake and other national parks by 1920, was recognized by the late 1930s as both harmful to wildlife and hazardous to visitors. Though the practice was probably unsurpassed in its ability to delight tourists (the bears were often given human names by park staff and reported on enthusiastically in the local press), the practice was, from the start, only detrimental to bears. Eventually visitation in the parks increased to the point where park personnel could no longer safely regulate encounters between bears and the public. Property destruction and injury were the inevitable results. Park Service efforts to reverse course and prohibit visitor contact with bears took decades to succeed. In the meantime, scores of so-called "troublesome bears" were killed or traumatized.[53]

The Later Years of Will Steel

A LAUDATORY PROFILE OF seventy-one-year-old Will Steel, entitled "The Guardian of Crater Lake," was published in the May 1926 issue of *Sunset Magazine*. The essay concluded with an oft-told anecdote that journalist A. Cooper Allen chose from several Steel shared with him on the occasion of their interview. In this tale, the fabulously wealthy and powerful railroad magnate E. H. Harriman, standing with Will Steel at the rim of Crater Lake, expressed his envy for the pure and

Will Steel, burdened by deep resentments during his later years, maintained his passion and enthusiasm for Crater Lake and its national park. (Courtesy NPS, CLNP Museum and Archives Collection.)

selfless life Steel had led in "fathering" Crater Lake National Park. Harriman said, according to legend: "Mr. Steel, I would give every dollar of which I am possessed if I could trade my life for yours!" The chronically short-of-cash Steel supposedly replied: "Mr. Harriman, if you had all your wealth right here in your hands, I would not trade with you."[54]

Just three years after the *Sunset* article appeared, Steel, writing from his cabin near Crater Lake, sounded a strikingly different note: "My heart is full of sorrow, the sorrow of a forgotten old man, broken and condemned to solitude. . . . I look across the little valley and see strangers and friends passing in review, but they know me not, neither do they care."[55]

These two scenes aptly portray the contrary winds that blew within the mind and heart of Will Steel. Such emotional crosscurrents, unquestionably common among human beings in all times and places, were especially strong, even tempestuous at times, in Steel's case. He believed passionately in the cause of preserving Crater Lake and sharing its wonders with as many people as possible. And over the course of his lifetime, he sacrificed willingly and unsparingly in the interests of that cause. Yet he was also haunted throughout much of his adult life by the conviction that he had never received fair recompense, material or otherwise, for his labors. In contrast to his own discontents, many of Steel's contemporaries, understandably impressed by the ample acknowledgments that *did* come his way, concluded that no amount of recognition or adulation would be enough to satisfy him.

As we have seen, Steel—wary of the inexorable advance of the National Park Service on "his" Crater Lake domain, and still smarting from the criticisms of Stephen Mather—vacated his job as Crater Lake National Park superintendent in favor of the new position of park commissioner in 1916. From the start, Steel seems to have embraced his role as commissioner less for its ostensible duties than for its weighty title and its implied license to come and go in the park as he pleased, without consideration of the new Park Service czar, Stephen Mather, or his hand-picked superintendents. Steel was able to pursue this course partly because his quasi-judicial duties as commissioner (for example, reprimanding the occasional park miscreant) were light. And as long as his contacts were confined to park visitors—explaining the volcanic origins of the lake and caldera, regaling novices with stories about his role in Crater Lake history, and so on—he got along fine. But when Steel brushed with the park's authorities, particularly with the superintendents who served between 1916 and his death in 1934, friction usually resulted.[56]

The causes of Will Steel's late-life unrest seem mostly psychological and personal. After all, the National Park Service, the Crater Lake National Park community, and the state of Oregon paid liberal homage to him. He was routinely included in park ceremonies of all sorts, he was honored repeatedly, he was given what amounted to a sinecure for the last eighteen years of his life (a post then inherited by his daughter, Jean Steel), and he probably received as much publicity during his lifetime as did Stephen Mather himself. (Stanton Lapham's book, *The Enchanted Lake*, published in 1931, was largely a paean to Steel.) But all the adulation was not enough to silence his inner torments. To his dying day, Steel held on to deep resentments, and he took umbrage easily.[57]

In a letter to Acting NPS Director Horace Albright in 1918, superintendent Alex Sparrow, on the job at Crater Lake for less than a year, already seemed at the end of his rope on the subject of Will Steel. Sparrow complained that the special treatment demanded by, and usually accorded to, Mr. and Mrs. Steel caused hardships for others living in the park. He also criticized Steel's casual work habits, and his acquiescence to his wife's insistence that they remain in the park no more than "four or five weeks" during the summer, even though Steel's job as commissioner obliged him to stay there throughout the tourist season.[58]

When Mather succeeded, step by purposeful step, in dislodging Steel's longtime friend A. L. Parkhurst from ownership and management of the private concession at Crater Lake in 1920, Steel's animosity toward Park Service officialdom intensified. He considered it unjust that Parkhurst was at first blamed for shortcomings in visitor services at Crater Lake (shortcomings that were, according to Steel, beyond Parkhurst's control), and then deprived of his investment just when his efforts were beginning to pay off. By 1922 Steel had reached the far more extreme conclusion that the government's treatment of Parkhurst had gone beyond unjust to scandalous and criminal. And he alleged as much in a fiery editorial published in the Portland *Oregonian* on May 1, 1922. Accusing Stephen Mather, by name, of "harassing" and maliciously persecuting Parkhurst, with the intention of "driv[ing] him from the park," Steel concluded with a sarcastic recommendation: "All Mr. Parkhurst needs at this time is to be let alone and all the National Park Service needs is a new head."[59]

Later that year, in a letter to President Warren G. Harding, Steel took dead aim at both Mather and Interior Secretary Albert B. Fall, alleging a conspiracy between the Park Service and the new concessionaire to deprive Parkhurst of fair compensation for his confiscated interests. Steel practically threatened Harding, in his demand for punishment of those who "perpetrated" the "high-handed crime" against Parkhurt, warning that "public sentiment will hold you responsible unless these criminals are summarily dismissed from the offices they have so conspicuously disgraced."[60]

In 1924 Steel published and distributed a pamphlet entitled *The Crater Lake Scandal*, consisting of his *Oregonian* editorial, his letter to President Harding, another supportive editorial by a private citizen, and a brief letter to Steel by Interior Secretary Hubert Work. The pamphlet drew enough attention to warrant discussion on the floor of the House of Representatives in February 1924, partly because it tapped into the sentiment of a growing number of citizens and members of Congress who believed the Park Service had become too strong, Stephen Mather too powerful, and the federal government too high and mighty.[61]

Steel's hatred of Mather even came to dominate his thinking about Crater Lake National Park as a whole. If Mather supported something, Steel was against it; if Mather opposed something, Steel was for it. It was just about as simple as that. Nothing demonstrates this near-

obsession more clearly than Steel's "change of heart" on the issue of
the park's proposed boundary extension and incorporation of Diamond
Lake. After supporting the idea actively while superintendent, Steel
went out of his way in 1926 to oppose what had become an important
cause to Mather, even citing the unrelated Parkhurst controversy in
explaining his opposition.[62]

Irretrievably embittered toward the Park Service establishment, Steel
launched a final Crater Lake campaign in 1932, the year his wife, Lydia,
died and just two years before his own death. In actively soliciting
support for construction of a tunnel through the rim of the Crater
Lake caldera to the water's edge, Steel gave a final push to an idea he
had promoted off and on since the mid-1920s. And like other positions
he took during the last two decades of his life, the tunnel plan was
probably conceived and advanced more because it was anathema to
the Park Service establishment than for any other reason. Though he
argued, with apparent democratic zeal, that "with such a road in
operation, instead of 1 percent of visitors going to the water there will
be 100 percent," his heart seemed more engaged in a rhetorical thrust
aimed at the Park Service: "Every visitor is equally interested with every
other American citizen in this park, and shall they be deprived of its
use by a few men with a little brief authority and possessed of a dainty
theory?"[63]

Steel garnered little support for the reckless idea. A favorable editorial
in the *Pacific Northwest Hotel News* revealed the sort of ideological
company he kept near the end of his life: "There has been entirely too
much aesthetic tomfoolery in Government interference with practical
engineering in the National park and forest areas on the Pacific Coast.
. . . Men in high positions have seen fit to entirely ignore
recommendations of Western business men and listen to the foolish
recommendations of impractical college professors, Mazama hikers,
landscape gardeners, and the like." Yet the endorsements Steel needed,
from area chambers of commerce and newspaper editorial boards, were
not forthcoming. Some even expressed their opposition vehemently:
Robert W. Sawyer, longtime influential publisher of the Bend *Bulletin*
and close friend of the late Stephen Mather, called Steel's plan a
"sacrilege."[64]

However, for all the tension and animosity between Will Steel
and Park Service officials during the last two decades of his life, Steel
remained committed to the basic NPS mission to promote public

Will Steel took the lead in advancing public knowledge about Crater Lake through such means as his privately published periodicals *Steel Points* and *Steel Points (Junior)*, shown here. (Courtesy NPS, CLNP Museum and Archives Collection.)

enjoyment and appreciation of the national parks. Even in the midst of sometimes-bitter controversies at Crater Lake, Steel spent most of his time in the park fulfilling that mission with energy and enthusiasm. For example, during the summer of 1921, the Medford *Mail Tribune* reported exuberantly on the recent changes in management at Crater Lake Lodge—changes, as we have seen, that Steel opposed fiercely. Part of the newspaper's glowing account included this rosy Steel vignette: "Will Steel, the father of Crater Lake, . . . is behind the counter to greet you, not as another customer, but as another candidate for initiation into the Mystic Order of Crater Lake enthusiasts."[65]

Such willingness to bury the hatchet, at least now and then, was demonstrated by Park Service officials as well. Emmett Blanchfield, who worked in several jobs at Crater Lake National Park in the early 1930s, recalled that superintendent Solinsky asked him to accompany "Judge Steel" on a hike up to Garfield Peak in 1931. This was one of Steel's last significant hikes in the park, and Solinsky feared for the frail septuagenarian's safety.[66]

Contrary winds continued to blow in Will Steel's mind and heart to the very end. Though forever unforgiving of Stephen Mather and other Park Service operatives who had, as he saw it, done him injustices, Steel was laid to rest in Medford's Siskiyou Memorial Park in 1934, clad in his National Park Service uniform, his casket borne by rangers of Crater Lake National Park.[67]

Education at Crater Lake

IF ONE THINKS OF EDUCATION, in the basic sense, as one person's readiness to teach and another person's willingness to learn, with enthusiasm playing the key role of catalyst, Will Steel stands out clearly as Crater Lake's first teacher (that is, its first non-Indian teacher). He knew his subject thoroughly, he sought students tirelessly, and he conveyed his lessons with irrepressible, infectious enthusiasm.

As the key organizer of the Mazama Club's program of popular lectures and scientific studies at Crater Lake in 1896, Steel helped determine how knowledge of the Crater Lake region would initially be construed and taught. Then, in the aftermath of that fertile summer, he played a prominent role in publishing the special "Crater Lake issue" of *Mazama*, which formalized and documented portions of the summer program. This book-sized issue of the club's journal served contemporaries as an informal guidebook to the region and acted as a sort of curriculum outline for future Crater Lake studies. Its inclusion of *some* subjects (botany, zoology, geology, and recent history, for example) and exclusion of others (regional Indian cultures, notably) helped set the Crater Lake education agenda for decades to come.[68]

Both before and after the Mazama Club convention, Steel, more than anyone else, wore the mantle of "Crater Lake historian." In this role, he devoted special attention to deciphering the sequence of early "discoveries" of Crater Lake by whites, and it was largely through his historical investigations and judgments that John Wesley Hillman and his party of 1853 were legitimized as first in that sequence. Over the years, and until the end of his life, Steel actively searched for and collected information pertaining to Crater Lake history. And during his stays in the park, no matter what his official job at the time, he delighted most in sharing his abundant knowledge with park visitors.[69]

UNTIL 1926, EDUCATIONAL EFFORTS at Crater Lake National Park were mostly informal and sporadic, consisting of presentations by Steel and others during boat tours of the lake and at various Rim Village sites. During the summer of 1926, however, Loye Miller, a naturalist from the University of California, Los Angeles, was hired by the Park Service to devise a formal educational program at Crater Lake, as he had done earlier at Yosemite National Park. Miller and a few part-time assistants staffed an information desk at the Community House, prepared small rock and botanical exhibits, and occasionally distributed printed material to visitors. Evening lectures on such subjects as the formation of Wizard

Island and the impacts of Mount Mazama's ancient glaciers were offered at Crater Lake Lodge and the Community House, and guided field excursions were available most days from the Community House.[70]

Biologist Earl U. Homuth, in his position as temporary ranger-naturalist, took charge of the park's educational program in 1928. Under his watch, the first issue of *Nature Notes from Crater Lake* was published in July of that year. Intended originally as a supplement to lectures and field trips conducted by park naturalists, *Nature Notes* subsequently published hundreds of short articles and essays, most written by permanent or seasonal park staff, on all aspects of the natural and cultural history of the region. The role and duties of park naturalists evolved further during the late 1920s and early 1930s to include managing museum and library development, organizing exhibits, and compiling research information.[71]

The educational program at Crater Lake was given a critical boost in the late 1920s and early 1930s by the involvement of eminent paleontologist John C. Merriam, a distant cousin of zoologist C. Hart Merriam, who had participated in the Mazama Club convention at Crater Lake in 1896. After becoming president of the Carnegie Institution in 1920, John Merriam, whose scientific links to Oregon dated from the late 1890s, had continued to pursue his interest in the extraordinary geologic history of south-central Oregon. When, as Carnegie president, he put in place an aggressive plan to develop educational programs in national parks during the 1920s, it was only natural that he would focus some of his personal attention on Crater Lake National Park.[72]

Merriam was well placed to help the park build both an educational program and the facilities to support it. In 1927, working with superintendent Charles Goff Thomson and naturalist Loye Miller, Merriam instigated early discussions of a museum and observation point on the rim of Crater Lake, which he envisioned as both an educational facility and an inspirational site. A few years later, after he had further developed his thinking about science education, Merriam concluded that an observation and teaching station on the rim of Crater Lake would be the perfect location nationally for conveying the ideas of "magnitude, power, movement, and development"—concepts he believed were essential to understanding geology and history as dynamic processes.[73]

The Nicholas J. Sinnott Memorial Overlook, dedicated in the summer of 1931, was the fulfillment of Merriam's vision. After playing a key role in obtaining the congressional appropriation needed to build the structure, Merriam added another $5,000 of Carnegie Institution money for exhibits and telescopes. In its initial configuration, the observation area overlooking the lake was equipped with nine exhibit stations. Field glasses and binocular telescopes were mounted between each exhibit stage to help tell the geological story of Mount Mazama and Crater Lake in step-by-step fashion.[74]

Crater Lake's mainstay educational features—Sinnott Memorial programs, nightly lectures, and daily field trips—helped establish the park's distinct identity and reputation in the 1930s. Naturalist Donald S. Libbey helped augment that reputation in the early 1930s by introducing a sixteen-stop, three-hour "rim caravan" auto tour and boat tours of varying lengths, all led by ranger-naturalists. On the strength of such programs at Crater Lake and other parks, the American public began to regard the national parks as vital centers of learning.[75]

Throughout the 1930s, Crater Lake attracted a strong contingent of seasonal naturalists, most from colleges and universities, to conduct summer educational programs for the public and to work cooperatively in short-term research projects. In the mid-1930s, the park began to host a range of more complex and longer-term scientific research efforts, including the geological investigations of Howel Williams, whose lectures and writings became a popular Crater Lake institution during the next decade. (In linking his studies of Mount Mazama and its caldera-forming eruption to Luther Cressman's archaeological work in the Fort Rock Valley in the later 1930s, Williams also contributed significantly to the dating of Oregon's earliest Indian cultures.)[76]

The arrival of John E. Doerr, Jr., as park naturalist in 1936 gave Crater Lake's educational program another surge of creative energy. His leadership lent momentum to the drive for a new central museum building at Crater Lake, and he continued to expand and build upon the park's fledgling research and core "interpretive" programs, as public education came to be called within the Park Service during the 1930s. The staging of an exhibition called "Interpretation of the Beauty of Crater Lake and Its Surroundings" in the interior museum room of the Sinnott Memorial in 1937 gave further realization to John Merriam's ideas and aspirations.[77]

The Visibility and Invisibility of the Klamath Tribes

As CRATER LAKE JOINED THE ELITE CIRCLE of national parks marketed energetically to the American public in the 1920s and 1930s, the native people who had known and lived in the area longest became nearly invisible to those who operated and those who visited the park. During the first half of the twentieth century, the Klamath, Modoc, and Yahooskin-Paiute peoples of the Klamath Reservation tried to maintain some semblance of their native cultural traditions and identities while adapting to legal and economic institutions imposed upon them. And because of both their industriousness and the inherent wealth of their reservation lands, they were reasonably successful. By mid-century, the peoples of the Klamath Reservation were as prosperous as any other native people living on reservations in the United States.[78]

Though the Indian people of the region were fairly easily ignored by the Park Service and its visitors, neither Klamath County nor the U.S. government could afford to ignore them. Throughout much of the first half of the twentieth century, the Klamath tribes took on the federal government in a legal struggle to reclaim more than one hundred thousand acres of reservation land—territory that had been granted, without their knowledge or consent, to a military road company before they signed the 1864 treaty. A tribal council, formed in 1909 and developed further over the next decades, gave direction to the tribes' legal and economic dealings and provided a means for official relations with the Bureau of Indian Affairs.[79]

The early tribal council also provided a forum for expressing contrary political views. During the 1920s and 1930s, opposing tribal philosophies—generally speaking, individualist versus collectivist—gave voice to political rifts that would eventually harden in the termination controversy of the 1950s. The individualist point of view, which tended to downplay the relevance of tribe, reservation, and native tradition,

Klamath Reservation schoolgirls, in neat western dress and orderly assemblage, at the reservation agency in the 1930s. (OHS neg. OrHi 53239.)

had become stronger as income from timber sales and the lease and sale of allotted lands to whites brought more cash into the reservation economy. (Those who espoused the individualist philosophy tended to be the more acculturated tribal members, some only recently returned to the reservation, drawn by the economic boom.) Though the added income and free-flowing cash obtained from the sale of communal resources promoted short-term prosperity on the reservation, native farming and ranching, as well as work incentives generally, were undermined in the long run.[80]

So, despite relative well-being, the Klamath tribes remained subject peoples, in dubious transition between a traditional way of life no longer feasible and a vague new way of life that seemed alternately unattainable and undesirable.

RANGER R. P. ANDREWS'S ACCOUNT of a "humorous" conversation with a "smart-cracking" Indian—published under the title "Indian Giver" in a 1933 issue of *Nature Notes from Crater Lake*—gives voice to a catalog of prejudices and stereotypes, and highlights the insensitivity and incomprehension that frequently ruled in Park Service-Native American relations until fairly late in the twentieth century.

The Klamath Reservation Indian in question—"dirty and unkempt" but smiling, unlike most of his sullen brethren—objected halfheartedly to the one-dollar Crater Lake entrance fee charged to his rickety Model-T Ford and its "motley ménage" of passengers, arguing that the entire park area once "belonged to Indians." Ranger Andrews countered that while the Indians may have moved freely on these lands in olden times, they did so with "sore feet," because they had "no way to travel." Andrews went on to explain to the Indian: "White man took Lake, gave Indian Ford." Then, as he handed over the entrance fee, the Indian driver purportedly chuckled and said: "You keep Lake, Indian take 'em Ford."

Both participants in this exchange, according to Andrews, played their roles with tongue-in-cheek levity. As the ranger saw it, the Indian's protest that "white man charges Indian one dollar to travel his own country . . . seemed to carry no conviction. He was not in earnest. He seemed to be repeating his tribe's old, old objection just to see what I would say."[81]

Chapter 6

Frustration and Achievement

1941-1969

The Park Service and World War II

BY THE TIME THE UNITED STATES entered World War II, Newton B.
Drury was firmly in place as the fourth director of the National Park
Service. Though still only twenty-five years old year in 1941, the Park
Service was widely regarded as an institutional success story. Indeed,
few could argue that the promotional efforts of Stephen Mather, Horace
Albright, and publicist Robert Sterling Yard had been anything short
of brilliant. By 1941 the American public was fully convinced of the
national parks' value to the country, and the National Park Service was
a well-established participant in the federal government's management
of public lands.

Bureaucratic security for the Park Service did not necessarily translate
into practical protection for the national parks, however, especially amid
the pressures of wartime privation and strategic necessity. The delicate
political and public-relations task of articulating the Park Service's
unique war contribution and defending its entrusted lands from
commercial and "national-defense" assaults fell primarily to NPS
director Newton Drury. His article "The National Parks in Wartime,"
published in August 1943, argued that the national parks could make
their greatest contribution to the war effort not by opening their
protected acres to lumbering, grazing, and mining but by providing
peaceful and inspirational refuge for a war-weary nation and its fighting
men and women. Reflecting later on the wartime experience, journalist
Freeman Tilden wrote: "Early in the spring of 1941 the Army
recognized the tonic possibilities of wild areas for soldiers on leave;
and as the war went on, the parks were used more and more for
convalescence and for the recuperation of jaded, shocked, and frustrated

young souls, as well as for maneuvers, tests of equipment, and training for Arctic and other climatic conditions."[1]

During the war years, Crater Lake National Park was visited by thousands of U.S. Army, Navy, and Marine personnel, most of them stationed in Klamath Falls or Medford. Fees were waived for the military visitors, and the scaled-down park staff scrambled to provide special assistance for them. If peace and tranquility were the qualities sought by military sojourners during their Crater Lake retreats, they had a far better chance of finding such solace after 1943, when the United States had become fully engaged in the war. In 1941, on the eve of American involvement, visitation at Crater Lake had reached an all-time high of 273,564; by 1943, attendance had plunged precipitously to 27,656, just about a quarter of that number from military personnel.[2]

The war's impact on national parks throughout the country was dramatic, with a system-wide drop in visitation of some 73 percent, but nowhere was the momentum of prewar growth more profoundly interrupted than in Oregon's sole national park. While Crater Lake's high elevation and remote location shielded it from the worst examples of wartime resource assault, such as the threatened logging of coastal Sitka spruce stands in Olympic National Park in 1943, its location was also partly responsible for the park's extraordinary drop in attendance of nearly 90 percent. Within the National Park Service, where visitation statistics reigned supreme, this unusually steep decline in tourism was bound to have far-reaching repercussions.[3]

The Crater Lake Community

AT THE TIME PEARL HARBOR WAS BOMBED, Ernest P. Leavitt was four years into his fifteen-year term as superintendent of Crater Lake National Park. His annual report for 1942 referred to an atmosphere of "confusion and bewilderment" brought on by the war. The sudden abatement of activity in the park—as public-works programs abruptly ended, tourism dropped off, and staff was radically reduced—must also have lent a kind of eeriness to the place. One rollback in park operations led to another, as the Park Service took note of Crater Lake's unusually sharp decline in visitation. After a strong start in its initial five seasons, the Crater Lake winter program was immediately curtailed, and the park remained closed from approximately mid-September to mid-June annually between 1942 and 1946. When Crater Lake's entire snow-removal fleet, several trucks, and other equipment and supplies were transferred to the U.S. Army in 1942, the park was deprived of some of its most essential tools of operation. Nothing could have signaled more forcefully Crater Lake's virtual hibernation for the duration of the war.[4]

Winter closures during the war years also reduced the park's already short summer seasons, as the effort needed to remove snow accumulations from fall, winter, and early spring consumed far more time than in years when snow had been removed gradually throughout the off-season. Excessive snow buildup and compaction during these years took an inordinate toll on park buildings, facilities, and landscapes, just when construction and development projects from the 1920s and 1930s were settling into attractive maturity. Partly because conditions at Crater Lake were allowed to deteriorate more than at other parks during the war years, the Park Service seriously considered extending the winter-closure policy into the postwar period. But the ardent objections of Oregonians—many from nearby Medford and Klamath Falls, where winter recreation enthusiasts had grown accustomed to the park's off-season attractions—quickly scuttled the idea.[5]

The war years also witnessed the penultimate chapter of the Steel era at Crater Lake National Park. When Will Steel died in office as park commissioner in 1934, his daughter, Jean Gladstone Steel, was immediately appointed to the position long held by her father. At the time of her appointment, Jean Steel was already well acquainted with the park, having spent most summers since childhood at Crater Lake with her mother and father. An accomplished horsewoman, she was an avid user of the park's bridle paths, both before and during her ten-year term as commissioner. But in 1944, after ten years on the job, Jean Steel acknowledged that the commissioner's duties had diminished well beyond their limited scope during her father's time, and she agreed to resign as a war-economy measure.[6]

THE NUMBER OF VISITORS TO CRATER LAKE bounced back rapidly after the war, as year-round park operations resumed in 1946. By the end of the next summer season, the park had already surpassed its previous attendance records, set during the years just before the war. Under superintendent Leavitt's direction, park staff and facilities, not yet recovered from wartime cutbacks and hardships, struggled to meet the demands of the postwar wave of tourists. In trying to reassemble both a permanent and a seasonal staff, reduced by 80 percent or more from resignation, transfer, and military service, Leavitt faced the obstacle of Crater Lake's growing reputation within the Park Service as an isolated outpost plagued by extraordinarily harsh living conditions. His annual report for 1949 noted the park's difficulty in recruiting permanent employees with school-age children, since Crater Lake had no public school, a deficiency that had in the past forced some families to cope with the additional stress and expense of maintaining separate households.[7]

The job of leading Crater Lake back to normalcy after the war was surely formidable, and it was a challenge perhaps better suited to a younger, more energetic man than Leavitt. For Doug Roach, who was working at Crater Lake when Leavitt arrived in 1937, the new superintendent immediately suffered by comparison to the departing David Canfield. As superintendent, the friendly and approachable Canfield showed his concern for park employees at all levels, frequently going out of his way to mingle with staff in the course of their work. By contrast, Roach considered Leavitt "pretty much of a desk man . . . an administrative type of individual." Likewise, Wayne R. Howe, who joined the Crater Lake staff as a twenty-five-year-old seasonal ranger in 1946, recalled that superintendent Leavitt seemed "terribly old," both in age and manner. "He was a baronial-type of person, [and Crater Lake] was his private fiefdom," Howe observed. Leavitt signaled his old-school Park Service roots unmistakably in his choice of uniform: shunning the long trousers adopted by practically everyone else in the postwar era, he wore puttees—leather leg wrappings secured by straps—characteristic of earlier decades.[8]

Katherine Leavitt, Ernest Leavitt's wife during his fifteen-year stint at Crater Lake, tried to compensate for her husband's aloofness with her own more outgoing personality. She was remarkably successful. After a few years at Crater Lake, Wayne Howe concluded that Katherine Leavitt was more interested in the park community and its staff than her husband was. Howe and his wife, Jean, recalled that Mrs. Leavitt "gave Christmas gifts to every child in the park," and the Howes found her to be a consistently kind and caring person. Katherine Leavitt and Lucille Sneddon, wife of assistant chief ranger Lee Sneddon, together established the park community's first primary school, which eight Crater Lake children attended during its initial year of operation in 1949-1950. And when Ruth Hopson Keen joined the Crater Lake staff for the 1947 season as the park's first female naturalist, "Kit" Leavitt (as Keen and other friends knew her) made a special effort to see that the young woman felt welcome and comfortable in her pioneer role.[9]

Such vivid and congenial personalities as Katherine Leavitt's have played a major role in shaping the quality of life and work at Crater Lake. Perhaps because of the extra challenges posed by weather and isolation, community life has been especially important for those who have lived there. Some residents, unhappy in the remote and exacting Crater Lake setting, have contributed to the park's reputation as an onerous assignment. But many others have found great and sustaining comfort in local friendships and community ties.

In describing the consolations of community support amid Crater Lake's sometimes trying conditions, Hazel Frost put it this way: "We had our neighbors [in times of need], because the people we lived with and the people we worked with and the people we played with were all the same people at Crater Lake." It was a small, tight-knit community, and Frost, who lived in the park with her ranger husband, Jack, from 1936 to 1943, felt privileged to be part of it. Similarly, James Kezer, a seasonal naturalist who lived in the park without family during the summers of 1951 and 1952, found great social solace in the mess hall, where he was able to chat with and befriend people of varying backgrounds, working in all sorts of jobs.[10]

The bonds of community support have been especially important to staff and their families living in the park throughout winters. Park

Crater Lake National Park ranger Rory "Slim" Mabery conducted "ski school" for the children of park employees in the late 1950s. Such activities helped forge community bonds in the harsh, remote environment of Crater Lake. (Courtesy National Park Service, Crater Lake National Park Museum and Archives Collection.)

employees have always had their jobs to keep them busy during these weather-bound months, but family members stuck at home during the long snow seasons have been more vulnerable to cabin fever. While the beauty of each year's new snowfall is widely acknowledged, many park residents have found the grimy, melting snow of spring tiresome and frustrating. Winter square dances and potlucks were invaluable morale boosters for Wayne and Jean Howe, particularly after the community mix was improved by a few departures and additions in the late 1940s. Wayne Howe recalled that Lou Hallock's arrival as chief ranger in 1949 was "like a breath of fresh air," transforming what had become "a really tough place to work" into a post that was difficult to leave.[11]

Puzzles and Paradoxes in Park Operations

IN LIEU OF NORMAL OPERATIONS and activities, the war years witnessed a profusion of Park Service studies and plans for future development at Crater Lake. Among several ill-conceived ideas then considered, a variation on Will Steel's rim-tunnel project was briefly revived and supported by superintendent Leavitt. Nearly all of the plans hatched at this juncture showed the typical Park Service preference for

Rim Village cluttered with automobiles, as shown here in the 1930s, was one outcome of the "protection through maximum access" formula— advanced by both Will Steel and his antagonist Stephen Mather. (Courtesy NPS, CLNP Museum and Archives Collection.)

construction, development, and tourist fulfillment over the values of conservation and natural-resource protection, a tendency perhaps intensified by the pent-up energies of Park Service engineers, builders, and landscape architects forced to defer their developmental urges until after the war.[12]

The permanent location of Crater Lake's administrative headquarters was debated vigorously during the 1940s. One analysis in 1943 concluded that the headquarters should be returned to the park's south entrance area (near Annie Spring), where lower elevation shortens the snow season and lessens obstacles to human activity. Many who took this position believed that the group of buildings that made up the Munson Valley park headquarters, though impressive in appearance, had already proved inadequate for winter administrative operations. And even though they had supposedly been built for summer use only, it now seems clear that the creative team of Thomas Vint, Merel Sager, and Francis Lange, and the builders they employed, erred in some aspects of original design and construction, since the structures were not even able to withstand routine seasonal snowfalls.[13]

Park Service officials all the way up to director Newton Drury became enmeshed in the puzzles of Crater Lake National Park's management and operations throughout the 1940s. Future development and activity in the rim region (Rim Village, in particular) presented the most complex and paradoxical set of issues. Will Steel had seen clearly, sixty years earlier, that the campaign to preserve Crater Lake would succeed or fail according to his success in publicizing and promoting access to the area's principal features, the great mountain lake and the surrounding caldera rim. And for all the ill will that flowed between Steel and Stephen Mather, the two men were in basic agreement on the "preservation through maximum access" formula. National Park Service decision makers, during the agency's first two decades, strove to lure as many tourists as possible to Crater Lake and its rim area, with little consideration of the long-term impact of crowds on this fragile area.[14]

But when the hard times of the Great Depression eased, and people began to return to Crater Lake in ever-greater numbers in the years just before World War II (annual attendance approached a quarter million by 1939-1940), some Park Service officials began finally to question the long-term viability of the "maximum access" formula at Crater Lake, where the maximum-access ideal was, to such a great extent, concentrated on a single feature. NPS concerns about possible deterioration of the rim area, however, were expressed not so much in specific decisions as in a general pattern of vacillation and ambivalence.

Beginning in the 1940s and continuing for decades, Crater Lake was caught in a welter of Park Service plans, proposals, initiatives, and studies. Many of these were contradictory in their recommendations or conclusions; most of them, in the end, produced no concrete results. By the time superintendent Leavitt finally retired in 1952, the park had seen only a few minor construction projects during the entire postwar period. The rim-tunnel chimera, which included, in its latest guise, a proposal for mechanical lifts to transport visitors to the lake, had been revived and then dismissed again. Removal of park headquarters to the south entrance area was recommended, rejected, and then taken up once more. Various versions of a year-round museum/visitor-contact center at Rim Village were proposed, but nothing much came of any of them. Park Service director Drury's announced anticipation of a "fluid" postwar development climate at Crater Lake now appears as a sardonic understatement.[15]

A SOURING OF RELATIONS BETWEEN the Park Service and the Crater Lake National Park Company, the park's concessionaire, further complicated the murky postwar environment. In addition to its own internal uncertainties, the Park Service was obliged to contend with the concessionaire's necessarily distinct motives and interests. In the aftermath of Stephen Mather's messy removal of A. L. Parkhurst, Richard Price and the new Crater Lake National Park Company had enjoyed relatively smooth sailing for more than a decade. Then, after surviving the Great Depression intact, the company was bolstered by the revival of brisk business in 1935-1936. ("Visitation" for the Park Service has always been "business" for the concessionaire.) When Price signed a new twenty-year contract with the National Park Service in April 1941, the United States was still officially a nonbelligerent in World War II. In a little more than seven months, Price and company would be virtually out of business for the next four years.[16]

Crater Lake Lodge, one of the concession company's main attractions, stood completely empty for three summers during the war. Toward the war's end, Park Service decision makers, with little regard for the company's point of view, began to discuss options for the rickety, fire-prone structure, including relocation, demolition, adaptation, and renovation. The company's suspicions of Park Service plans for the lodge and the prime site it occupied were soon smoothed over, though, by the rapid return of tourists to the park. The summer of 1946 presented the Crater Lake National Park Company with the "finest

Crater Lake Lodge, inelegantly sprawling and tattered by the 1950s, was still appreciated by most visitors. An architectural-engineering report in 1953 identified structural weaknesses in the building that would eventually lead to its closure.

business" in its history, according to Price. But at the same time, with visitors again patronizing the lodge in such impressive numbers, Park Service officials renewed their anxious musings about structure's safety.[17]

Over the next several years, until Price sold his interest in 1954, a series of threats and compromises passed between the Park Service and the concession company. In 1953 an architectural-engineering evaluation, referred to as the Haner Report, estimated that $72,000 would be needed to correct the lodge's septic system, roof hazards, dry rot, vulnerability to fire, and general structural weaknesses. When the father-and-son team of Harry W. "Pop" Smith and Harry C. Smith bought the Crater Lake National Park Company in 1954, they inherited a prosperous set of concessions (including transportation, a gasoline station, food and souvenir sales, and fishing, boating, and camping services) and a major headache in Crater Lake Lodge.[18]

Complexities of Resource Management

MANY VISITORS TO CRATER LAKE through the years have been only vaguely aware that the park consists of more than the lake, Rim Drive, and Rim Village. For the hard-pressed Crater Lake ranger force, though, the vastness and variety of the park have been inescapable facts of everyday life. In the 1940s, chief ranger J. Carlisle Crouch continued his efforts to formalize the roles and functions of rangers throughout

The Watchman Lookout and Trailside Museum, built with great ingenuity on a prominent peak in 1931, has played an important role in Crater Lake National Park's evolving fire-education program. (OHS neg. OrHi 103398.)

Known as the Kiser Studio when it was built in 1921, this stone and log building was taken over by the National Park Service in 1929. Called the Exhibit Building in later years, the handsome but small structure has been a primary Rim Village contact point for visitors and park staff. (Courtesy NPS, CLNP Museum and Archives Collection.)

Crater Lake National Park. Much of his energy was directed toward the increasingly complex (because of expanding visitation and the introduction of year-round operations) challenge of serving the park's 249 square miles with the limited staff available. Crouch's recommendations—for locating campgrounds close to park boundaries and ranger stations, for building a permanent ranger station at Rim Village, for assigning rangers to the lake and its shores, among others— were aimed largely at promoting ranger-tourist contacts in the park, thereby increasing the likelihood of serving and protecting the clientele.[19]

Crouch was equally preoccupied with fire prevention. Though somewhat at odds with the goal of maximizing contacts between rangers and visitors, since it required rangers to patrol remote sections of the park, the emphasis on fire control was also driven by the priority of visitor satisfaction. When the park's annual attendance dropped off dramatically during the war years, the diminished ranger force focused even more intensively on fire prevention and suppression. Superintendent Leavitt and chief ranger Crouch knew well that the tourists would eventually return, and that they would not be pleased by the sight of acres of burned trees or a lake shrouded in smoke.[20]

O. W. "Pete" Foiles, who worked as a ranger at Crater Lake National Park from 1939 to 1942, and Wayne Howe, a Crater Lake ranger between 1946 and 1950, recalled how snow ruled much of their personal and professional lives, especially during long winter seasons when the park was kept open for a modest but steady stream of snow enthusiasts. Ski clubs from Medford and Klamath Falls entered the park mostly on weekends, setting up their own ski tows on Garfield Peak and on slopes in the northern park region. A commercial ski tow geared to more casual skiers operated in the Rim Village area. Fender-benders related to weather and busy weekend traffic required the regular attention of rangers, who also maintained a first-aid hut at the rim for treating a variety of ski-related injuries. Weekday duties often involved shoveling snow from heavily traveled areas at the rim and patrolling backcountry regions in the versatile Tucker Sno-Cats.[21]

In the face of postwar attendance that broke prewar records, superintendent Leavitt struggled to restore Crater Lake's permanent and seasonal staff to at least prewar levels. As part of that effort, he lobbied for reappointment of a park commissioner to succeed Jean Steel, who had resigned during the war. Leavitt faced opposition from Oregon's federal judiciary and from federal budget overseers, who questioned the need for commissioners in fourteen national parks in the late 1940s. Although Leavitt eventually prevailed, and a new Crater

Lake commissioner was appointed in the early 1950s, the position finally withered away entirely in the 1970s.[22]

The labor squeeze at Crater Lake caused Leavitt to remark as early as 1941 that staffing stood dangerously "below a minimum required to perform satisfactorily even the most essential services." Still, the superintendent was compelled to set priorities and assign staff with the personnel at his command. Protecting the park's natural resources ranked consistently below catering to tourist expectations, even in years when tourist counts plummeted. For example, park officials were unable to do much more than remark weakly upon the perennial embarrassment of wildlife slaughter beyond the park's boundaries during winter migrations, attributing the problem to Klamath Reservation Indians ("natural-born hunters [who] recognize no closed season") and to "'old-timers' [who] consider they are justified in killing a deer, an elk or a bear any time they get a chance."[23]

After generations of bears had been conditioned to expect easy food from park garbage pits and sometimes even from park staff, the virtual shutdown of operations during the war years led to diminished food supplies and hungry bears. Superintendent Leavitt astonishingly attributed the resulting "depredations" of "ill-tempered" and "dangerous" bears to the animals' unwillingness "to get out and rustle their own living." Bears, of course, paid the price for such human folly, as some eighty-seven of the creatures were destroyed in 1943 alone at Crater Lake, Yellowstone, and Yosemite national parks. The so-called bear problems resumed at Crater Lake after the war, as a newly established garbage-disposal site again began to attract both bears and tourists eager to view them.[24]

An episode of concentrated lake research—most of it conducted between 1934 and 1940 by seasonal naturalists J. Stanley Brode and Arthur Hasler, in cooperation with permanent naturalists John Doerr and Donald Farner—produced the first systematic body of scientific information about Crater Lake, including a detailed account of its aquatic life. Among other findings, Hasler and Farner determined that rainbow trout and coho salmon (the latter probably introduced inadvertently) were then reproducing naturally, and that stocking the lake with hatchery fingerlings was an ineffective way to maintain the existing fish population. Though twenty thousand additional rainbow trout were planted in 1941, the lake was never again stocked with fish after that year.[25]

In 1948 superintendent Leavitt cited lake research results from the previous fifteen years in an effort to explain the park's recently changed policy on sport fishing. Until further research offered more definitive

The encouraged presence of bears in tourist areas of national parks was a difficult habit to break for an agency bent on tourist promotion. Here a Crater Lake National Park employee tantalizes a group of adult bears in the 1940s. (Courtesy NPS, CLNP Museum and Archives Collection.)

Superintendent Ernest Leavitt and chief ranger Carlisle Crouch pose proudly in 1940 with fish taken from Crater Lake. Eight years later, after Leavitt ruled that the park would no longer encourage recreational fishing in the lake, promotional pictures of this kind ceased. (Courtesy NPS, CLNP Museum and Archives Collection.)

guidance, Leavitt ruled that the park would no longer encourage (but nor would it *dis*courage) fishing in the lake. The Park Service allowed individual superintendents to depart from what was still the dominant agency policy of encouraging recreational fishing in national parks, if the superintendent "determined that the lake or stream was of 'greater value without the presence of fishermen.'" Leavitt's halfhearted ruling, though, was rooted less in his deference to the preliminary results of lake research than in his conclusion that the cost of maintaining a recreational fishing program could no longer be justified by the amount of tourist interest.[26]

Although the long-term impact of fish on the ecological health of Crater Lake remained unclear, the harm that would result from sewage seeping into the lake was indisputable. Nevertheless, in response to rapidly escalating visitation during the postwar years, the Park Service decided to "upgrade" sewage-disposal facilities in the Rim Village area by installing a septic-tank drain-field system near Crater Lake Lodge. Limnologist Douglas W. Larson has argued that "park managers made no attempt to determine if sewage [from the new system] was entering the lake," even though "it was known that sewage water percolated through drain-field soils" of the kind found at the Crater Lake rim.[27]

"Mission 66" at Crater Lake

CRATER LAKE'S POSTWAR STRUGGLES were mirrored, to varying degrees, in the predicaments of national parks across the country. After postponement of both development and basic maintenance during much of the 1940s, the postwar resurgence in tourism overtaxed the capacities of parks before Congress could agree to replenish the NPS budget. A widely read article in the October 1953 issue of *Harper's Magazine*, entitled "Let's Close the National Parks," served as a wakeup call for the American public. The author, popular journalist and historian Bernard DeVoto, detailed deplorable conditions in some of the best-known national parks and recommended a complete shutdown until Congress proved ready to provide the support needed to keep the parks safe and habitable, for tourists and NPS employees.[28]

Conrad Wirth, who had been director of the National Park Service since 1951, harnessed the furor surrounding DeVoto's article to conceive and promote a program of massive government investment in the national parks. Eventually given the name "Mission 66," the ten-year plan was packaged to conclude in 1966, the year of the Park Service's fiftieth anniversary. Wirth, a protégé of former NPS director Horace

Albright, had risen through the agency's ranks during the thirties and forties, earning high marks for his successful channeling of Civilian Conservation Corps resources into the national parks. Both his experience with the CCC public-works programs and his overall political education as an NPS administrator helped Wirth sell the Mission 66 idea to the Eisenhower administration and to Congress in 1955 and 1956. The NPS director formally announced the program to upgrade national park facilities and staffing at a Washington, D.C., banquet in February 1956, and some of the $1-billion bonanza began to trickle through the Interior Department and into the parks shortly thereafter.[29]

Wirth garnered broad support from Congress partly by emphasizing that the benefits of Mission 66 would be shared among all states with Park Service properties. The program proved true to its promise of sharing, but the sharing was hardly equal. Expenditures of the Mission 66 largesse naturally reflected the agency's priorities, and NPS priorities in 1956 were still largely based on the formula devised and practiced by Stephen Mather and Horace Albright forty years earlier: invest most generously in parks and attractions likely to draw the greatest patronage. By the time Mission 66 funds began to flow, Crater Lake was no longer

Mazama Campground was one of Crater Lake National Park's principal additions during the "Mission 66" decade (1956-1966) of massive federal investment in the national parks. (Courtesy NPS, CLNP Museum and Archives Collection.)

counted among the system's actual or potential superstars, and the park's fate during the Mission 66 decade clearly demonstrated that subordinate ranking.[30]

◯

As Crater Lake National Park staff historian Stephen R. Mark has noted, "With the initiation of Mission 66, park officials fully expected that construction of a visitor center and a winterized Sinnott Memorial would begin [in the Rim Village area] in 1957." But throughout the Mission 66 period, the park was tantalized with plans and proposals rather than transformed in any fundamental way. Crater Lake's failure to capture funding for its three most coveted improvements (the Rim Village visitor center, the adapted Sinnott Memorial, and a park museum) is partly attributable to a lack of continuity and political punch in the superintendent's office during this period. From 1956 to 1966, five men occupied the position, four of them first-time superintendents. Perhaps partly as a result of Ernest Leavitt's long tenure as Crater Lake superintendent toward the end of his Park Service career, the park took on the reputation as a distant pasturage either for auditioning rookie superintendents or phasing out veterans.[31]

Replacement of the steep and treacherous Crater Wall Trail with the more easily traversed Cleetwood Cove Trail represented a significant gain for visitors venturing from rim to lake, but the improvement was relatively minor by Mission 66 standards. Other Mission 66 developments—construction of the new Mazama Campground near Annie Spring, trail renovations, sewer and water system "improvements," road reconstruction, and housing—were also modest when compared to the massive investments in visitor centers and museums made elsewhere. Although substantial Mission 66 monies were spent at Crater Lake, the park's identity remained essentially the same, as it settled into a second tier of American national parks.[32]

Annual visitation at Crater Lake during the 1960s averaged nearly half a million, with a peak attendance of 592,124 in 1962—healthy but unspectacular figures for the burgeoning postwar period. Studies of visitor use during the decade gave further evidence that Crater Lake would probably continue to lag far behind the national park standouts— Yellowstone, Yosemite, Mount Rainier—for the rest of the century. A 1968 analysis reaffirmed that "Crater Lake National Park is a stopover rather than a terminal destination area," with an intensely seasonal pattern of use (around 75 percent of visitation occurs between Memorial Day and Labor Day). A 1964 study had already determined that 83.4

Crater Lake's intensely seasonal pattern of use, combined with overwhelming visitor concentrations in the rim and lake area, have put continuous pressure on key areas of the park environment, as suggested in this photo of a crowded Rim Village parking lot on Labor Day, 1961. (Courtesy NPS, CLNP Museum and Archives Collection.)

percent of the park's visitors came from just three states: California (45 percent), Oregon (29 percent), and Washington (9.4 percent). And the same study showed that while 15 percent of summer visitors stayed overnight, 60 percent spent just one to four hours in the park.[33]

Classification of Crater Lake as a "natural area" in 1964, toward the end of the Mission 66 decade, ostensibly signaled that "the park would [henceforth] reflect as little evidence of human activity as possible." But this essentially administrative measure served an even more important strategic purpose: in providing an implicit explanation for why Crater Lake had not seen the dramatic changes promised by Mission 66, it gave temporary cover to Park Service officials who had doubted that major investment in Crater Lake would pay off in increased visitation, as well as to the few who believed, for ecological reasons, that the Crater Lake rim area should be restored to natural conditions rather than developed further.[34]

When superintendent J. Leonard Volz, in the mid-1960s, revived the issue of moving park headquarters to the south entrance vicinity, this timeworn topic became grist for years of further discussion. Park historian Mark has speculated, with a touch of humor, that Volz's enthusiasm for the south entrance was related to his having been the first park superintendent to live in Munson Valley for an entire winter, following disposal of the Medford winter headquarters in 1964. Though the Munson Valley complex of administrative buildings had been adapted for year-round use in the mid-1950s, Volz might well have been taken aback both by the amount of snow and its survival well into spring. In any case, the issue soon became caught in a tangle of complex proposals that eventually came to nothing.[35]

The seemingly mundane matter of administrative locale took on a new guise in 1969 when the NPS Klamath Falls Cluster Office was formed to preside over Crater Lake National Park and Oregon Caves, Lava Beds, and John Day Fossil Beds national monuments. The "reform," finally abandoned in the early 1980s, was widely scorned in later years (except perhaps by the plan's executive masterminds). Lines of authority within the new administrative setup became significantly muddied for park personnel, who were sometimes stumped on the basic question of who was in charge: was it Crater Lake's superintendent, or was it the general superintendent at the Klamath Falls office? Dick Brown, chief park naturalist at Crater Lake from 1966 to 1970, called the scheme "a stupid waste of money," as well as a frequent nuisance for Crater Lake staff involved in such routine tasks as trying to locate files that had been moved to Klamath Falls. Administrative officer Marvin Nelson decided to retire partly as a result of the Cluster Office change: "After we went to Klamath Falls, it was just too much. I was eligible to retire and told them they could have it." Much of the criticism of the move came because Crater Lake lost ten staff members to the Klamath Falls office, including key personnel who had only recently been assigned to the park year-round after abandonment of the Medford winter office.[36]

怒

HARRY W. AND HARRY C. SMITH operated the Crater Lake National Park Company for only five years before selling out to Ralph O. Peyton and James M. Griffin in 1959. During the brief Smith era, relations between the concessionaire and the Park Service warmed somewhat. The Smiths were not much more responsive to NPS prodding than their predecessors had been, but they were more amiable in their style of resistance. An addition to the Rim Village cafeteria was completed in 1956, and Crater Lake Lodge received cosmetic remodeling during 1957-1958, but few of the recommendations of the Haner Report (with its $72,000 price tag) were carried out, and the long-neglected need for an automatic fire-protection sprinkling system in the lodge remained unattended. Nonetheless, many at Crater Lake hated to see Pop Smith and his son leave. Naturalist Ted Arthur remembered the Smiths as "great individuals . . . very approachable . . . cooperative, and not pushy.

[They were not] out to further commercialize the area, but to present a good facility [and] good food."[37]

When Peyton and Griffin bought the company from the Smiths in 1959, the contract for concession services was due to expire the next year. Negotiations between the concession company (now called Crater Lake Lodge, Inc.) and the government included a Park Service proposal to purchase Crater Lake Lodge for possible conversion to a visitor center and museum. According to this proposal, the concessionaire, with cash from the sale, would then build a new facility somewhere in the Rim Village area. Negotiations stalled, however, over the thorny issue of location: Crater Lake Lodge, Inc., sought a site for the new lodge much closer to the caldera rim than the Park Service found acceptable. A five-year contract renewal extended the status quo through 1965, but then a one-year renewal was made contingent on the concessionaire's installation of an automatic sprinkler system in the old lodge. A partial sprinkler system, covering mostly the lobby, was finally installed in 1967.[38]

While the relationship between the Park Service and Crater Lake Lodge, Inc., remained uneasy throughout most of the 1960s, disputes and suspicions between the parties were generally invisible to the public. Many Park Service officials were "scared to death" of the lodge during these years, fearing a major conflagration and loss of life. After having lived through the sometimes acrimonious discussions over the concession company's reluctance to install a comprehensive fire-protection system, Wayne Howe admitted that he would have felt safer sleeping "out in the street" at that time. Judged by the 1965 edition of the park handbook, however, peace and harmony prevailed, as the Park Service touted the full range of concession services, from lodge to coffee shop, from boat landing to gasoline station. And, in fact, the relationship between Park Service and concessionaire was sound enough to foster a new thirty-year contract, signed in 1967.[39]

In the same year, the Park Service was also able finally to consummate its long-discussed purchase of Crater Lake Lodge from the Peyton and Griffin concession operation. A lease arrangement allowed the concession company to continue managing the lodge while NPS decision makers pondered the long-range fate of the structure and site. In the meantime, park officials were able to carry out a few long-ignored safety measures. Then, buoyed by their new contract, Peyton and Griffin in early 1968 announced a $2-million, nine-year building program for Crater Lake. Most of what was announced never materialized, however, as relations between the Park Service and Crater Lake Lodge, Inc., settled into a frequently contentious, sometimes antagonistic pattern. Park Service officials tended to view the concession owners (the irascible Ralph Peyton, in particular) as obstinate and money-hungry; concession company officials saw Park Service figures as impractical and anti-business.[40]

Challenges to the Park Service Ranger Ideal

FROM THE FOUNDING OF THE FIRST national park in 1872, to the formation of the National Park Service in 1916, to the continued diversification of the national park system throughout the twentieth century, the national parks and other Park Service attractions have been managed and supported by workers in a variety of occupations. During much of that time, however, the park ranger—a prototypical sturdy, white male wearing the trademark "Smokey Bear" hat—epitomized the National Park Service for most Americans. This idealized park ranger image, like so many other NPS conventions, was invented and refined during Stephen Mather's landmark term as director in the early twentieth century.[41]

Mather and his public-relations machine successfully marketed a ranger-dominant version of the Park Service a decade or more before recruitment and training were able to bring agency practice in line with this ideal. By the time the pioneer director retired in 1929, rangers (sometimes referred to as "Mather men") occupied center stage in National Park Service image projection. But the significance of these consummate NPS professionals went well beyond image. Park Service historian Richard West Sellars has observed that by 1929 "rangers and superintendents had coalesced as a distinctive group with a strong sense of identity and a common understanding of how national parks should be managed."[42]

At Crater Lake, this powerful association was perhaps best exemplified in the nearly ten-year professional relationship between superintendent Ernest Leavitt and chief ranger Carlisle Crouch. By the time Crouch left the park in 1947 to become assistant superintendent at Blue Ridge National Parkway, the Crater Lake ranger force, through the key position of chief ranger, was closely allied with the superintendent's office and involved in nearly every aspect of park operations. The all-encompassing scope of ranger duties was a significant point of pride and protectiveness for rangers at Crater Lake and throughout the Park Service. In fact, rangers were so loathe to relinquish any of their acknowledged duties that when chief ranger Carlock E. Johnson spelled out the position's responsibilities at Crater

This neat alignment of the Crater Lake National Park ranger force in front of the Rangers' Dormitory (now the Steel Center) in 1941 conveys a sense of the "ranger ideal" that was marketed by the Park Service throughout much of the twentieth century. (Courtesy NPS, CLNP Museum and Archives Collection.)

Lake in 1955, he included "fish planting," which had not been done since 1941, by rangers or anyone else.[43]

Rangers, as a profession, also clung to and perpetuated an image of national parks as rugged frontier outposts softened by elegant tourist facilities. They portrayed their role within these unique domains as scout, soldier, backcountry survivalist, resort host, camp counselor, and selfless do-gooder, all rolled into one. Throughout the 1950s and 1960s, rangers guarded their masculine province against the encroachments of other occupations, frequently documenting their versatility and professional supremacy in detailed administrative reports. Amid the wide-ranging cultural changes of the 1960s, a few women began to penetrate the inner sanctum of the ranger profession. But their arrival was fraught with controversies, including great tempests over suitable uniforms for female rangers. As historian Polly Welts Kaufman has pointed out, even as women made inroads into traditionally male jobs, the "male-defined culture of the Park Service" persisted, and woman "pioneers" frequently felt pressure to conform to masculine models. Women did not claim NPS leadership roles of any kind until the 1970s.[44]

Rangers defended their historically advantageous position in other ways as well. Sellars has argued that when NPS director Conrad Wirth placed Park Service biologists under the direction of rangers and foresters in the late 1950s, he formalized an alliance (between rangers and foresters) and a dominance (of resource management over research science) that was already well established. Rangers enjoyed a favored institutional niche in relation to Park Service educators and interpreters as well. In reminiscing about George C. "Doc" Ruhle, Crater Lake's chief naturalist between 1940 and 1953, ranger Wayne Howe explained that "naturalists and rangers just plain didn't get along . . . weren't supposed to get along. . . . That's the way it was. . . . The ranger force was *the* force; the naturalist force was a kind of subsidiary force."[45]

The Reawakening of Science

ALTHOUGH THE INSTITUTIONAL DOMINANCE of rangers continued to color Park Service resource management in the 1950s and 1960s, the knowledge and perspectives of biologists, botanists, and ecologists began to seep into some national park policies. The ecological approach to nature, fashionable among scientists and certain intellectuals in the 1930s, was reinvigorated with popular appeal and political potency in the 1960s, partly on the strength of such best-selling environmental exposés as Rachel Carson's *Silent Spring* (1962) and Paul Ehrlich's *The Population Bomb* (1968). In addition, two prestigious documents published in 1963—the *Report of the Advisory Board on Wildlife Management in the National Parks* (known as the Leopold Report) and a National Academy of Sciences study (known as the Robbins Report)—posed challenges to reigning Park Service policies on development, resource management, and science, policies that many believed had reached their logical conclusions in carelessly planned and executed development projects during the Mission 66 period.[46]

At Crater Lake, scientifically grounded guidelines for the treatment of bears—prohibitions against feeding, controls on garbage and garbage dumps, education of campers—were finally articulated and followed during the 1950s and 1960s. At the same time, even while wildlife biologists argued that "bear problems" in the national parks were a direct result of policies allowed or promoted by the Park Service, official NPS statements on the subject were still more likely to cite the danger of "troublesome bears" than to admit past errors.[47]

Willingness of the Park Service to amend its traditional fish-management policies came even more grudgingly, at Crater Lake and elsewhere. Though the lake had not been stocked with fish since 1941, and fishing had tapered off since that time, many NPS professionals continued to regard sport fishing as an important recreational option for all national park visitors. Consequently, aquatic biologist O. L. Wallis was assigned in 1958 to study fish reproduction in Crater Lake, and to determine whether stocking should be resumed. Wallis's recommendation—that the park reject "additional plantings of fishes and other organisms" in Crater Lake and in park streams—was rooted in sound biology, but his report was cleverly packaged in a brand of reasoning likely to appeal to the more traditional, non-biological perspective of the Park Service. Wallis argued that because of the lake's relative inaccessibility, as well as other factors peculiar to the park, only a small percentage of the fish planted over time had been caught. Thus, the scientist maintained, undue costs and other complications for non-fishing visitors would probably outweigh whatever benefits might come from resuscitating an active sport-fishing program at Crater Lake.[48]

Scientific knowledge about Crater Lake accumulated slowly during the second half of the twentieth century. Questions surrounding the lake's fish population became less central to scientific investigations— except perhaps the basic question of how the artificial presence of fish might affect the lake's complex web of life. Among other findings, scientists began to discover an amazing array of diatom species, rare invertebrates, and mosses living at startling depths. In 1959, scientists from the U.S. Coast and Geodetic Survey probed the Crater Lake

A plankton net is lifted from Crater Lake onto a research vessel in the summer of 1967, part of Oregon State University professor John Donaldson's early lake-studies work at Crater Lake National Park.

basin with more than four thousand echo-soundings, an exercise that yielded data for a topographic map of the lake bottom. The soundings also confirmed the presence of two submerged volcanic cones and established a new maximum lake depth of 1,932 feet, 64 feet less than that recorded in 1886. Then, between 1961 and 1964, the U.S. Geological Survey conducted tests and research that, according to limnologist Doug Larson, "established permanent and frequent baseline records for lake temperature, lake surface elevation, and water chemistry for use as a comparison with future data."[49]

With baseline data on Crater Lake finally available, John Donaldson, a fisheries professor at Oregon State University, established a pioneer lake-studies program in cooperation with the National Park Service in 1966. Donaldson, who received a research grant from the Interior Department's Office of Water Resources Research, invited three Oregon State graduate students (including Doug Larson) to participate in his Crater Lake investigations during the summer of 1967. Because of its unique properties as a "closed basin," Donaldson viewed Crater Lake "as the ideal limnological benchmark with which to compare other Oregon lakes," Larson has written. Work by several scientists in the late 1960s substantiated earlier reports about the lake's exceptional water clarity and provided additional baseline information for tracking the lake's clarity over time.[50]

Ostensibly in the interests of forest protection, entrenched Park Service fire-suppression and insect-eradication policies remained in effect at Crater Lake during the 1950s and 1960s, even as these policies were increasingly challenged by science and questioned within the Park Service itself. NPS professionals had begun to experiment with "prescribed" and "controlled" burns at various sites in the late 1950s, but a paragraph in Crater Lake's master plan for 1964 detailing the park's fire history for the previous thirty years made clear that park officials at Crater Lake were still preoccupied with their ability to suppress fires at all costs.[51]

LIKE THE EARLY ECOLOGY MOVEMENT, the cause of wilderness preservation burned brightly in the 1930s before dimming during the war years and into the early 1950s. The wilderness campaign then revived in the later 1950s, partly in response to concerns about excessive development and misuse of natural areas during the Mission 66 period. Conrad Wirth, Mission 66 architect, unwittingly contributed momentum to the wilderness cause in 1957 with publication of *The*

Long after scientists had challenged the effectiveness of insect-eradication efforts in forests, most national parks continued the practice. Here Crater Lake National Park personnel burn the bark of ponderosa pines in an effort to control the spread of bark beetles in 1960. (Courtesy NPS, CLNP Museum and Archives Collection.)

National Park Wilderness, a large-format color brochure intended, implausibly, to portray Mission 66 as a boon to wilderness preservation. Wirth, already sensitive about criticisms of Mission 66, hoped to head off the efforts of wilderness advocates to extend their zeal into national park areas; instead, he attracted even greater scrutiny of the national parks.[52]

Although the Wilderness Act of 1964 targeted U.S. Forest Service and Bureau of Land Management land policies far more than those of the Park Service, parts of the law did refer specifically to wilderness preservation in national parks. Moreover, the act defined "wilderness" in ways that offered new interpretations of the Park Service's legislative mandate to maintain national park lands "unimpaired" for the enjoyment of future generations. Because the proposed legislation threatened to constrain the Park Service in the management of its backcountry regions, the NPS leadership opposed it. And in claiming that the wilderness bill would be redundant in its application to the national parks, NPS spokesmen took the position: "We prefer to continue defining and managing wilderness in our own way, and *our* way allows for compatibility between wilderness and development."[53]

Once the Wilderness Act became law in 1964, the Park Service position on the legislation shifted from outright opposition to official neutrality. NPS leaders soon found themselves contemplating how the park system might be forced to comply with the act's requirement that "every roadless area of five thousand contiguous acres or more in the national parks, monuments and other units of the national park system" be assessed for "suitability or nonsuitability" as wilderness. At Crater Lake, several years of NPS analysis culminated in a plan proposing four areas of the park, around 104,200 acres (nearly 60 percent of the park's surface area), as wilderness. Park officials hoped initially that these four areas could simply be designated as wilderness, without further requirements to comply with the Wilderness Act's specific definitions of wilderness.[54]

As the 1960s came to an end, and as the costs of the Vietnam War began to have budget repercussions throughout the federal government, National Park Service leaders anticipated a set of even more demanding compliance obligations, these associated with the National Environmental Policy Act of 1969. Although the law's specific regulatory requirements for the Park Service remained unclear in 1970, the legislation helped convince NPS leaders that they could no longer afford to think of the national parks as "distant, serene enclaves of natural landscape architecture," in the words of geographer Lary Dilsaver. Other powerful players from outside the Park Service would henceforth contribute to shaping the NPS system.[55]

Interpreting Crater Lake

GEORGE C. "DOC" RUHLE, Crater Lake's chief naturalist between 1940 and 1953, inherited an active and resourceful interpretive program when he came on the scene. Until the demands of war brought a halt to "nonessential activities" in the fall of 1942, Ruhle managed to maintain the educational program's momentum. In 1941, he convened an advisory committee—chaired by R. W. Leighton of the University of Oregon and including Ruhle, Luther Cressman, Howel Williams, and others—to support scientific and educational work at the park. And in the summer of 1942, just before the interpretive branch shut down altogether, he oversaw one term of a new training school for park interpreters. In these and other aspects of science studies and public education at Crater Lake, John C. Merriam continued to offer valuable inspiration and political support until his death in 1945.[56]

In 1946, when Crater Lake reopened year-round and Doc Ruhle returned from a four-year stint in the navy, eight seasonal naturalists were hired to work under his direction. While these new members of the interpretive staff were schooled, along with the park's rangers, in a revived postwar ranger-training program, the bulk of their education in interpretive work came from practical contact with Ruhle and other naturalist colleagues.[57]

Ruhle revived contacts between Crater Lake National Park and the University of Oregon during the postwar period, taking advantage of John Merriam's links with both institutions and drawing on the interest generated by the prewar advisory committee chaired by the university's R. W. Leighton. The Crater Lake Field School of Nature Appreciation, modeled after a similar program at Yosemite National Park and offered by the University of Oregon for the first time during the summer of 1947, presented an innovative five-week course featuring the cross-disciplinary approach championed by Merriam. One of the course instructors, Ruth Hopson Keen, became the first woman naturalist at Crater Lake a short time later.[58]

Ruhle, who held a Ph.D. in chemistry (hence the nickname "Doc"), was entirely comfortable working with men and women with advanced degrees or specialized training in the sciences. In fact, he went out of his way to hire such people as seasonal naturalists at Crater Lake. Before 1957, the year when alarm over the Russian Sputnik satellite helped generate new sources of funding for individual scientific research in the United States, highly qualified scientists often looked for science-related employment in national parks during the summertime academic off-season. Biologist James Kezer, who worked as a naturalist with Ruhle during the summers of 1951 and 1952, recalled that half or more of the seasonal staff from those years held Ph.D.s. Even more impressive, according to Kezer, was Ruhle's rare ability to recognize the limits of his own knowledge and to prosper from the expertise of those who worked under his direction.[59]

THE CRATER LAKE NATURAL HISTORY ASSOCIATION, a nonprofit scientific and historical society, was founded in 1942 to promote exhibits, publications, and other forms of public education germane to the park. As a support group organized outside the formal structure of the Park Service, the association's aims could more easily stretch beyond typical Park Service ideas and practices. For example, one of the group's stated constitutional objectives—"to study living conditions, past and present, of the Indians of the region, to encourage their arts and crafts, and to perpetuate their structures, customs, traditions, legends, etc."—carried the potential for meaningful educational innovation and perhaps even political rapprochement with the area's oldest inhabitants. If the association had been able to pursue this goal with energy and determination at mid-century, they might have initiated an important break in Crater Lake's long-term indifference toward the region's native population. But additional decades would have to pass before park officials, staff, and support groups would seriously pursue such an objective.[60]

The association, thriving in the postwar period, published *Nature Notes*, sponsored lectures, sold printed materials, and took an increasingly active role in supporting small-scale research and publication efforts. During the 1950s and early 1960s, the association published several works on the park's natural history by Crater Lake interpretive staff. Profits from sales of these publications and others (more than $7,000 in 1964 alone) supported more research and publishing, provided critical funds for augmenting the park's library, and helped fill gaps in the park's federal budget appropriation.[61]

FOR MOST OF THE THIRTEEN YEARS Doc Ruhle served as park naturalist, he believed that a multipurpose museum would eventually take shape at Crater Lake to serve as a hub for the park's interpretive program well into the future. From the early 1940s to the early 1950s, Ruhle wrote, revised, and rewrote prospectuses for this much-anticipated facility, which, many hoped, would mark Crater Lake's return to top-tier status among U.S. national parks. When Ruhle left Crater Lake in 1953 for a new assignment at Hawaii Volcanoes National Park, the museum project was still under active discussion, and a version of the prospectus was finally approved in 1957.[62]

But the museum was never built. Like other major construction proposals of the time, this one succumbed to uncertainty within the Park Service over whether to adapt existing Crater Lake structures to current needs or build new ones, as well as to basic indecision over the most appropriate locations for the three main categories of human activity in the park: administrative, recreational, and educational. Moreover, as pointed out earlier, some NPS decision makers in the postwar period were beginning to conclude that major investments at Crater Lake, such as the proposed museum project, would never pay off in increased visitation.

Ruhle had nonetheless managed to reestablish a strong postwar interpretive tradition at Crater Lake. During the summer months,

Visitors consult a Park Service booklet while enjoying their self-guided hike along the picturesque Castle Crest Wildflower Garden Nature Trail, near the Munson Valley park headquarters. (Courtesy NPS, CLNP Museum and Archives Collection.)

evening talks on natural history were featured at Crater Lake Lodge and the Community House in Rim Village, and geology presentations were given every day at the Sinnott Memorial. Free printed materials were offered for self-guided hikes to Garfield Peak, through Castle Crest Wildflower Garden, to the lake, and along the rim; twice-a-day guided boat tours of the lake and a guided automobile caravan tour of the crater rim also continued to be popular attractions. Visitors at the park's entrance stations were encouraged to begin their tours at the Exhibit Building (formerly the Scenic America Company's Kiser Studio, which the Park Service had acquired in 1929 from the financially strapped Fred Kiser), where brief exhibits and displays helped orient newcomers. At the Sinnott Memorial, another popular starting point, a naturalist with field glasses and a large relief map gave geology talks and helped point the way to the lake trail and other attractions.[63]

At the time Ruhle left in 1953, and in subsequent decades, the interpretive program relied more on the character and ingenuity of the staff than on fancy facilities and state-of-the-art teaching tools. Still, Crater Lake facilities, while hardly modern, were impressive in their own way. The Sinnott Memorial, though small, was unmatched as a site for talks on Mount Mazama and Crater Lake geology. Likewise, the Exhibit Building served as a cramped but fairly efficient location for dispensing basic information, selling literature, and displaying small plant and animal specimens. The Community House, with its

Seasonal naturalist Norman Wild uses a projected image of Crater Lake's Phantom Ship to make a geological point in an evening talk at Rim Village's Community House in 1955. (Courtesy NPS, CLNP Museum and Archives Collection.)

insubstantial frame construction and rugged setting, was nearly impossible to protect against the rim's harsh winter weather. Nonetheless, with its picturesque fireplace and cozy appointments, the Community House, even in poor condition, provided comfortable shelter for summer evening presentations. The Watchman Lookout afforded a small but stunning spot for viewing the entire park, and a particularly apt setting for small displays on forest ecology. Finally, the handsome Administration Building in the Munson Valley park headquarters area furnished essential office, storage, and laboratory space for the interpretive staff.[64]

This rustic Rim Village sign advertised Crater Lake National Park's free, naturalist-guided auto-caravan tour of Rim Drive, a daily attraction during the busy summer season. (OHS neg. OrHi 80834.)

ᗢ

THE CRATER LAKE INTERPRETIVE PROGRAM of the 1940s, 1950s, and 1960s, reflecting priorities and pressures typical of the Park Service during these decades, encouraged staff to pursue independent "projects," without allowing them much time to do so. Most of the naturalists' forty-hour workweek was given over to public contact, in both planned and spontaneous settings. Independent projects, sometimes referred to as "research," were to be accomplished outside scheduled work hours. Most naturalists, whether out of professional devotion or sheer interest, found time to pursue such projects, which usually brought them into gratifying contact with the park's landscapes and life forms. And in carrying out this fieldwork, they were able to enrich their public presentations and equip themselves for useful contributions to *Nature Notes*. But most such projects were relatively casual and short term, and did not have the rigor and duration of true scientific research.[65]

Not until the later decades of the twentieth century did the Park Service begin, haltingly, to recognize and promote the potential of national parks as "scientific laboratories"—unique realms of study for scientists both within and outside the Park Service. Throughout most of the twentieth century, science and science research struggled against competing programs within the Park Service for a "favorable place in the sun," to cite an apt botanical metaphor used by NPS biologist Lowell Sumner. The struggle has been mostly uphill, as the strong tourist orientation of the National Park Service has favored the resource-management approach of rangers and foresters over the research-science and ecological approach of scientists and interpreters. This bias, which sometimes expressed itself in the form of suspicion toward higher levels of academic training, was rooted in a false opposition between the "practical" approach of rangers and the "theoretical" approach of scientists. Dick Brown, who worked at Crater Lake as a naturalist and a research biologist in the 1950s and 1960s, recalled the discomfort of some Crater Lake superintendents with permanent or seasonal staff who, they feared, might be "too academic."[66]

Nonetheless, in the decades between 1940 and 1970, the permanent and seasonal naturalist corps at Crater Lake, with their different educational backgrounds (from college zoology majors to Ph.D.s in biology), fulfilled the NPS interpretive mission of teaching basic science and natural history concepts within natural settings as well as any other national park interpretive staff in the United States. Crater Lake interpreters gained a reputation for excellence within the National Park

Service, and their achievements helped propel the NPS to the forefront of beyond-the-classroom education in the United States in the second half of the twentieth century. As far as Dick Brown was concerned, "excellence" meant the best possible "delivery of the park story" in the various venues in which interpreters and visitors came together at Crater Lake. Interpretation was directed, broadly speaking, at the elusive "typical visitor," and most interpreters strove to reach as many people as possible with clear, broadly intelligible presentations. While interpretive talks sometimes missed their mark with audiences at the extremes (those profoundly uninformed or uninterested, or those already well informed), Park Service interpretation, at Crater Lake and elsewhere, has generally excelled in reaching the vast middle ground of intelligent, curious visitors.[67]

The entertainment portions of Park Service programs (piano playing, skits by concession employees, "campfire songs") sometimes belied the seriousness of purpose that underlay the educational mission. At Crater Lake, for example, interpreters with Ph.D.s in science led songs just like all the other interpreters, because such group activities were a "required . . . part of the regular routine." At the same time, Crater Lake interpretive staff of this era never forgot the overriding, earnestly educational purpose of their work. Providing reviews and critiques of the tape-recorded presentations of interpretive staff was an important part of Dick Brown's role as park naturalist, and work evaluations of that era had potentially serious repercussions. (It was generally accepted that a high evaluation at Crater Lake during these years really meant something within the NPS system.) Bruce Black, chief naturalist at Crater Lake between 1959 and 1963, invested substantial time and effort in his evaluations of seasonal and permanent employees, and he considered this "quality-control" function one of the most difficult and meaningful parts of his job.[68]

Ted Arthur, who worked as a Crater Lake naturalist from 1958 through the 1960s, felt thankful for the guidance he received as a member of the interpretive team: "I owe a great debt of gratitude to Dick Brown, who was extremely patient with me, would take me out in the forest and identify trees, plants, and birds, gave me a lot of material to read, [and] encouraged me to hear other people's campfire programs." Likewise, after F. Owen Hoffman joined the Crater Lake interpretive staff fresh from college in 1966, he soon felt part of an educational tradition that was both demanding and deeply gratifying. In acknowledging the two professional naturalists—Glen Kaye and Ted Arthur—responsible for his training, Hoffman recalled: "They took everything so seriously that you knew you were about to enter a profession as opposed to something . . . on the order of clerk or tour guide. They gave us each two weeks' time to rapidly learn about the plants, animals, and the geology of the lake. We spent two weeks in training prior to being permitted to put on the uniform. After that time, we would audit the talks and walks of the more veteran naturalists."[69]

Ᏸ

THE CRATER LAKE INTERPRETIVE PROGRAM, by all accounts, operated at a high professional level during these years, and was effective as far as it went. But the park story conveyed to the public—the blend of information, scientific ideas, and natural-history concepts typically presented by the interpretive team—was, in some respects, narrow. Dick Brown remarked in later years: "Crater Lake just wasn't historical enough, and my orientation was not to history. . . . I think I had a blossoming of concern that more wasn't being done about the historical record that was being lost with the death of . . . people who had real history of Crater Lake in their heads."[70]

The general neglect of the human historical record in Park Service interpretation was even more pronounced in the area of Indian culture and history. Will Steel and some of his contemporaries had energetically compiled information about the region's recent history, but the story of the area's oldest inhabitants was largely overlooked. A few presentations developed by Ted Arthur in the late 1950s and early 1960s provided an exception to the general shortchanging of native history in Park Service interpretation at Crater Lake. When Arthur came to Crater Lake in 1958, his interests leaned in the direction of history and social science (so much so, in fact, that he was somewhat baffled at having been hired as a naturalist). Then, while at Crater Lake, he became fascinated by the Klamath Reservation and the tribal termination process then unfolding. When Arthur asked Dick Brown about the possibility "of giving an evening program on the Indians of the area," he received an enthusiastic go-ahead. Arthur conducted interviews with tribal members, including several conversations with well-known elder and Tribal Council chairman Seldon Kirk, and he compiled a slide collection on Indian artifacts, basketry, and history. His presentation incorporating native cultures and history was called "Crater Lake through the Years."[71]

The Crossroads of Tribal Termination

POSTWAR DECISION MAKING ABOUT the future of Crater Lake National Park was, as we have seen, rarely forthright. But for all the ambivalence and second-guessing, Park Service strategists were able to simplify their task somewhat by largely ignoring the area's Indian population. Between 1940 and 1970, the peoples of the Klamath Reservation became increasingly separated from Crater Lake. The once-sacred mountain lake, now ruled by the federal government and its National Park Service agents, had become a playground for white Americans in their automobiles. The Klamath Indians, meanwhile, contending with the U.S. government on several fronts and struggling for acceptance in a largely inhospitable society, increasingly lost touch with their culture's traditional forms of religious expression. At a time when the Indians no doubt needed spiritual consolation more than ever, Crater Lake had become unattainably remote, part of a separate world.

Tribal members of starkly different outlooks generally agreed that the apparent prosperity of the Klamath Reservation peoples on the eve of World War II was frail and most likely impermanent. More than seventy years of reservation life had been more effective in undermining traditional native cultures than in inculcating the values and behaviors of the dominant Euro-American culture. The Klamath people, as a whole, remained poorly educated and ill prepared for assimilation into a society that, in many ways, dictated their fate. Widespread "cultural confusion" among the reservation population translated into high rates of alcoholism and psychological despair. Although Klamath leaders agreed that change was needed, especially in the tribe's relationship to the U.S. government, potential courses of change either remained obscure or were bitterly disputed among tribal members.[72]

Those who, before World War II, had preached individualism and gradual disengagement from the tribe and reservation were even more strongly committed to that course after the war. Led by Wade Crawford, who had advocated a form of nontribal individualism among the Klamath since the 1920s, returning war veterans resolved to push their people beyond the one institution—the reservation—that seemed most to symbolize their subservience. In rejecting the reservation, many also turned away from the tribe, which both helped to define the reservation and epitomized a way of life that seemed more and more irrelevant to the demands of the future. Although some prominent voices continued to embrace the tribe and its traditions, Klamath postwar spokesmen conveyed an overall impression of dissatisfaction with the reservation.[73]

In the early 1950s, native discontent with reservation life converged with a vein of American political sentiment favoring bold government action to bring about Native Americans' assimilation into American society and an end to their "dependency." According to this politically popular line, the gradualist approach to assimilation offered by reservations had been ineffective, largely because "wardship status and the isolation of reservations had kept Indians from enjoying their full rights as U.S. citizens." House Concurrent Resolution 108, passed by Congress in 1953, called for termination of federal supervision of certain Indian tribes, a change in legal status that would end federal aid to the tribes and remove their exemption from local taxes. While native political factions argued about the exact formula for managing or dividing assets upon dissolution of the tribe, by 1954 most Klamath Reservation peoples were resigned to termination in one form or another.[74]

The Klamath Termination Act signed by President Dwight D. Eisenhower in August 1954 allowed tribal members born before that date either to maintain a joint interest in tribal assets or to withdraw and receive a cash payment for their share of corporate assets. This formula served to further divide an already confused and fragmented people: in addition to the obviously different economic interests of

This meeting of the Klamath Tribal Council's executive committee took place just a few months after the Klamath Termination Act was signed by President Eisenhower in 1954. (OHS neg. CN 012356.)

those who remained within the tribe and those who withdrew, those born after August 1954 were deprived of their tribal birthrights without compensation of any kind. Four more years passed before eligible tribal members were allowed to vote to remain (474 votes) or withdraw (2,154). The actual termination order was then postponed another three years, until August 1961, as government officials and tribal leaders considered testimony and evidence that the reservation peoples, because of deficits in education and employment skills, and because of racial prejudice, were unprepared for termination.[75]

While the origins of and responsibility for Klamath tribal termination are difficult to pin down, the effects of the policy were clearly devastating. Living conditions steadily worsened for Klamath County Indians over the next two decades, and the psychological trauma suffered by hundreds of people as a result of losing their homeland was immense. Tribal identity weakened, and people who had once felt part of something larger than themselves now seemed more adrift and alienated than ever before. Though the termination policy was quickly recognized as destructive, the federal government failed to restore tribal legitimacy until 1986. In the meantime, tribe and reservation, so recently scorned as symbols of subjugation, began to appear to many as long-lost friends—and as the strongest potential links to a restorative native tradition.[76]

Chapter 7

Trauma and Recovery

1970-1985

∽

The Hartzog Era at Crater Lake

BY 1967, WHEN HE NAMED Donald M. Spalding as Crater Lake National Park's sixteenth superintendent, George B. Hartzog, Jr., reigned supreme as the seventh director of the National Park Service. Appointed in early 1964 by President Lyndon Johnson, Hartzog served through 1972, when he finally fell victim to President Richard Nixon's pique. Hartzog was one of the most decisive and authoritative directors in Park Service history. He coolly viewed the competition for money and "turf" among federal agencies as a kind of white-collar combat, and he deployed his NPS troops like a commanding officer bent on total victory.[1]

The bureaucratic warfare waged by Hartzog on behalf of the National Park Service between 1964 and 1972 was made especially fierce by budgetary hardships imposed by a real war in Vietnam. As a whole, the NPS fared reasonably well during these difficult, polarized years: its domains were extended, its ranks were diversified, and its appeal was broadened, at least slightly. But most appraisals of Hartzog focus on his passion for the NPS and his willingness to act boldly (for better or for worse) rather than on specific achievements. Known as an executive with a single-minded determination to get things done, Hartzog was not shy about ruffling feathers.[2]

But for all the passion and boldness flowing from Washington, D.C., during the Hartzog era, Crater Lake National Park entered the 1970s as a neglected second sister among the great western national parks. As Hartzog shepherded the Mission 66 renewal program through its final two years, culminating in the fiftieth anniversary of the Park Service in 1966, Crater Lake's three most coveted development projects were mired in limbo. Then, when Hartzog assigned Donald Spalding to Crater Lake in 1967, the NPS director instructed the new superintendent to manage southern Oregon's park only as time permitted. Spalding's main charge was to get California's Redwood National Park, with its magnificent, politically potent northern coastal forests, up and running.[3]

Spalding naturally found it impossible to give his full attention to Crater Lake: "I was never able to do the job that should have been done [there]," he later admitted. Hartzog accentuated his snub of the Oregon park by jauntily directing Spalding to devise a new master plan for Crater Lake in his "spare time." And, in typically blunt fashion, Hartzog ordered that the new plan include a formula for relocating park headquarters and housing from Munson Valley to a lower-elevation site on the western slope of Mount Mazama. Though this was not an absurd idea in itself, Hartzog's directive showed little appreciation for the proposition's complicated history. But Spalding, who as "superintendent-in-absentia" had not spent enough time at Crater Lake to gain much of a feeling for the park's history himself, was not inclined to argue with the domineering Hartzog. He did manage to oversee the creation of a new master plan for Crater Lake, which included specifications for Hartzog's mandatory headquarters relocation. However, this plan, like so many others before it, went unfulfilled.[4]

Introduction of the Klamath Falls Cluster Office in 1969 compounded the park's management and operations problems in the 1970s. The additional troubles came about not so much because Crater Lake lost its superintendent, Donald Spalding, to the Cluster Office (he had not been deeply involved in the park up to that time, anyway), but because other key park personnel were displaced and lines of authority were further clouded. After Spalding assumed his duties as general superintendent in the Klamath Falls office, a new and untested administrator, Einar L. Johnson, was appointed superintendent of Crater Lake. But Johnson's stay, in keeping with the pattern of recent superintendents, was short. In 1973, he yielded the job to Richard H. Sims, a neat, soft-spoken, indecisive man who would occupy the hot seat at Crater Lake during the park's greatest crisis.[5]

The Water-Contamination Crisis of 1975

THOUSANDS OF OREGONIANS probably first became aware of their state's only national park in 1975 when Crater Lake hit the headlines with a major public-health scare. The origins of the upheaval lay in the most basic human biological needs. Providing for such requirements—water, most fundamentally—had from the start been a major challenge at Crater Lake National Park. As that challenge was answered over time, with more complex solutions responding to greater numbers of visitors, a parallel challenge emerged: the sanitary and safe disposal of waste. For most of the park's lifetime, the engineering needed for these necessities had gone largely unnoticed. But for a brief time during the late spring and early summer of 1975, the engineering failed, and the park's systems of water supply and waste disposal intersected perilously.

Sometime in May 1975, a clogged sewer line near Crater Lake Lodge caused raw waste to overflow and mix with snowmelt running into Munson Springs, the park's main source of water at that time. By June, contaminated water was flowing throughout Crater Lake's water-supply system, and by the middle of June park residents and employees were becoming ill with gastroenteritis. When visitors began to report similar illnesses in July, news of the outbreak became impossible to contain. After the cause of the contamination was finally pinpointed on July 10, the NPS closed Crater Lake National Park to the public. During a three-week shutdown, the park's water system was flushed, sanitized, and refilled with potable water. Though visitors began to trickle back into the park on August 1, the lodge remained closed for the rest of the season. Fallout from the episode depressed tourism at Crater Lake, where visitation dipped to 427,252 for the year, as well as throughout Oregon. The morale of the Crater Lake workforce plummeted as months of investigations gave rise to unseemly finger pointing and brought embarrassment and personal humiliation to several key people connected with the park.[6]

Oregon's senior U.S. senator, Mark O. Hatfield, took the lead in the government's investigation of the incident. Because the fiasco had become a national news story, carrying with it public accusations of government negligence and cover-up, the U.S. Senate committee hearing that convened in Medford City Hall in September was under great pressure to determine responsibility for the mess. Hatfield's grilling of witnesses was painstaking and aggressive, and park superintendent Richard Sims, in particular, seemed beaten down by the questioning. (In the wake of the investigation, the Park Service immediately reassigned both Sims and chief ranger Jim Wiggins.) In the end, though, the committee's report focused more on the shortcomings of the National Park Service and Congress than on the culpability of individuals. As Senator Hatfield put it bluntly in his summary of the committee's findings: "Had Crater Lake been adequately staffed, this episode would not have occurred."[7]

Employee morale at Crater Lake National Park plummeted in the wake of the water-contamination crisis of 1975. Here staff and their families line up for vaccinations and blood tests. (Courtesy National Park Service, Crater Lake National Park Museum and Archives Collection.)

Many in the Park Service, however, blamed concessionaire Ralph Peyton for the disaster, claiming that he ignored early signs of danger among seriously ill concession employees, and that he bullied superintendent Sims into postponing action in hopes that the rash of sickness would disappear without creating harmful publicity. The committee report, while soft-pedaling Peyton's personal responsibility, did recommend an increase in "supervision and control of concession activities." Subsequently, in a 1978 lawsuit, Peyton and his company were found guilty of "wanton misconduct" for their failure to warn guests of the illnesses among concession employees, but by that time the Portland entrepreneur had sold the Crater Lake concession rights to the Canteen Company of Oregon for $1.9 million.[8]

While the Hatfield committee report focused on Crater Lake's weaknesses at the time of the water crisis (among other criticisms, the report pointed out that only sixteen of the park's twenty-four authorized permanent positions were filled), the contamination problem was, in another sense, traceable to questionable decisions made a decade earlier. Although the hoped-for massive investments in park infrastructure never materialized at Crater Lake during the Mission 66 decade, millions of dollars were spent. And as these appropriated monies were quickly dispatched, at Crater Lake and elsewhere, criticisms of shoddy and intrusive Park Service "improvements" became more numerous.[9]

Sometimes the shoddiness was not immediately evident, as with the new sewage system installed at Crater Lake in 1965, supplanting one that had drained for years into the park's east canyon. Events over the next thirty years would show, however, that placement of this new septic-tank apparatus near Crater Lake Lodge, with the drain field suspended close to the park's main water source, jeopardized both the lake and the park's visitors and employees. In fact, in a later round of legal wrangling, Ralph Peyton successfully charged the National Park Service with negligence in its installation of the sewage system in 1965. Concluding that the Park Service bore primary responsibility for the water-contamination incident in 1975, courts awarded Peyton just over $1 million in damages in 1981. Although the 1976 Hatfield committee report gave little attention to the Mission 66 deficiencies brought into view by this later litigation, the Oregon senator was instrumental in launching a General Accounting Office study in 1980 that found glaring health and safety problems throughout the national parks, many traceable to hurried, substandard "improvements" during the Mission 66 period.[10]

The Uncertain Fate of Crater Lake Lodge

THE PARK SERVICE HAD CROSSED SWORDS frequently with concessionaire Ralph Peyton even before the water crisis of 1975. One of the more visible controversies had surfaced in 1973, when the concession company constructed an employee dormitory at a prime Rim Village site just south of Crater Lake Lodge. Park Service officials, who regularly took pains to appease the hard-bargaining and prickly Peyton, first went along with the plan, but then reversed course following high-profile objections made by environmental groups. Although construction of the unattractive dorm building (known as the Rim Dormitory) went ahead, the incident caused Interior Secretary Nathaniel Reed, supported by Oregon's U.S. Senator Robert Packwood, to call a halt to further construction of concession facilities at Rim Village. This action added to a general climate of constraint during the 1970s, as Park Service officials resigned themselves to compliance with new federal laws mandating public involvement in national park planning. Even in the midst of this new climate, though, the NPS continued to toy with proposals to alter or remove Crater Lake Lodge and other Rim Village structures, and to build replacements.[11]

In this new era of enhanced public involvement, the longtime disparity between public and Park Service regard for Crater Lake Lodge

The original Crater Lake Lodge, circa 1975, showing signs of terminal vulnerability under the stress of another season's snow load. (Courtesy NPS, CLNP Museum and Archives Collection)

was bound to become more apparent. Park Service officials had for decades openly scorned the lodge, considering it both a public danger and a blemish on the natural beauty of the crater rim. The structure still stood in 1975 largely because the Park Service habitually found it hard to take decisive action, especially when it involved Crater Lake's rim area. Meanwhile, the public—especially Oregonians—continued to support the lodge enthusiastically. Public reaction to the Park Service's weak commitment to Crater Lake Lodge first expressed itself strategically in the 1970s, in a drive to add the structure to the National Register of Historic Places. The Park Service, obliged to heed this popular effort, began to shift its calculations about the old lodge within a broader framework of intended development at Rim Village.[12]

By 1977, for example, a general plan for Rim Village called for maintaining the lodge as a first-class hotel in an overall scheme that included a new visitor center, "restored green space" (eight to twelve acres), and removal of rental cabins to make way for smoother pedestrian and auto traffic. Still, not all Park Service officials were resigned to the prospect of Crater Lake Lodge perched indefinitely on the lake rim. A skeptical Frank J. Betts, whom the Park Service had brought in as superintendent to restore order following the crisis of 1975, ordered a new structural inspection of the lodge in 1978. Another inspection in 1980 determined that basic structural and safety improvements would likely cost around $2.4 million, and the General Accounting Office report of the same year, inspired by Senator Hatfield, emphasized the lodge's fire-safety deficiencies and its need for extensive renovations.[13]

By the early 1980s, though, Oregon's strong historic-preservation community, and the public at large, were mobilized behind the cause of rehabilitating the lodge, now more than sixty years old. The structure was formally placed on the National Register of Historic Places in 1981, and rehabilitation work was scheduled to begin in 1982. But the Park Service balked again after a revised cost assessment, which took into account slope deterioration undermining the building's foundation, raised the estimated cost to more than $6 million. In 1984 the Park Service began openly to advocate demolishing the lodge as part of a broader plan to reduce development at Rim Village. But the fully engaged public responded to the news in protest via newspapers, the Historic Preservation League of Oregon, and the state legislature, demanding a reconsideration of the project's costs and a reversal of the decision to erase this cherished bit of Oregon's past.[14]

The frustrated and puzzled attitude of the Park Service toward Crater Lake Lodge during the 1970s and 1980s is well represented in the recollections of two park superintendents from those years. James S. Rouse and Robert E. Benton, whose views on the management of Crater Lake National Park differed in most other respects, generally agreed about the lodge. Both men found the public's sentimental attachment to the structure incomprehensible, but both also understood that in the later twentieth century a mobilized public could have its way with the formerly self-contained Park Service on many issues. The typically reserved Rouse minced no words on the point: "I didn't go along with the public who felt the lodge was such a great cathedral and all of that. It was nothing but an old barn that developed without any sound planning. . . . After its torn and tattered history, especially with all the safety and fire concerns, my feeling was that it had served its purpose. It probably never should have been built there in the first place. A visitor doesn't need to turn over in his bed and look out the window to see the lake." And the typically forthright Benton was true to form on the subject: "If you're making judgments based on dollars, to redo the old lodge made no sense at all. It was made out of crap the day they built it, and sixty years didn't do it any good."[15]

In contrast to the controversies surrounding Crater Lake Lodge, some renovation of historic structures was done with little disagreement during these years. Three key components of the Munson Valley park headquarters—the Rangers' Dormitory, the mess hall, and the

Administration Building—were restored beginning in 1985 and 1986. The work required extensive shifting of offices, workspaces, and storage areas, but for most park staff the temporary inconvenience was offset by the delight in seeing these vintage structures, each more than fifty years old by then, restored architecturally and adapted for contemporary use. And while schemes for new hotel accommodations in the park remained tangled in the cross-purposes of the Park Service, the concession company, the state's historic-preservation community, and environmental groups during the 1980s, plans for expanded campgrounds went ahead with far fewer complications. (At the insistence of Park Service director George Hartzog, in 1967 Crater Lake had become the first national park to introduce the much-debated practice of concession-operated fee campgrounds.)[16]

The Elusive Concept of Wilderness

VISITATION TO CRATER LAKE bounced back strongly after the dismal 1975 season, fueled by national Bicentennial enthusiasm in 1976 and 1977. Even with unprecedented visitor counts of more than six hundred thousand in each of those two years, a survey of those entering the park in 1977 confirmed earlier evidence that attendance would probably soon settle again into the five to six hundred thousand range. Crater Lake was, and would continue to be, according to the survey's analysis, "principally a day-use area . . . [frequently] part of a north-south trip which includes visits to other areas." Of the small percentage of visitors who stayed in the park overnight, about two-thirds camped in Mazama Campground. Rim Village and Rim Drive continued to be the park's overwhelmingly dominant attractions, and winter use and travel into backcountry areas remained light.[17]

Even though expectations of Crater Lake as a tourist destination were firmly modest by 1980, the park's consistent annual visitation of more than a half million people, its predictably severe weather, and its complex natural and built environments demanded vigilant management and custodianship. As Park Service decision makers looked ahead to the last quarter of the twentieth century (and to the park's one-hundredth anniversary in 2002), a few general resolutions emerged: overall land use for in-park development would decrease; principles of rustic design would be strictly observed in future construction; and development would be confined to Rim Village, Munson Valley, the Mazama and Lost Creek campgrounds, the maintenance area near the south entrance, and the Cleetwood Cove area of the rim and lake. All other areas of the park would retain, or in some cases be restored to, their "wilderness" character.[18]

THE WEB OF FEDERAL LEGISLATION binding the Park Service in the 1980s and 1990s had first begun to take shape decades earlier. In the years leading up to passage of the Wilderness Act of 1964, the NPS maneuvered to defend its autonomy. As suggested in the previous chapter, director Conrad Wirth's attempts to exempt his agency were so clumsy that the wilderness legislation that finally emerged in 1964 was aimed more at the Park Service than it probably would have been otherwise. Still, NPS observance of the act in the decades that followed was, for the most part, irresolute and unenthusiastic.[19]

The general attitude of Park Service officials toward the law—especially insofar as it threatened to impinge on the agency's discretion in its own backcountry regions—is captured neatly in the remarks of Robert E. Benton, Crater Lake's superintendent between 1984 and 1991. Benton, an ideological and temperamental protégé of NPS director George Hartzog, recalled that Hartzog, who began his nine-year tenure just months before the Wilderness Act was passed, "thought the Wilderness Act, as related to the National Park Service, was kind of stupid. He didn't think it was right. . . . We never did get out of the Wilderness Act what might have aided the parks a lot. . . . A classic example might be Crater Lake. Crater Lake's Organic Act [enabling legislation] is totally adequate to protect the resources of Crater Lake if the superintendent's got any guts. . . . Yet, there was a desire to put some wilderness on top of Crater Lake because it would give it an extra layer of protection. What a bunch of bullshit! You don't need that extra layer of protection."[20]

For decades after passage of the act, the urge to retain maximum independence guided the NPS stance on wilderness. In pursuing that primary objective, Park Service officials sometimes used contradictory and transparently self-serving arguments. Wayne Howe, a ranger at Crater Lake National Park from 1946 to 1950 and an NPS administrator later in his career, remarked in a 1988 interview that "when the Wilderness Act finally came in, there were many of us in the Park Service who said, 'This is a farce. We are a wilderness, anyway. We manage our backcountry as a wilderness.'" Later in the same interview, he admitted: "I thought [the wilderness recommendations for Crater Lake were] kind of silly. . . . This is not a wilderness area. And very frankly, I still do not consider it a wilderness area." In other words, depending on audience and circumstance, the Park Service was prepared to argue that wilderness legislation as applied to the national parks was redundant, since national park backcountry regions were already managed as wilderness; or that wilderness legislation applied to national parks was nonsensical and inappropriate, because national parks are *parks*, not wilderness areas. [21]

ONE OF THE MOST PERPLEXING outcomes associated with the Wilderness Act (perplexing because it appears to defy the generally accepted image of Park Service foot dragging in response to the new law) occurred at Crater Lake National Park in the summer of 1970, just months before mandatory public hearings were to be held on the long-awaited NPS wilderness proposal for Crater Lake. Seven historic backcountry cabins, dating from the Civilian Conservation Corps period of the 1930s, were gutted and removed by Park Service staff during the summer. This precipitous action was apparently taken to comply with the Wilderness Act, even though no one then seemed certain about how the law would apply to the national parks.[22]

James Rouse, who then worked in the NPS Pacific Northwest regional office in Seattle, vaguely attributed the action to director

This backcountry patrol cabin stood in the Bear Creek area of the northeast park. Built in the 1930s with Civilian Conservation Corps labor, the cabin was destroyed in 1970 amid confusion over the Wilderness Act's mandates for national parks. (Courtesy NPS, CLNP Museum and Archives Collection.)

George Hartzog's "decree that we were not going to have wilderness that had manmade facilities in it." Robert Benton, a dogged defender of Hartzog and a consistent critic of Rouse (who, in the late seventies and early eighties, preceded Benton as Crater Lake's superintendent), denounced the destruction of the backcountry cabins. "We lost some very neat historical stuff at Crater Lake," Benton recalled. "Whoever was worrying about Crater Lake at the regional [Seattle] or park level . . . tore them down or burned them or both. All seven of those backcountry cabins were deliberately destroyed, not because it was ever thought out whether they needed to be destroyed," but because of some imagined inconsistency between the cabins and the Wilderness Act.[23]

At the time the historic cabins were demolished, Crater Lake had no superintendent. Donald Spalding had moved on to head up the Klamath Falls Cluster Office, and Einar Johnson had not yet arrived to take his place. Although Spalding, as general superintendent, apparently signed off on the decision, the debacle appears to have been more the product of deep-seated confusion within the Park Service about the requirements of the Wilderness Act than the result of anyone's purposeful decision. Since those requirements, to some extent, remain cloudy today, and since the park's own formal wilderness proposal had not yet even undergone public review when the deed was done, the destruction of the cabins appears rash, to say the least, and perhaps even negligent. In later years, the episode has proved to be an embarrassment to Crater Lake National Park and to the Park Service, because of what was lost, certainly, but also because of how responsibility has been so difficult to pinpoint.

Hearings on the park's wilderness proposal did eventually take place in Medford and Klamath Falls during January of 1971. In the course of the public-review process, the Wilderness Society, the Sierra Club, and other environmental groups criticized aspects of the Park Service proposal for inadequately safeguarding park wilderness areas; other interests, such as the Oregon state game and fish commissions and the U.S. Forest Service, supported the NPS plan. A modified proposal was later approved by Park Service director Ronald Walker and sent to Congress by the Nixon administration in 1974. Six years later, when the park's area was expanded by nearly twenty-three thousand acres, Congress still had not acted on the proposal. As a result of the added acreage, though, the park's wilderness plan was adjusted in 1981 and again in 1986. At the beginning of the twenty-first century, Congress had still not acted on Crater Lake's latest wilderness recommendation, and the park still had no formally designated wilderness areas, as defined by the Wilderness Act. Ironically, though, Congress's failure to act and the resulting lack of official wilderness designation has probably had little impact on the park's management of its backcountry areas.[24]

IN THE YEARS BETWEEN HIS EMERGENCY intervention at Crater Lake in 1975 and 1980, Senator Mark Hatfield and his staff had continued their active involvement in national park issues, spurring the influential and largely critical 1980 General Accounting Office study of park facilities. In advocating legislation in 1980 to expand Crater Lake National Park by some 22,890 acres, Hatfield argued that preservation of the park's lake and rim, geological features, and ecological communities would be enhanced. A report on the proposed boundary revision from the Senate Committee on Energy and Natural Resources, chaired by Washington's Senator Henry M. Jackson, showed Hatfield's imprint: "The proposed minor changes would improve the park boundary by more closely following the topographical features of the land area. It would also add to the park key natural features associated with the geological formations in the park."[25]

Located less than a mile from each other near the northwestern boundary of Crater Lake National Park, Sphagnum Bog (above) and Crater Springs (opposite) are two of several rich natural areas added to the park in the boundary expansion of 1980. (Courtesy NPS, CLNP Museum and Archives Collection.)

Though the boundary expansion of 1980 was not monumental, it *was* significant. James Rouse concluded that the addition of natural features (including the Sand Creek drainage, Bear Butte, Sphagnum Bog, Crater Springs, Spruce Lake, and Thousand Springs), as well as the cooperation with "external interests" that the boundary-expansion legislation fostered, were among the strongest achievements of his tenure as superintendent. Rouse's agreement with U.S. Forest Service representatives (the "external interests") on revised park boundaries was, indeed, the product of sensible give-and-take. (The area added by the 1980 legislation included parts of three different national forests.) But the agreement was probably more a testament to Senator Hatfield's substantial influence on the Forest Service, a traditionally strong federal presence in Oregon, than to the negotiating skills of Park Service officials. For more than two decades, Hatfield played the key political role in forging a lucrative partnership between the Forest Service and commercial timber interests in Oregon, and the Forest Service was not likely to cross him in order to hang on to several thousand acres abutting Crater Lake National Park.[26]

The Slow Advance of Science

IN SEARCHING FOR AN IMAGE to describe the role of science in national parks during the last quarter of the twentieth century, one is drawn to the paradoxical half-empty, half-full glass of water. Assessments at century's end ranged from woefully inadequate ("half empty") to vastly

improved ("half full"), but nearly all observers agree that science had come to play a greater role in 1990 than it had in, say, 1960. It is also widely acknowledged that federal environmental legislation—the Wilderness Act (1964), the Endangered Species Act (1973), amendments to the Federal Air Pollution and Water Pollution Control acts, and, most important, the National Environmental Policy Act (1969)—drove the evolution of that more prominent role.[27]

Commentators who have stressed the "half empty" status of science have done so partly because the Park Service, by most appearances, has admitted science to the national parks only reluctantly and grudgingly. Although NPS officials have rarely criticized the overall intentions of science-based environmental legislation, they have frequently balked at application of the legislation to national parks, arguing that the parks are already managed properly. NPS leaders did incorporate a few science positions into the vast workings of the Denver Service Center, established in 1971 to coordinate planning, design, and construction throughout the NPS system. These science jobs, according to Park Service historian Richard West Sellars, were included in an otherwise development-oriented office to help ensure (or give the appearance of) compliance with science-based regulations, especially those contained in the National Environmental Policy Act.

However, as Sellars points out, "allocations of staff and funds to address ecological concerns were meager" when compared to the Denver Service Center's "several hundred employees devoted to planning, designing, and constructing national park facilities." And through the sheer volume of compliance work heaped upon them, Park Service scientists were given the unmistakable message that their main objective was to "meet minimal regulatory requirements of the law in order to avoid litigation over noncompliance." As a result, they often found themselves in the ethically uncomfortable position of "justifying decisions already made" and "rubber-stamp[ing] . . . plans pouring out of the Denver office," as Sellars puts it.[28]

Though more compelled by federal law than freely chosen by the Park Service, science did gradually assume a greater role within the national park system during the last quarter of the twentieth century. In 1970, North Cascades National Park joined with the University of Washington to establish a university-based scientific research office. This first of the cooperative park studies units, as they came to be called, served as a model for similar setups between national parks and universities across the country, including one that linked Crater Lake National Park and Oregon State University's College of Forestry in 1975. Such collaborations gave the National Park Service a low-cost but credible means of demonstrating its heightened attention to science. In the 1970s and 1980s, forestry projects and lake research were undertaken at Crater Lake by dozens of Oregon State students working on master's degrees.[29]

As science gained greater visibility within the NPS bureaucracy, science-based policies became more evident in the individual national parks. At Crater Lake, for example, park officials inched ever closer to acknowledging that "bear problems," past and present, were the result of human blunder rather than bear recalcitrance. In keeping with this new outlook, the park's revised bear management plans of 1974 and 1980 asserted scientifically sound intentions to undo the damage of previous policies (most related to allowing unnatural food sources) and "to restore and maintain the natural integrity, distribution, abundance, and behavior of the endemic black bear populations."[30]

A Crater Lake fire management plan introduced in 1977 featured a principle that biologists had been touting for two decades or more: fire is an important natural ecological factor in the preservation of native plants and animals. As with other aspects of science-based environmental policy, this altered approach to fire was largely forced upon the Park Service by the work of individual scientists and the lobbying of environmental groups. Sequoia National Park took the lead in the late 1960s. Departing from the long-established NPS practice of fire suppression, the California park introduced "prescribed burning" to simulate natural forest processes. Reflecting this trend, the 1977 Crater Lake plan recognized "management of fire" as an important tool for restoring "primeval forest composition" and for reducing the "probability of unnaturally intense or catastrophic wildfires caused by unnaturally high fuel accumulation."[31]

The change in fire policy signaled an even more fundamental reorientation in the goals of NPS resource management during the 1970s. In national parks throughout the country, Park Service officials stated their determination to maintain natural, pristine conditions in park ecosystems as much as possible. Crater Lake's natural resources management plan of 1982, built around the ecosystem principle (which presumes a web of distinct relationships connecting living organisms and nonliving features of distinct environments), committed the park to policies of restoring and protecting natural ecosystems, analyzing and understanding natural resources, and teaching and interpreting natural processes. While these stated goals were not remarkable for their time, they represented a sea change when compared to resource policies proclaimed and practiced thirty years earlier.[32]

OF COURSE, STATING resource-management goals is one thing and achieving them is another, as late-twentieth-century controversies at Crater Lake clearly demonstrate. In 1971, shortly after scientists accomplished the dangerous and unprecedented feat of measuring and recording data on the lake during winter, the promising lake-research program started in 1966 by Oregon State University professor John Donaldson came to an abrupt halt. Then, following seven relatively barren years in lake studies, Doug Larson, a former student of Donaldson's and now a limnologist working for the U.S. Army Corps of Engineers, returned to Crater Lake to conduct an independent research program under the NPS Volunteers-in-the-Parks program. Larson's research between 1978 and 1983 focused on the lake's more than one hundred species of phytoplankton. Other researchers during that time added important details to the accumulating knowledge of the lake's unique array of plant life. Still others offered the first explanations of how heat from two suspected thermal springs on the floor of the basin is distributed throughout the lake.[33]

While conducting his independent research, Larson also launched a program to measure and monitor the lake's clarity over time. (Next to its famous blue color, Crater Lake's remarkable clarity has probably contributed most to its historical reputation.) Larson compared clarity measurements taken in the summer of 1978 with those taken ten years earlier, when he and other scientists on Donaldson's team had confirmed measurements of the lake's exceptional clarity recorded in 1937 and 1957. To his surprise, Larson found that the lake's optical clarity had "decreased by roughly 25 to 30 percent." Well aware of the park's embarrassing water-contamination episode three years earlier, he had worried since the late 1960s that the lake's exceptional properties might eventually be degraded by the impact of hundreds of thousands of annual Rim Village visitors. In light of this preliminary evidence, Larson and other scientists started to ask whether an increase in plant nutrients in the lake—perhaps related to sewage leaching from the park's septic tank drain-field system—had fostered unusual abundances of phytoplankton (microscopic, single-cell plant species), which had, in turn, reduced the lake's clarity. A similar unexplained clouding of nearby Waldo Lake, which shares important technical properties with Crater Lake, deepened the suspicions of Larson and others.[34]

When alerted to Larson's findings, Crater Lake staff, with the notable exception of resource management specialist Mark Forbes, reacted with "nervous skepticism," according to Larson. At the close of the 1978 summer season, Forbes arranged a meeting between Larson and superintendent James Rouse, during which Larson summarized his research. The meeting went poorly, as Larson recalled in an interview: "Throughout our conversation, he . . . never really paid much attention to what I was saying. That is, until I got to the word *sewage*. Then he suddenly looked up and became quite interested in what I had to say." When Larson went on to voice his concern that sewage might be entering and degrading the lake, Rouse stated flatly that contamination of the lake by sewage was a physical impossibility, but offered no evidence to support his conviction. John Salinas, then a Park Service interpreter working with Larson on his lake-research project, felt that Larson's warning about lake contamination in the late 1970s drew a head-in-the-sand response from the Park Service: "[They] didn't want to hear [about] any of this. It sounded bad."[35]

While Larson continued to record declines in clarity over the next few years, Rouse and most other park managers minimized the possibility of danger. "Mark Forbes . . . was really the only one who encouraged my work and expressed interest in what was going on. The other people just seemed indifferent, and some people actually felt threatened," Larson remembered. Although park officials offered little encouragement or technical support, they did allow Larson to carry on his research as a volunteer through the 1981 season. During that time, the researcher shared his results with park staff and, via annual progress reports, with NPS regional officials in Seattle.[36]

In late 1981, Oregon Congressman Denny Smith became aware of Larson's theory that sewage contamination might be causing a decrease in Crater Lake's clarity. Then, in December, an article in the Portland *Oregonian* reported Larson's ideas to a wider audience. The *Oregonian* story, which implied that the Park Service had so far failed to investigate

Led by limnologist Doug Larson during the summer of 1980, the crew on a borrowed pontoon boat prepares for another day of collecting samples and conducting experiments on the lake.

the possibility of contamination, included assurances from Rouse that the Park Service was concerned about findings of diminished lake clarity; but the superintendent also made clear his strong skepticism about Larson's theory. The park's water-supply and sewage system had, indeed, been improved after the 1975 water-contamination fiasco, as Rouse maintained, but parts of an antiquated septic-tank sewage system were still located just a few hundred feet from the lake—a fact that Rouse was either unaware of or unwilling to admit. Thus, despite the superintendent's repeated claim of "physical impossibility," sewage might well have been percolating into the lake in 1981.[37]

With public focus on the issue intensifying, Congressman Smith led a legislative effort to force the Park Service to investigate the contamination hypothesis, "and to immediately implement such actions as may be necessary to assure the retention of the lake's natural pristine water quality." Amid this heightened interest, the Park Service finally launched a lake-studies program of its own. As John Salinas described it, "The Park Service wanted to have a monitoring program in place. They didn't want to be told to start a program." Thus, in early 1982 the Park Service regional office asked Doug Larson to set up a formal lake-monitoring program at Crater Lake, initially devoting just 10 percent of his paid professional hours to the NPS work. Larson agreed to the plan enthusiastically, partly because he had all along hoped to land a limnology job at Crater Lake.[38]

During the summer of 1982, Larson, now officially a part-time employee of the Park Service, tackled the job of formally establishing Crater Lake's monitoring and research program. Because of both interest and need, he soon found himself volunteering time beyond the 10 percent agreed to by his primary government employer, the Army Corps of Engineers. Although the first season's work went smoothly, a meeting in the NPS Seattle regional office during the fall revealed signs of future discord. Since the latest season's research results showed the same trend of optical loss evident since 1978, Larson saw no reason to modify his sewage-contamination hypothesis. However, Larson's contacts in the regional office suddenly became "uneasy with any discussions about sewage and optical loss," even though they had previously been aware of his ideas. It was as if the Park Service administrators had hoped that by including Larson in the NPS "family," he would join the damage-control effort and cease all discussion of sewage contamination.[39]

Larson was prepared to contend with healthy scientific skepticism. In fact, he believes he tried to maintain his own skepticism about the contamination hypothesis. But he was not prepared to deal with "outright denial"; nor was he willing to participate in a whitewashing of the whole matter. Only free scientific inquiry could illuminate the controversy and disagreements, Larson contended, but he soon concluded that no one in the Park Service "was willing to take action" to bring that about. Park Service geologist J. F. Quinlan recommended a dye-injection procedure to trace the course of the presumed wastewater seepage, and Larson himself proposed a test to measure whether lake algae were growing in response to septic-tank leakage. But Park Service officials refused to authorize either of these detection methods. Larson reflected years later that as attitudes hardened in 1983 and 1984, he began to realize that his status with the Park Service had grown "very shaky." But he was determined not to back off and allow the issue to be "swept under the rug," even at the risk of losing his chance to become Crater Lake's full-time limnologist.[40]

By the end of the 1983 research season, Larson was more convinced of his contamination hypothesis than ever. Recent analyses of a spring flowing from the caldera wall into the lake revealed "roughly ten times more nitrogen [often an indicator of human waste] than any of the other forty or fifty springs tested." Moreover, geologic maps of the caldera suggested that "spring 42," as it was designated, stemmed from

High nitrogen levels in "Spring 42," which flows into the lake from its source (shown here) on the southwestern caldera wall, heightened the suspicions of some that sewage was contaminating Crater Lake.

"a groundwater aquifer flowing directly beneath the septic tank drain-field system." This discovery appeared to strengthen the possibility of a link between septic wastewater and the lake. Still, the Park Service declined to conduct the tests recommended by Quinlan and Larson. And without such tests, the limited historical data on lake clarity were inadequate to prove whether recent findings of diminished clarity were unusual or part of a normal, longer-term cycle.[41]

Finally, in 1984, impelled by Larson's work and Congressman Smith's legislation, the Park Service opened a full-time professional limnologist position at Crater Lake. Larson applied for the job. Though he was eminently qualified, having done much of his Ph.D. work at Crater Lake in the late 1960s, and having launched the lake-research program there in the late 1970s, Larson lost out to a competitor with no Crater Lake experience (also, coincidentally, named Larson). He was gravely disappointed and somewhat bitter about the rejection, but not completely surprised, considering what had passed between him and Park Service officials.[42]

In the fall of 1984, while still absorbing this rebuff, Larson received a letter from NPS regional director Daniel Tobin. In the course of thanking him for his contributions to Crater Lake research, Tobin emphasized that Larson was no longer in charge of the lake-research program. Larson reflected later that he had "always viewed that letter as a nice way of saying, 'Get your ass out of there. We don't want you around anymore.'" In a 1997 interview, former superintendent Rouse weakly explained what was, in essence, Larson's dismissal from the job he had inaugurated: "Doug had done some very good research, but it wasn't in the same direction that we were going in the [Park Service] program. . . . We felt that the way Doug was oriented was not the course . . . needed for Crater Lake." Larson's coworker John Salinas saw a definite connection between Larson's controversial theory and his failure to land the job he had pioneered. Larson "was branded as a non-team player," Salinas recalled. "He did everything he could with the Park Service, but he kept hitting the closed door."[43]

The Crater Lake Limnological Studies Program that resumed under aquatic biologist Gary L. Larson after 1985 was, in its basic outlines, the same program Doug Larson had built from the ground up. Its avowed objectives—to collect data for use as a benchmark for future comparisons; to augment understanding of the lake's complex life processes; to establish a long-term monitoring scheme—were essentially those established and pursued by Doug Larson and his colleagues since 1978. Doug Larson's work during the summer of 1985,

Crater Lake National Park employee John Salinas (left) poses in the early 1980s with Doug Larson aboard a research boat on Crater Lake. Larson, in the late 1970s and 1980s, launched the park's first serious, sustained effort to study and monitor the lake.

his last at Crater Lake, focused on the transition to his successor, Gary Larson. Salinas recalled that Doug Larson "was essentially dropped from the program [after Gary Larson was hired]. One day he was there and the next day he was gone." Though his removal was partly the result of personal choice (he could no longer hope that his volunteer and part-time work would result in a permanent job), Salinas noted that Doug Larson was "never really asked to do anything in the park" after 1986. In any case, while the "new" Crater Lake limnology program proceeded to study the lake in 1986 and beyond, the Park Service, according to Doug Larson, "continued to stall on the issue of sewage contamination."[44]

Decline and Revival in Interpretation

THE EARLY 1970S, A BARREN TIME for lake-related research, were also years of poverty in educational and interpretive programs at Crater Lake. In research, education, and most other aspects of its operations, the park seemed to sleepwalk through this period, moving inexorably toward the public-health and public-relations disaster of 1975. Staffing and infrastructure during these years were seriously undernourished by the Park Service, which itself was suffering amid stringencies of the Vietnam War era.

A cheery interpretive prospectus compiled by Crater Lake and regional staff in 1972 and published by the NPS Denver Service Center in 1973 glossed over basic deficits in interpretive staff and facilities in favor of presenting a conceptually confused "new approach" to public education in the park: "All that we experience in the natural world is changing, and is the product of change. . . . Interpretation should contribute to an awareness of how, if we do not learn to understand and guide the forces of change which we are capable of perpetrating, we may be engulfed by great upheavals in our world and our lives. . . . If the skeletal components of fact and theory are skillfully articulated [in interpretation], and firmly bonded by a relevant concept—a more lasting and meaningful response to the Crater Lake experience will result."[45]

A more basic "upheaval" affecting Crater Lake's educational programs had taken place in 1969. F. Owen Hoffman, who had thrived at Crater Lake in the 1960s as a young seasonal interpreter on chief naturalist Dick Brown's topnotch team, took his first permanent Park Service job at Zion National Park in 1969 (after hoping, but failing, to land a full-time post at Crater Lake). Hoffman later recalled: "I found that from the training I got as a naturalist at Crater Lake, I was immediately one of the best interpreters at Zion. Their program was not anywhere close to being at the same professional level as the program at Crater Lake." However, the quality of Crater Lake's interpretive program was then already in decline. A massive staff exodus in 1969, brought about partly by Park Service director George Hartzog's decision to reduce the number of permanent interpreters at Crater Lake and a few other national parks, led to an erosion in the park's interpretive program that took the better part of a decade to repair.[46]

The 1960s and 1970s were a time of widespread doubt and questioning within the field of NPS interpretation. Mission 66 expenditures had brought high-profile visitor centers and state-of-the-art interpretive tools to several national parks, but the quality of person-to-person interpretive work during these years was often found wanting. Some critics theorized that the fancy bells and whistles of the modern visitor centers and interpretive media had undermined the traditional personal touch of Park Service interpretation. In any case, this general pattern was bound to play out somewhat differently at Crater Lake, where no major Mission 66 investments in interpretive infrastructure were made, and (perhaps consequently) where a strong person-based interpretive program persisted through most of the 1960s. Not until the interpretive staff was allowed to wither in the early 1970s did Crater Lake join the general downturn.[47]

The exodus of skilled interpretive staff from Crater Lake, which began in 1969 and continued for a few more years, resulted in a decline in interpretive service that was soon evident to observers. In 1973, the same year Crater Lake's dubious interpretive prospectus appeared, the Park Service conducted a study of "personal interpretation" in Pacific Northwest national parks. The investigator found "poor communication skills, poor morale, lack of employee understanding of Service goals, insufficient training, recruitment and rehire of incompetent seasonals, and inexperienced supervisors." The survey turned up "no programs in the excellent category." By contrast, just a few years earlier Crater Lake's interpretive program had been indisputably "in the excellent category," and was considered something of a paragon within the Park Service.[48]

A member of the park staff uses the spectacular vantage point of the Sinnott Memorial Overlook to point out a feature of the Crater Lake caldera. The Sinnott Memorial has been a perennially effective park location for the tried-and-true methods of person-to-person interpretation. (OHS neg. OrHi 103400.)

Conditions grew worse before they improved. The water-contamination crisis of 1975 brought the park to a low point in its history. Then, while still reeling from that disaster, park staff had to contend with all-time high numbers of visitors during the 1976 and 1977 seasons. In the aftermath of the 1975 crisis, the Park Service acted quickly to vacate and fill the park's two top positions with strong leaders: Frank Betts as superintendent and Dan Sholly as chief ranger. The two men sometimes fought each other tooth and nail, but they managed to return order to the park and to begin the long process of restoring confidence and morale.[49]

☙

JOHN SALINAS WAS A HIGH SCHOOL science teacher in Grants Pass, Oregon, when he was hired as a seasonal interpreter at Crater Lake in 1978. He recalled: "There was no interpretive staff at that time; there was just no one out there." But with a new chief and assistant chief of interpretation, as well as a talented new seasonal staff, soon to arrive, Crater Lake's educational program and workforce were shortly on the mend. Both Salinas and seasonal ranger Larry Smith remembered fondly that James Rouse, who began a six-year tenure as superintendent in 1978, gave important reinforcement to this comeback with his strong support of interpretive work. By the late 1970s and 1980s, Crater Lake's interpretive program had returned to the straightforward, commonsense educational formula of its banner years: try to make complex scientific issues enjoyable and clear to audiences of intelligent, curious people.[50]

For five years Salinas thoroughly relished his work in Crater Lake's resuscitated interpretive program: "I really enjoyed my job with the Park Service—doing the boat tours, leading walks, and giving talks. Probably the duty I enjoyed most was in Mazama Campground. Coming on duty later in the day, around noon, and preparing for the evening program. I did a circuit of the whole campground, walking it, inviting folks to the evening program. Then I set up the amphitheater, started the fire, and greeted folks." Sometimes as many as four hundred people attended these evening programs, Salinas recalled. In addition to offering such conventional subjects as "Crater Lake Geology" and "Plants and Animals of the Park," Salinas cooked up an evening program entitled "The Winter Scene," in which he delighted in reminding summer guests that the park was "buried in snow" for nearly nine months of the year. A typical five-day summer workweek for Salinas included an evening program, a boat tour, a "living history" presentation, a day of roaming and talking to visitors in Rim Village, and then perhaps another boat tour.[51]

As the twentieth century advanced, the number of history-based sites (national historic sites, national battlefields, and others) within the NPS system surpassed the traditional nature-based sites. Starting tentatively in the 1930s and then accelerating through the rest of the century, the Park Service acknowledged historic preservation as an important part of its mission and incorporated history as a legitimate branch of interpretation, even at nature-based parks and sites. Ostensibly reflecting this greater recognition of history, "living history" (portrayals of historical characters and reenactments of historical scenes) became fashionable in Park Service interpretive programs of the 1960s and 1970s.[52]

"Living history" at Crater Lake focused on the single character of John Wesley Hillman, the southern Oregon gold prospector whose small party stumbled on to its "discovery" of Crater Lake in 1853. John Salinas, one of several Hillman performers at Crater Lake, believed strongly in the educational value of these reenactments, measured primarily by his sense of the size and responsiveness of audiences. Many historians, meanwhile, have criticized "living history" as a lazy approach to teaching history, one that dodges the central challenge (analogous to that faced in teaching natural history) of making complex historical *ideas* enjoyable and clear to audiences of intelligent, curious people.

Gary Hoskins, on horseback with period clothing and paraphernalia, plays the character of J. W. Hillman, addressing Rim Village audiences on his "discovery" of Crater Lake in 1853. Such "living history" performances were popular at Crater Lake in the 1960s and 1970s but have since been phased out. (Courtesy NPS, CLNP Museum and Archives Collection.)

While the Park Service has done away with "living history" at Crater Lake and many other sites, NPS educators and interpreters have never really solved the puzzle of how to convey history to their audiences in a compelling way.[53]

☙

DURING THE LAST QUARTER of the twentieth century, Crater Lake's museum and library collections became important adjuncts to the park's interpretive program. Partly as a result of Will Steel's historical interests and accumulative instincts, reaching back to the park's turn-of-the-century origins, Crater Lake by mid-century possessed a rich array of artifacts, documents, and printed materials. Possession is one thing; organization and preservation for use is another. Not until Dick Brown's era as chief park naturalist in the 1960s was much effort given to the enormous chore of organizing and cataloging the park's geological, botanical, zoological, and photographic collections.[54]

Motivated largely by federal mandates associated with the National Historic Preservation Act of 1966, the Park Service bureaucracy began to encourage national park staffs to pay greater attention to park histories and historic structures. For example, in 1979 a Park Service analysis of major historical themes at Crater Lake included the long-neglected subject of regional Indian cultures. The report also recommended completion of a park historic resource study and an administrative history, projects that were tackled during the 1980s.[55]

The greatest boon to historical studies at Crater Lake, though, came from the initiative of Robert Benton, the park's superintendent from 1984 to 1991. Benton, undoubtedly the most fiscally resourceful superintendent in the park's hundred-year history, engineered the hiring of a park historian in 1987—a remarkable achievement at a time when few natural-area parks such as Crater Lake supported such a position. Benton believed that "history had to be brought into the foreground . . . had to be made a viable part of the Crater Lake operation," in part to guard against such travesties as the destruction of the historic backcountry cabins in 1970. Benton also gave Crater Lake's unusually strong library a boost. Although the Crater Lake Natural History Association had for decades underwritten the park's acquisition of books and other printed materials, a suitable physical space for the library was not made available until the mid-1980s. Now occupying quarters in the renovated Rangers' Dormitory (Steel Center), Crater Lake's growing library falls under the direction of the park historian.[56]

Re-Tribalization among the Klamath Peoples

THE DRIVE TO UNDO the Klamath Termination Act of 1954 had begun almost immediately after passage of the legislation, as many former Klamath Reservation Indians vehemently denied that their people had chosen termination freely. Ideological and generational rifts worsened by provisions of the legislation took time to overcome, but the obvious damage done by termination began to incite and unify the Indians by the 1970s.[57]

Claims against the federal government, as well as other legal contests with both federal and state government, helped keep tribal embers burning during decades when, legally speaking, no tribe existed. The Indians achieved an important victory in the federal courts in 1974 when traditional treaty rights were upheld in a long-simmering dispute over native hunting and fishing practices on former reservation lands in the Winema National Forest. (A parallel attempt by the Klamath to claim treaty-protected hunting rights in a portion of Crater Lake National Park was unsuccessful.)[58]

As a by-product of the successful legal effort to defend hunting and fishing rights, in 1974 several Indians held the first Klamath General Council meeting since the tribe's termination two decades earlier. Then in 1975 tribal government as a whole was reconstituted to oversee the Klamaths' recently upheld treaty rights and to represent the tribe in its dealings with local, state, and federal governments. These developments

Klamath Restoration queens Alisha Gentry (top) and Lahoma Schonchin participate in the annual August Klamath Restoration Celebration in Chiloquin, marking the anniversary of the federal government's restoration of tribal status to the Klamath Tribes in 1986. (Courtesy Klamath Tribes.)

led to a de facto re-tribalization, even as the pursuit of formal tribal restoration remained hesitant. Klamath leaders worried about the burdens of renewed federal control as well as their people's lack of a land base, since most of the traditional native land base had been relinquished by treaty in the nineteenth century and reservation lands had been "sold" to the government in the twentieth.[59]

The personal crusade of Edison Chiloquin provided regional natives with an important rallying cry in the years between tribal termination and restoration. Even though some native people considered him eccentric and too much the "old-fashioned Indian," most Klamaths applauded Chiloquin in his long fight with Congress and the U.S. Forest Service to obtain title to lands once occupied by his grandfather's village. Rejecting both the principle of tribal termination and the resulting government payments for his share of tribal lands, Chiloquin struggled for more than a decade to defend his right to use 580 acres of traditional tribal lands absorbed into the Winema National Forest. In 1985, Congress finally granted Chiloquin and his heirs a trust deed to these 580 acres for use in preserving Klamath heritage. By that time, though, Chiloquin had grown skeptical of his fellow Indians' willingness to adopt traditional ways.[60]

Gaining additional confidence from such pan-Indian political forces as the National Congress of American Indians, the American Indian Movement, and the Indian Self-Determination Act of 1975, and buoyed by the restoration of tribal status to other Indian peoples in the United States, the Klamaths moved toward formal tribal restoration in the late 1970s and early 1980s. Finally, on August 27, 1986, President Ronald Reagan signed the Klamath Restoration Act, which returned federal protections to surviving Klamath, Modoc, and Yahooskin-Paiute tribal members and their descendants. This legislation marked an important turning point in the native peoples' potential to reunite with their traditional cultures.[61]

Formal restoration of tribal status represented only a stage in the lengthier process of cultural re-tribalization, however. Government recognition immediately brought health, education, economic-development, and housing benefits, which helped relieve poverty, alcoholism, and despair among the Indians. But the former Klamath Reservation peoples still faced the difficult task of redefining "tribe" in the post-termination era. Re-tribalization and the sometimes-painful cultural introspection required to bring it about have inevitably contributed to divisions among the peoples of the reconstituted tribe.[62]

The Kla-Mo-Ya Casino, opened in 1997, was the first major economic enterprise of the restored Klamath Tribes. The name is a combination of the first two letters of the three peoples—the Klamath, the Modoc, and the Yahooskin-Paiute—who constitute the Klamath Tribes. (Courtesy Klamath Tribes.)

For example, debate over the Klamath Economic Self-Sufficiency Plan, a mandatory requirement under the 1986 restoration act, generated competing ideas about economic aspects of Klamath cultural survival. After extensive deliberation in the 1980s and 1990s, the tribe opted to construct a casino as one of its major economic self-sufficiency measures. While the Kla-Mo-Ya Casino, which first opened its doors in 1997, has served as a model of Klamath economic ingenuity, it is surely not the sort of cultural expression envisioned by Edison Chiloquin in his fight to regain use of former tribal lands.[63]

Other branches of tribal government have taken steps more in keeping with the hopes of traditionalists. The tribe's Culture and Heritage Department has helped reintroduce the sweat lodge, giveaway, and fish ceremonies, as well as the powwow. These rituals have sometimes taken traditional Klamath, Modoc, or Yahooskin-Paiute forms, and sometimes have assumed more pan-Indian aspects. The tribes spent $500,000 for a private Indian artifact collection in 1986 and are, at the time of writing, trying to raise another $9 million to build a museum for display of the collection. (The Native American Graves Protection and Repatriation Act of 1990 provided the Klamath Culture and Heritage Department with legal grounds for acquiring additional Indian artifacts.) Meanwhile, overt religious expression in the post-restoration period has remained predominantly Christian. Perhaps only through a revival of shamanism would the Klamath be able to fully renew their traditional spiritual bond with Crater Lake.[64]

Chapter 8

New Directions

1985-2000

The Renaissance of Crater Lake Lodge

As some Indians of the region sought paths back to Crater Lake via restoration of tribal status, other Oregonians freshened their links with Crater Lake through a drive to save and restore Crater Lake Lodge. By the mid-1980s, the public had spoken unmistakably of its desire to preserve the lodge. And while the federal government, which owned the old structure, reluctantly recognized this general acclamation, NPS planners still hoped to satisfy the public with a preservation formula consistent with overall Park Service plans. But when structural inspections in the late 1980s revealed that the lodge was in dire condition, it became clear that the building probably would not last as long as the Park Service would need to come up with a solution. After keeping the old lodge open for the 1988 season against the advice of consulting engineers, the Park Service finally closed it in 1989 amid warnings that portions of the structure could collapse at any time.[1]

Public hearings on four alternative plans for Rim Village and Crater Lake Lodge had been held in Klamath Falls, Medford, and Portland in 1988, and from these forums NPS regional director Charles Odegaard gauged correctly that Oregonians would settle for no less than a fully renovated lodge equipped to accommodate overnight guests in a manner resembling its traditional practice. Other aspects of Odegaard's Rim Village plan were largely ignored by the public in its celebration of victory over what many perceived had been the Park Service's intention to demolish the lodge. But when the structure suddenly closed before the 1989 season, with no money yet budgeted by the Park Service for its reconstruction, the force of public opinion rose again. Within a month, members of Oregon's congressional delegation delivered an appropriations bill that funded planning and

Closed in 1989, Crater Lake Lodge here remains empty on the eve of restoration work, begun in May 1991. The building was, in effect, "deconstructed" before reconstruction efforts began. (Courtesy National Park Service, Crater Lake National Park Museum and Archives Collection.)

design work for the lodge ahead of all other aspects of the Rim Village plan.[2]

In the year and a half before the start of reconstruction work in 1991, architects were forced to confront the puzzles that underlay the project. The new Crater Lake Lodge, it soon became apparent, would require "reinvention" more than restoration. Since the lodge had never been finished in the first place—and was, in any case, a "building full of contradictions . . . and idiosyncrasies"—architects and planners had no historical model to emulate. Instead, the rehabilitation was based on their vision of how the building might have looked if it had been completed, as some had hoped it would be, in the 1920s or 1930s. Nearly everything added to the structure after 1930 (annexes, false ceilings, cosmetic remodeling) was done away with in the reconstruction, and only about 10 percent of the original lodge was reused. But as far as the public was concerned, the rehabilitation effort had been undertaken to "save" and "restore" the old lodge.[3]

The four-story structure reopened with great fanfare in 1995. Built on a steel-reinforced foundation of native volcanic rock, the new lodge is topped by a lovely forest-green roof buttressed with steel to withstand heavy snow loads. Its brown-shingled exterior now encloses accommodations equipped with telephone jacks, bathrooms, and central heating, all compliant, at long last, with public safety codes. The main interior spaces—rooms, dining area, lobbies—are oriented toward the

The "reinvented" Crater Lake Lodge reopened amid celebration in 1995 after a reconstruction investment of about $30 million. The government's substantial expenditure was a tribute to the force of public sentiment in contemporary National Park Service affairs. (Courtesy NPS, CLNP Museum and Archives Collection.)

lake, reflecting the original source of historical and contemporary enchantment with the site and the building. The approximately $30 million spent on the new Crater Lake Lodge was far more than the Park Service would have allotted without the intervention of powerful public sentiment and political clout.[4]

THOUGH THE RECORD OF CRATER LAKE Lodge, Inc., since taking over the park concession in 1976 had been mixed, that record was as good as any achieved by earlier concession providers. The company had enjoyed a "honeymoon" of a few years following the traumatic water-contamination crisis of 1975 and the departure of unpopular Ralph Peyton as principal concession owner. But not long after Robert Benton arrived as superintendent in 1984, he judged the Crater Lake concession "a complete disaster." With the lodge closed after 1988, many of Benton's complaints focused on the company's operation of Mazama Campground. In his annual report for 1990, his last as superintendent, Benton noted that the concessionaire had received "an unsatisfactory rating" for its overall performance and was guilty of "contract non-compliance" for specific failures at Mazama Campground.[5]

The park's relations with the concession company recovered in the early 1990s with the appointment of Richard Gordon as general manager. After Gordon's second year, superintendent David Morris reported that the company's performance had improved dramatically. According to Park Service officials, this was largely the result of Gordon's decision to remain in the park for most of the busy season, personally supervising concession business. (The company's offices are in White City, some sixty-five miles southwest of the park.) While Gordon believed that the company's ability to make a profit and satisfy visitors was seriously impeded by the lodge's continued closure during his first three seasons on the job, these three years of limited service appear to have given him valuable time to get the concession back on track. In fact, with the reopening of Crater Lake Lodge in 1995, concession services—from the lodge dining room and cafeteria to the boat tours—began again to show signs of strain.[6]

After 1997, Crater Lake Lodge, Inc., operated the park concession without a contract, authorized instead by year-to-year letters of renewal from the federal government. When the last thirty-year agreement expired in 1995, a new fifteen-year contract came under negotiation. (This "between contract" status is fairly common for Park Service concessionaires today. At Crater Lake, in consideration of the company's loss of contractual security, the Park Service temporarily waived the usual 2 percent franchise fee paid by the company to the government.) In 2000, general manager Dick Gordon affirmed that Crater Lake Lodge, Inc., "expects to be the continuing concession," but a little more than a year later the company announced that it would leave the park after October 31, 2001.[7]

The working relationship between the park and Crater Lake Lodge, Inc., was constructive and relatively trouble-free after 1995. Occupancy and visitor satisfaction at Crater Lake Lodge, Mazama Campground, and other concession outlets were generally high, and the profile of seasonal concession staff at Crater Lake improved remarkably after the early 1990s. From a predominance of college-age employees, the summer staff of some 230 gradually became a mixture of young and old, with maturity and stability added to the force as a result. Retirees in summertime recreational-vehicle migrations, for example, have shown increasing interest in seasonal work at Crater Lake. In addition to their established job skills, most of these retired seasonal workers bring their own "housing" in the form of recreational vehicles—an added bonus for both park officials and the concessionaire, who have struggled over the years to provide housing for seasonal employees.[8]

The Pressure-Cooker Regime of Robert Benton

CRATER LAKE CONCESSION SERVICES were not alone in attracting Robert Benton's critical eye in the mid-1980s. In a 1994 interview with park historian Steve Mark, Benton speculated that the Park Service had assigned him to Crater Lake in 1984 because of his track record in "cleaning up really bad messes." If that was, in fact, the rationale of Park Service executives for sending Benton to Crater Lake, the new superintendent soon found little to contradict their conclusion that a "mess" really did exist there. Even though improvements had been made since the early 1970s, Benton's assessment of conditions at Crater Lake in the mid-1980s was bleak. From the maintenance crew ("probably the sorriest in the National Park Service") to the park's housing for permanent and seasonal employees ("a travesty"), Benton judged that "Crater Lake had just been allowed to go to hell."[9]

Benton's 1994 interview contains strikingly harsh criticisms of fellow Park Service professionals, especially those who had immediately preceded him at Crater Lake; likewise, his self-congratulations for accomplishments during his Crater Lake years is sometimes overbearing. Nonetheless, while Benton does not come across as an especially likeable personality, his candor is refreshing and many of his conclusions are compelling. The interview as a whole serves as a demonstration of character traits he considered necessary for superior achievement in the NPS system of his day. Benton believed that if he, as Crater Lake superintendent, could provide a model of personal

Robert E. Benton, Crater Lake's intense, fiscally resourceful superintendent between 1984 and 1991, helped bring about vital improvements in the quality of life and work for Park Service employees at Crater Lake National Park. (Courtesy NPS, CLNP Museum and Archives Collection.)

diligence and tenacity, and if he could build a staff of like-minded professionals, housed properly and given decent working conditions, he would be able to move "this fine, old park into the mainstream of the National Park Service," as he put it in his annual report for 1987.[10]

Benton emphasized that his success in improving park housing and in introducing such amenities as satellite television was rooted in simple determination: "The quality of housing in a national park is directly dependent upon the superintendent's willingness to have good housing. If he wants it, he'll get it. If he doesn't want it, he won't." By the same token, according to Benton, it fell to him to make certain that staff had decent work areas: "You can't expect people to work in a damn tent, and we had some pretty awful stuff. . . . We had to have buildings that people could work in. . . . We had to have cars. We had to have equipment." In pursuing such goals in a tight-fisted, potentially unresponsive bureaucracy, a superintendent must be willing to step on toes and make enemies, Benton maintained: "Being a superintendent is not a pleasant life if you want to do it right. It may be wonderfully self-satisfying, but not pleasant. You take a lot of abuse. . . . We had to go and push on every facet at Crater Lake with an awful lot of aggression. We did not proceed with any sense of diplomacy or delicateness. . . . We were only gonna get one real crack at bringing Crater Lake into the modern age, kicking and screaming."[11]

The upgrading and improvements in housing and facilities during Benton's years at Crater Lake (1984-1991) were remarkable.

During Bob Benton's era as superintendent, this key maintenance and service building in the Munson Valley park headquarters area was transformed from an unsightly garage to a modern support facility. (Courtesy NPS, CLNP Museum and Archives Collection.)

Inferior housing for seasonal employees was demolished before these comfortable replacement quarters were constructed on the same site, in the Sleepy Hollow region of park headquarters. (Courtesy NPS, CLNP Museum and Archives Collection.)

Substandard housing for seasonal employees was demolished and replaced by some of the best of its kind in the National Park Service. Housing for permanent employees was renovated. The Rangers' Dormitory (now the Steel Center), the mess hall (the Canfield Building), and the Administration Building (the Sager Building)—three of the most prominent structures in the Munson Valley historical district—were redesigned as headquarters for the interpretive program, the ranger force, and the administration, respectively. While the sheer volume of new development during Benton's time may not have matched construction during the public-works era of the 1930s or the Mission 66 period of the 1950s and 1960s, the impact of the Benton-era improvements on the everyday lives of park employees was unprecedented.[12]

In the most basic sense, Benton fought for these changes because they were needed. But his analysis of why the need was so desperate sheds light on important historical features of both Crater Lake National Park and the National Park Service. As Benton began his tenure at the Oregon park, he was warned that "Crater Lake may be the most difficult area in the National Park Service to live in." He soon confirmed this caveat with studies by Park Service sociologists and his own observations, which were surely as well founded as those of any of his predecessors (among the twenty-four superintendents in Crater Lake's one-hundred-year history, he maintained the longest continuous residence in the park). Armed with statistics and other evidence that showed unusually high incidences of violence, divorce, alcoholism, and poor morale among year-round residents, Benton resolved to make changes that would improve living and working conditions in the park. He expressed his leadership commitment succinctly: "National Park Service people are not second-class citizens, so by God they aren't going to live like it!"[13]

Benton's recipe for success as a national park superintendent consisted of one part determination ("to hustle a buck"), one part courage ("guts," in his graphic idiom), and one part political savvy. The political savvy part did not include diplomacy, to be sure, but rather the foresight to have plans in place and the capacity to act quickly. As he put it, in typically salty fashion: "You'd be surprised how much money we got at Crater Lake because we had plans and some other area didn't. I used to manage to screw some of the other parks out of an awful lot of coin because I had the plans and they didn't." According to Benton's formula for effective leadership, one success builds on another. After a few consecutive successes, everyone ("teammates" and "competitors" alike) begins to *expect* success from you. At the point when everyone else expects you to succeed, you have gained the psychological edge in achieving success.[14]

Benton believed emphatically that he succeeded in his seven years as superintendent, though he also acknowledged a few failures and several problems left unattended: "Crater Lake was simply so big, so immense in the number of problems that had to be addressed, that there was absolutely no way that any one superintendent was ever going

The old Rangers' Dormitory nears completion in 1986 as the renovated Steel Information Center, home of Crater Lake National Park's library and interpretative offices. (Courtesy NPS, CLNP Museum and Archives Collection.)

to be able to be there long enough to get it all done." In his mind, by the early 1990s he had laid the groundwork to enable the park and its staff "to compete in the National Park Service" after his departure. Since "living in the park isn't too bad anymore," Benton felt confident that Crater Lake would be able to attract competent staff and hold on to them long enough to produce some good. At the same time, though, he estimated that the park would always need a strong leader, and he had come to question whether most contemporary superintendents understand the Park Service well enough to be strong leaders: "You have superintendents who don't really know what the Park Service is all about. . . . They are being made superintendents for all the wrong reasons, and I think it is showing. . . . Now we end up with a lot of folks who don't know sheep shit from Arbuckle coffee about the Park Service."[15]

The Intersection of Politics and Science

THERE IS NO DENYING that Bob Benton had his hands full in the mid-1980s. Not long after he arrived at Crater Lake, he got word through sources in the Bureau of Land Management that private exploratory drilling for geothermal energy was likely to begin soon in the Winema National Forest, adjacent to the park. This rumored threat to Crater Lake's water quality—as Benton publicly characterized the geothermal project—became real in 1985 when the California Energy Company received approval for a test-drilling program. Bureau of Land Management and Forest Service officials, under increasing pressure from the Reagan administration to open public lands to private enterprise, contended that the drilling could be done without damage to Crater Lake. Benton countered that since the region's geothermal waters were relatively unexplored, drilling *did* pose a potential threat to Crater Lake (which many believed held thermal springs at its bottom). As the disagreement intensified over the next few years, Benton seemed to welcome the fight: "There was nothing that ever happened on the geothermal issue that I wasn't aware of. If there was, and I found out later, I'd have had somebody scalped. I had to know, practically minute-by-minute, object-by-object, that whole doggone program . . . . That was such a tremendous political issue that I had to know blow-by-blow."[16]

Benton viewed the geothermal controversy as essentially political, and he knew he would need strong political allies to prevail. He took little time to decide that NPS regional director Charles Odegaard was

According to superintendent Bob Benton and others, exploratory drilling for geothermal energy in the mid-1980s in Winema National Forest, adjacent to Crater Lake National Park, posed a threat to the well-being of Crater Lake. (Courtesy NPS, CLNP Museum and Archives Collection.)

not up to the task. Benton explained: "Since [Odegaard] doesn't have a [Park Service] background, he didn't know that he could go to the wall with those bastards and win. From his standpoint, if one of those lackeys—and that's what they were, Reagan lackeys—called him up, he didn't know that he could tell them to go to hell. . . . Odegaard simply didn't have the guts to go to war." Benton found his requisite political ally in Oregon's senior U.S. senator, Mark Hatfield, an influential voice of moderation in the Republican party during the Reagan years. "Hatfield was key to our salvation," Benton recalled. He "helped us a lot, and some of his staffers were absolutely wonderful in finessing what Odegaard was catching from these lackeys. Yes, Hatfield people . . . were there to be counted on. . . . [Hatfield] was a major, major player."[17]

In 1986, the California Energy Company, which had leased seventy-six thousand acres of national forest land, drilled a pair of four-thousand-foot test holes just four miles from Crater Lake and less than a mile from the park's southeastern boundary. If test results turned out positive, the company hoped to build a hydrothermal power plant on the leased property, using piped underground steam to power turbines and produce electricity for the San Francisco area. Early tests were promising, and the drilling continued in 1987. That year, however, much to Benton's delight, both the Sierra Club and the Oregon Natural Resources Council successfully appealed to the Interior Department

Crater Lake National Park aquatic biologist Mark Buktenica prepares to dive in *Deep Rover*, the one-person submarine used in 1988 and 1989 to explore the bottom of Crater Lake for evidence of hydrothermal springs. (Courtesy NPS, CLNP Museum and Archives Collection.)

for a temporary halt to the test drilling, on grounds of potential environmental damage to Crater Lake.[18]

As battle lines were drawn in the geothermal affair, Benton was determined to buttress his political counterattack with a scientific underpinning. Under the auspices of the park's Limnological Studies Program, Benton accelerated a plan to search for thermal vents on Crater Lake's floor. While the existence of such vents had long been theorized, the threat of geothermal drilling near the lake gave new urgency to finding them. Their scientifically demonstrated existence, Benton calculated, could be used to obtain formal protections against any further exploration in the Crater Lake vicinity. Using a remotely operated submersible vehicle, Oregon State University oceanographers Jack Dymond and Robert Collier began an initial phase of lake-bottom exploration during the summer of 1987. The scientists did detect small vents on the lake's bottom, as Benton hoped they would, and concluded that the vents were hydrothermal.[19]

California Energy Company scientists immediately challenged this finding. Company geologist Joseph LaFleur derided the park's quest for "mythical hot springs," but further explorations in a one-person submarine, the *Deep Rover*, during the summers of 1988 and 1989 added weight to Dymond and Collier's earlier conclusion. On the strength of evidence from the submarine work in 1988, Senator Hatfield sponsored a bill that added Crater Lake to a list of national parks containing "significant geothermal features." The legislation also gave the Interior Department authority to stop geothermal exploration outside the park, if the interior secretary had scientific evidence that such drilling would harm the lake. With Hatfield lending important aid to the Crater Lake cause, Benton spoke confidently in 1988 about the park's position in the geothermal standoff: "No way are the American people going to stand still for Crater Lake's features being in any way disturbed. [This legislation adds] a measure of protection."[20]

🕲

IN 1987, JUST AS THE GEOTHERMAL controversy was escalating, Doug Larson brooded about the Park Service's unwillingness to act upon his warning that sewage might be degrading Crater Lake's celebrated clarity. Aware that he had become something of an outcast in the park, Larson began writing letters to Oregon politicians and journalists in an effort to publicize the threat. If the Park Service refused to act upon his warnings and his advice, he reasoned, perhaps publicity and even popular protest could compel action.[21]

In the fall of 1987, an editorial and article published in the Eugene *Register-Guard*—both showing the imprint of Larson's arguments and concerns—brought the issue into broad public view. Far less conspicuous, but just as significant, a Park Service report in the fall of 1987, based on the findings of a panel of scientists, conceded that "elevated nitrate concentrations" in springs entering the lake were probably caused by the septic-tank leach field in the Rim Village area. This key science-based report went on to recommend shutdown and replacement of the suspect sewage system. However, as the *Register-Guard* reporter observed, superintendent Benton was "defensive on the [water] clarity subject and castigates reporters for taking such an interest in it." While the newspaper editorialized that the Park Service "must find out for certain whether any sewage is reaching the lake, and if so, how much is getting there and how long it takes," Benton, preoccupied with the geothermal fracas, referred to the controversy as a "red herring," adding sarcastically that "it is not the thing I lie awake nights thinking about."[22]

At the same time Benton sought to play down the issue, he acknowledged that the Park Service should "do something about" the portion of the old sewage system that remained precariously close to the lake: "I'm not willing to say that sewer system is causing a problem to Crater Lake, but we're not gonna take a chance." However, Benton's proposed action, included as part of a yet-to-be-approved park plan, was hardly on a fast track for completion. F. Owen Hoffman, a former Park Service employee then working as an environmental scientist for the Oak Ridge National Laboratory, knew from experience that proposed actions buried in "projected" Park Service plans were probably not imminent. After reading the *Register-Guard* article, Hoffman wrote a letter-to-the-editor emphasizing the urgency of learning "whether or not sewage nitrate is entering the lake; for if it is, immediate action should be taken by the Park Service. Superintendent Benton instead appears to be opting to postpone action until approval of a [pending] plan, a process that could well last a decade or more." The *Register-Guard* editorialized in September 1987 that Benton's casual reassurances about the sewage issue were not apt to satisfy most Oregonians. Though Benton regularly criticized the Park Service and his fellow employees on a range of issues, in this instance he bristled in response to a campaign of criticism aimed at several decades of Park Service policies and officials, including himself, retreating into an "us-versus-them" defensiveness.[23]

Just days after publication of the *Register-Guard* editorial, Benton wrote to Colonel Gary Lord, Doug Larson's boss at the Army Corps of Engineers, announcing that Park Service officials "question whether or not Doug Larson is using government time to present various papers and to discuss his particular theories involving Crater Lake clarity. . . . We are curious as to whether or not Dr. Doug Larson is, in fact, speaking for the Army Corps of Engineers or on his own behalf, and, as mentioned above, is this activity being condoned by the corps." The Army Corps investigated Benton's charge of professional misconduct, causing Larson considerable distress. But several weeks after Benton's letter, Colonel Lord responded to the Crater Lake superintendent, assuring him that Larson had "always informed reporters that he is speaking as an independent researcher," not as an Army Corps employee, on the subject of Crater Lake, and that he had "not abused Government work time." Before Benton's vindictive letter, Larson clung to the belief that he was enmeshed in a scientific debate with political overtones. After the Benton letter, he concluded that science had been overtaken by politics, public relations, and personal animosity. Benton's clumsy attempt to silence Larson ended up galvanizing him.[24]

THE INTERMIXING OF POLITICS and science during this time became starkly apparent in the way the sewage-contamination and geothermal-exploration debates converged. Cal Energy representatives argued that the Park Service, in a cynical effort to curtail geothermal exploration through "discovery" of fanciful thermal springs on the lake's floor, wasted public money that could have been spent on determining, once and for all, whether sewage was entering and degrading the lake. For his part, superintendent Benton maintained that Cal Energy apologists used the trumped-up issue of lake contamination to divert attention from their potentially damaging geothermal plans. Meanwhile, Doug Larson, increasingly marginalized (if not vilified) by the Park Service, found unlikely allies in Cal Energy scientists, who were exceedingly supportive of his concerns about lake contamination, even though he quietly opposed their geothermal drilling on the park's boundary.[25]

In the midst of his letter- and essay-writing activism, Larson continued his contributions to science. Invited to give a paper at an American Association for the Advancement of Science symposium on Crater Lake at Oregon State University in June 1988, Larson presented "Limnological Response of Crater Lake to Possible Long-Term Sewage Influx," coauthored with biologist Clifford Dahm and botanist Stan Geiger. After the meeting, as the AAAS was preparing to publish the symposium's papers in a volume entitled *Crater Lake: An Ecosystem Study*, superintendent Benton and other Park Service officials pressured the book's editors to exclude the Larson paper. Larson explained: "Fortunately, the senior editor, Ellen Drake, who is an oceanographer at OSU, publicly stated that there would be no censorship of this book." The editors, in their introduction to the volume, referred obliquely to the Park Service's efforts to eliminate Larson's voice from the published volume. Acknowledging that scientific controversies at Crater Lake during the 1980s had given rise to "a complex situation involving people from industry, government agencies, scientists and other individuals" (surely an understatement), they proclaimed, with some justification, that *Crater Lake: An Ecosystem Study* presented science expunged of "political taints."[26]

By 1990 superintendent Benton began to feel certain that the war against geothermal exploration had been won. His annual reports for 1991 and 1992 did not even mention the threat, and in early 1991 the Bureau of Land Management announced a two-year suspension of test drilling on the park's boundary. Pushed forward by Senator Hatfield, the BLM suspension was intended to allow the interior secretary time to determine whether Crater Lake possessed hydrothermal features significant enough to warrant a permanent ban on geothermal exploration in the area. Although superintendent David Morris's annual report for 1993 announced that the two-year ban on geothermal exploration near the park had been lifted—presumably because the evidence for Crater Lake's thermal features was still inconclusive—the

California Energy Company was by then in full retreat. The company, undoubtedly convinced that the potential gain was no longer worth the effort, announced indefinite postponement of its geothermal explorations at the Winema National Forest site.[27]

IN 1991, THIRTEEN YEARS AFTER Larson had first alerted the Park Service to the danger of sewage contamination from septic tanks near the caldera rim, and four years after a panel of scientists recommended abandonment of the system, the last vestige of the Rim Village septic-tank sewage system was finally shut down. Significantly, the superintendent's report for 1991 noted that this shutdown represented "a big first step in eliminating pollution threats to Crater Lake." Neither Benton nor his successor, David Morris, ever *publicly* conceded such a strong potential link between park sewage and lake contamination.[28]

In the spring of 1992, superintendent David Morris, responding to a recent op-ed article by Doug Larson in the Portland *Oregonian*, denied that "significant amounts of sewage" had ever entered Crater Lake. Morris also signaled the Park Service's emerging public-relations strategy by announcing that a soon-to-be-published ten-year scientific study of the lake would explain how "water clarity rises and falls in cycles due to a variety of reasons." As the ten-year report neared publication in 1993, Morris became even bolder in his assertions, claiming that scientists had determined that "the lake is still pristine," and that "no man-induced reduction in clarity" had taken place.[29]

The Crater Lake scientists who contributed to the ten-year report identified sewage contamination (often referred to, in such scientific discourse, as "nutrients from anthropogenic sources") as just one of several factors that *could have* affected water clarity in the past. But no single factor or combination of factors, they concluded, had affected water clarity permanently. Moreover, since the suspect sewage system had been removed in 1991, the historical factor of sewage contamination could never be documented or quantified. Larson criticized the ten-year report for its failure to "address Congress's original concerns about the pollution and consequent degradation of Crater Lake," and for conclusions that stretched beyond the evidence. In response to Morris's boast that "the lake is still pristine," Larson remarked: "To say that leach field never caused any problem was a whitewash. If it wasn't a problem, why remove it at the cost of $3 million?"[30]

Doug Larson continues to write occasionally about the Crater Lake sewage-contamination controversy and his role in it. Although he remains critical of Park Service practices, current Crater Lake managers, to their credit, seem far less preoccupied with Larson. For example, William M. "Mac" Brock, chief of resource preservation and research at Crater Lake, speaks respectfully of Doug Larson's contributions as a researcher at Crater Lake, even characterizing his theory as reasonable in light of the information Larson had at the time. But Brock also insists—perhaps with more certainty than is warranted, given the relatively short span of serious lake monitoring and research—that data collected over the last fifteen years show that the Larson hypothesis was wrong. Brock points out that the apparent reduction in clarity first observed by Larson in the late 1970s now appears to be "well within the range of fluctuations we know today to be normal"—variations rooted in complex lake processes known as "physical mixing" and "chemical cycling."[31]

Thus the link that Larson hypothesized between sewage contamination and permanently diminished clarity in Crater Lake is, on the basis of evidence, legitimately disputed. However, Larson's broader contention that sewage entered the lake over years by way of contaminated groundwater was very likely correct. And while exact amounts of sewage contamination and specific harmful effects are impossible to determine, common sense suggests that *any* contamination posed the risk of damage, and, for that reason, any contamination was too much. In any case, quite apart from the damage that sewage contamination might have caused, a lake inhabited by tens of thousands of non-native fish and populated by hundreds of gas-fueled motorboat cruises each year is in no sense "still pristine," as superintendent Morris claimed in 1993.[32]

To some observers, the "Larson hypothesis" is largely irrelevant to an assessment of Doug Larson's overall impact on the scientific study of Crater Lake. Owen Hoffman, a graduate student colleague of Larson's in the late 1960s who went on to earn his Ph.D. in ecology, sized up Larson's contribution in this way: "I think it's obvious that Doug is the instigator, if not the founder, of the ten-year research program. He was brave enough to bring the Crater Lake story to the attention of the public." John Salinas, who has worked at Crater Lake as a seasonal interpreter, resource manager, and limnologist since the late 1970s, described how his contact with Larson in the late 1970s permanently changed his life: "Doug's personality was attractive to me for some reason. He was very encouraging, respectful, and open with all the things he was doing. Doug was really a teaching limnologist, and he shared his work with the whole staff." While allowing that Larson had "a way of alienating people," and thereby causing some to turn away from his ideas for personal reasons, Salinas emphasized that those who do lake research today "are appreciative that this program came about because of [Larson's] early work. They are really happy that world-class research is being done on a world-class lake. Without Doug's actions, they wouldn't be doing research at Crater Lake."[33]

As for Larson himself, his adherence to the contamination hypothesis is beginning to loosen. His writing on the subject in popular forums remains largely polemical, but in conversations, interviews, and scientific formats he is cautious, thoughtful, and judicious on the subject. Larson concedes that as the issue became highly politicized in the 1980s, and as he suffered personally and professionally from the attacks of Park Service officials, he became, at times, an activist and an advocate as well as a scientist. Now, however, he is prepared to see his hypothesis disproved (as any reputable scientist should be), even while he continues to rankle over two questions. Why did Park Service officials meet his initial warnings with such nervous hostility? And why did the Park Service delay action for nearly fifteen years before correcting the sewage problem? Though he may never receive satisfactory answers to these questions, Larson finds great satisfaction in two achievements at Crater Lake in the 1980s and 1990s: replacement of the antiquated leach-field sewage remnant in Rim Village in 1991; and the Limnological Studies Program—begun in 1983 and renewed in 1993—through which Crater Lake has been seriously monitored and studied for the first time in its history.[34]

Now nearing the end of a second decade of lake research and monitoring, the Park Service will soon face a major crossroads. Will the agency support long-term research and monitoring of Crater Lake independent of federal legislation that forces its hand? Doug Larson's advice on this question points both to the future and the past: "Crater Lake National Park should have a lake-monitoring research program that is base-funded every year. It should be done routinely. . . . This would provide some way of knowing if the lake is indeed deteriorating due to some natural or anthropogenic cause. I think it should be done because future investigators will benefit from having a long-term and thorough historical record with which to compare their data. This was something we never had when hypothesizing that the lake had changed. If we had had this record, maybe this whole issue wouldn't have happened."[35]

NOW THAT THE OBVIOUS THREAT of a sewage system perched near the crater rim has been removed, scientists can more justifiably focus on other potential threats to Crater Lake's clarity and composition, such as automobile and boat emissions, contamination from springs (some perhaps still corrupted by residue from the old sewage system's drain field), climate change, air pollution, and non-native lake species. The current Limnological Studies Program has chosen to investigate these threats by way of basic scientific research into "what makes the lake work," in the words of lead investigator Gary Larson. In addition to a long-term monitoring scheme set up to allow future comparisons of temperature, water chemistry, clarity, microorganism populations, and fish life, this "holistic" approach demands fundamental understandings of the biological, chemical, and physical features of the complex lake ecosystem.[36]

In 1995, the addition of a new research vessel, the *Neuston*, boosted scientists' technical capabilities. Five years later, in July 2000, the most spectacular science vessel ever to enter Crater Lake was dropped to the surface by a U.S. Army Reserve helicopter. In a joint effort of the National Park Service, the U.S. Geological Survey, and the University of New Hampshire's Center for Coastal and Ocean Mapping, a sophisticated multi-beam sonar device (one of seven such units in the world) was mounted on the bottom of a twenty-six-foot boat, the *Surf Surveyor*, and deployed by scientists to shoot sound waves at the lake's bottom. Fans of sonar energy emitted from the instrument combined to generate some thirty million soundings of the Crater Lake basin, with the reflected sound waves then translated by computer into detailed digital images of the lake basin's contours and composition.[37]

The park's resource chief, Mac Brock, hailed this "historic event" for the extraordinary speed and precision brought to a task—the mapping of Crater Lake—that had, until the summer of 2000, proceeded slowly over more than a hundred years. Just hours after the boat was retrieved from the lake, the technology produced a preliminary map of the caldera. A final map, far more detailed and sophisticated than anything preceding it, was completed in just weeks. Characterizing the progression from a hundred soundings taken in 1886 (via lead weight and piano wire) to several thousand obtained in 1959 (with primitive sound-echo technology) to the thirty million produced in 2000, Brock invoked the image of human eyesight advanced, in two giant steps, from myopia to twenty-twenty acuity. In essence, the multi-beam sonar device has given scientists the ability "to see Crater Lake without the water."[38]

The maximum depth measurement obtained during the five-day survey was 1,958 feet, 26 feet greater than the maximum figure from 1959. But more valuable even than the precise depth information is the overall picture conveyed by this remarkable technology's

The data produced by the July 2000 multi-beam sonar sounding of the Crater Lake basin will contribute to the deciphering of such complex geological puzzles as Crater Lake's Redcloud Cliff, on the east caldera wall. (Courtesy NPS, CLNP Museum and Archives Collection.)

"backscattered" sound energy. The combined data, which have illuminated previously obscure vents, landslides, and formations on the caldera's underwater surface, will almost surely produce fresh interpretations of the volcanic history of Mount Mazama and Crater Lake. Brock predicted that over the next ten years, as geologists and other scientists examine and digest this wealth of new information, our understanding of "how Mount Mazama was formed, collapsed, and gave rise to Crater Lake," and how the lake's "ongoing processes" vary over time, will be broadened immeasureably.[39]

Tilting toward Science

SUSTAINED SCIENTIFIC INVESTIGATION and monitoring of Crater Lake did not really get started until the 1970s, seemingly late in the park's hundred-year history. But this delayed application of science at Crater Lake is consistent with the general pattern described by Park Service historian Richard West Sellars: "The infusion of an ecological and scientific perspective . . . constitutes the most substantive difference between late-nineteenth-century and late-twentieth-century natural resource management in the [national] parks."[40]

The slow advance of scientific study at the lake was even more pronounced elsewhere in the park. An official natural-resources management plan issued in 1986 identified Crater Lake National Park as "primarily a natural resource area, managed in such a manner as to allow natural processes to occur." But this resounding endorsement of ecological principles was more aspiration than fact. Progress in achieving several of the plan's goals—promoting native plant and animal species and allowing natural processes to flourish, fostering scientific research, limiting environmental threats at the park's boundaries, rehabilitating disturbed areas—was still barely perceptible in 1986.[41]

In 1992, a report from the inspector general's office of the Interior Department found "failings" in science-based ecological protections at Crater Lake and thirty other national parks. Superintendent David Morris cited the report's conclusion that native bull trout were close to extinction in Crater Lake National Park as a "warning that more needs to be done to understand the park's ecosystems and to protect them." The dilemma for the Park Service in 1992 remained not unlike what it had been in 1932: given a broad (and some would say contradictory) legislative mandate, the NPS faced too many obligations with too little money. Still, during the last decade of the twentieth century, the Park Service, which had tilted for most of its history toward development, use, and visitor satisfaction, began to tilt more toward protection, preservation, and ecological science. In response to stepped-up internal and external urgings, the NPS became more explicitly a "preservation organization," and this lent new gravity and urgency to identified ecological "failings."[42]

Despite explicitly new priorities, the tilt toward protection, preservation, and ecological science at Crater Lake has been slow and gradual. Just as the Limnological Studies Program was given an initial push by federal legislation mandating greater scientific attention to the lake ecosystem, federal laws have prodded other aspects of the park's research and preservation efforts. For example, the Endangered Species Act of 1973 has hovered over Crater Lake National Park's struggle to restore bull trout to park streams, as well as its efforts to survey and monitor such threatened species as the northern spotted owl, the lynx, the wolverine, and various amphibians.[43]

❦

A SURVEY OF CRATER LAKE National Park's Sun Creek in 1947 found some three thousand bull trout; forty-two years passed before the next survey, in 1989, counted only one hundred thirty fish. Scientists concluded that the bull trout had been nearly wiped out by a competitor species, the brook trout, which for decades was stocked in park streams to promote recreational fishing. Initial restoration efforts focused on constructing barriers on lower Sun Creek to prevent migration of the non-native brook trout into the park's portion of the stream. Brook trout already living in Sun Creek above the barriers were killed by electroshocking and poisoning. In 1996, with the number of adult bull trout rising modestly in Sun Creek, the recovery program was extended to Lost Creek. By 1997, the park could claim at least tentative victory, as the ratio of bull trout to brook trout had improved dramatically in the middle and upper reaches of Sun Creek. But the outcome remains uncertain. The fate of this program demonstrates once again that rescuing a species is so much more difficult than imperiling it in the first place.[44]

With the hiring of a fire management officer in 1990, Crater Lake signaled its intent to use scientifically endorsed "controlled fire" techniques as part of its larger effort to restore natural conditions to the park's native forest and plant communities. Just two years earlier Crater Lake firefighters had lost control of a prescribed fire, resulting in the burning of around one thousand acres of park property and another thousand acres of national forest land (the Prophecy Fire of 1988). Partly because of that failure, and because of even more conspicuous failures in other national parks, controlled fires have been used sparingly at Crater Lake. However, the addition of a fire management officer to the Crater Lake staff has helped improve cooperation with Forest Service officials from the three national forests adjacent to the park. And partly as a result of this general rapprochement, the park has had fewer disagreements with the Forest Service on other matters, such as clear cutting on the national forest side of park boundaries.[45]

Improved cooperation with the Forest Service has also helped Crater Lake's staff gain better control of park boundaries, and this, in turn, has helped improve overall resource protection. Crater Lake National Park's perimeters have always been somewhat ill defined and permeable, but expansion in 1932 and again in the early 1980s compounded the problem. Illegal deer and bear hunting, cattle grazing, mushroom poaching, and timber theft became more serious threats, in part because the altered Crater Lake boundaries were not properly surveyed, identified, and marked. As superintendent Benton commented in his annual report for 1989: "It seems incredible that Crater Lake does not know the location of its boundaries."[46]

The goal of restoring natural conditions to the park's native forest and plant communities was bound to remain unrealistic until better surveys and inventories were carried out. Progress was made in this direction during the 1990s: inventories of rare species were taken, the park's checklist of plants was expanded, and surveys of disturbed sites requiring revegetation were made. These ongoing efforts were buttressed by an overarching attempt to classify the park's vegetation zones with the aid of satellite imagery, and to develop digitalized maps and computerized spatial data for the entire park.[47]

Serving Visitors and Researchers at the Turn of a New Century

SINCE THE LATE 1980s, the Steel Information Center in Munson Valley has acted as the park's only year-round visitor-contact station. The building currently houses the park's main information desk, a theater offering regular presentations of a Crater Lake video, brief exhibits, book and merchandise sales, a post office, the park library, staff offices, and storage areas for collections. Visitors who manage to find the Steel Center (signs leading to it are easy to miss) can count on receiving good guidance. However, more than half of those who enter the park during the busy season either are unable to locate the Steel Center or intend to go directly to Rim Village, where crowds have overburdened the small Exhibit Building for decades. These conditions have limited the orientation capacities of the Crater Lake staff's ability to deliver basic information to potentially receptive visitors.[48]

For visitors who linger in the park longer than it takes for a quick look at the lake and a brief encounter with the cafeteria and gift shop, chances for exposure to Park Service educational programs increase. And for those who opt for an overnight stay, the likelihood of hearing

Evening programs in the Mazama Campground amphitheater provide a strong link to Crater Lake's outstanding interpretive tradition; such programs also appear to serve twenty-first-century visitors effectively. (Courtesy NPS, CLNP Museum and Archives Collection.)

Superintendent Bob Benton in 1988 presides at the dedication of the Superintendent's Residence as a national historic landmark, one of many Benton-orchestrated efforts to highlight the park's historical character. (Courtesy NPS, CLNP Museum and Archives Collection.)

talks from Park Service interpreters becomes even greater. Typical summer-season (June 22-Labor Day) educational offerings include boat tours of Crater Lake; evening campfire programs at the Mazama Campground amphitheater; children's programs at Mazama Village and Rim Village; backcountry hikes on the Garfield Peak Trail and walks in the Discovery Point, Mount Scott, Godfrey Glen, and Annie Creek areas; geology and lake-science talks at the Sinnott Memorial; walks through the Munson Valley and Rim Village historic districts; and limited exhibits at several indoor and outdoor sites. While natural history and popular science remain the focus of interpretive presentations, over the last ten years park educators have given greater attention to Indian peoples of the region; the history of regional exploration, conflict, and settlement; Will Steel and his crusade to make Crater Lake a national park; and the period of national park administration.[49]

As the park approached its centennial year in 2002, a new Visitor Services Plan included a Rim Village "visitor contact station" as one of its essential elements. In addition to offering a state-of-the-art space for interpreters to meet visitors within sight of the lake, the new plan promised expanded exhibit areas. Partly in anticipation of an enlarged exhibition program, Crater Lake hired its first full-time museum curator in 1993. Since that time, new collections have been acquired and a few small exhibit areas filled while the painstaking work of organizing, cataloging, and archiving existing collections has inched forward.[50]

In addition to managing the library, editing *Nature Notes*, and adding to the park's administrative history, the park historian, since the early 1990s, has devoted much time to compiling information on historical buildings and sites and to overseeing the park's compliance with federal legislation protecting them. Much of this work has involved the historic properties of Rim Village and Munson Valley, but more recent research and archaeological surveying have focused on a portion of the historic Fort Klamath-Jacksonville wagon road that passes through the park.[51]

The accomplishments of Crater Lake's historian and curator in the 1990s have vindicated superintendent Robert Benton's strategy to enhance the park's visibility, political strength, and money-procurement powers by highlighting its historical identity. Even though Crater Lake has always been known primarily as a natural-area park, Benton shrewdly saw potential bureaucratic advantage in playing on Crater Lake's historical character as the sixth oldest national park, home of some of the most impressive historic architecture in the entire national park system. Aside from their inherent value in documenting and preserving the park's history, the positions of curator and park historian thus appear to have "paid off" for Crater Lake much as Benton had hoped.[52]

Changing Relations between the Park Service and Indians

As American Indians began to voice their cultural and tribal interests more aggressively during the 1960s and 1970s, the perspectives of native Americans, past and present, began to creep into the considerations of National Park Service officials. This trend was reinforced by a host of new federal laws, passed and amended during the sixties, seventies, and eighties, requiring certain government agencies to assist native peoples in preserving their historic properties and cultural traditions.

Mandates of the National Historic Preservation Act, the National Environmental Policy Act, the Archaeological and Historic Preservation Act, the American Indian Religious Freedom Act, and the Archaeological Resources Protection Act led directly to the Native American Relationships Management Policy of the National Park Service, announced in 1987. This landmark shift in NPS organizational intent has gradually pushed the agency toward policies of real respect for Indian cultures, eventually engendering efforts to promote tribal cultures as living components of national parks and their histories.[53]

Chapter 9

Challenge and Opportunity in the New Century

The Klamath Tribes and the Contemporary Park

INDIAN LEADERS WHO POWERED the drive to restore federal recognition to the Klamath Tribes in the 1970s and 1980s knew well that President Reagan's signing of the Klamath Restoration Act of 1986 represented only a partial victory. The law reinstated government services that relieved some of the worst social ills plaguing the Indians in the post-termination period. But by the early 1990s, native leaders had begun to stress that only through restoration of former tribal lands would the Klamath Tribes be able to achieve economic self-sufficiency. Though the authors of the 1986 legislation had not intended the return of reservation lands as part of tribal restoration, the Restoration Act's requirement for an economic self-sufficiency plan gave the Indians an opportunity to present their land-repatriation argument as part of that mandatory plan.[1]

In fact, tribal reacquisition of 690,000 acres of the former Klamath Reservation—land that became part of the Winema and Fremont national forests following termination of the tribes in 1954—is the key premise of the Klamath Economic Self-Sufficiency Plan. Though these 690,000 acres make up less than one-twentieth of the traditional homelands claimed by the Klamath, Modoc, and Yahooskin-Paiute peoples, native strategists contend that the returned lands, after about thirty years of restored tribal management, could provide the necessary base for economic self-sufficiency and cultural regeneration. The Indians argue that their economic strength and cultural well-being were rooted historically in a communal land base (first, the traditional tribal lands and, later, the reservation lands), and that their future strength and well-being must be similarly grounded in communal lands. The formal economic self-sufficiency plan spells out how the 690,000 returned acres would be managed for the sustainable economic, cultural, and spiritual benefit of the Klamath peoples in the twenty-first century.[2]

Although the drive to repossess former reservation lands is aimed solely at U.S. Forest Service acreage, the native campaign has complicated regional politics for National Park Service managers. Reflecting changes in federal law, evolving NPS policy, and sheer individual initiative, Crater Lake officials have tried (especially over the last decade) to step up their engagement and cooperation with regional neighbors—Klamath tribal leaders, local government representatives, national forest officials, university presidents, and others. Naturally, the emergence of a contentious regional issue, such as the Klamaths' bid to reacquire former reservation lands, makes a policy of impartial outreach all the more difficult.[3]

Ongoing disputes over water rights and allocations in the Klamath Basin—involving primarily ranchers, farmers, environmentalists, recreationists, government officials, and Indians—have further sharpened the tenor of contemporary regional politics. While Crater Lake National Park has not been a principal antagonist in the crossfire of claims on the region's scarce water, droughts of the past several years have led some downstream contestants to question even the comparatively small volume of water used by the park from its Annie Spring source. Pressed by this challenge, Crater Lake managers have mobilized—assembling stream-flow data on park drainages and, through research into Crater Lake's legislative history, documenting "the most advantageous priority dates" for the park's water rights—to assert the park's priority claim to the water it needs.[4]

Amid this agitated and sometimes antagonistic political climate, Crater Lake officials—impelled by the Park Service's 1987 Native American Relationships Policy, by additional amendments to the National Historic Preservation Act made in the 1990s, and by the Clinton administration's "sacred sites" executive order—have begun to take careful steps to redress decades of neglect of neighboring native peoples by their Park Service predecessors. In August 2000, in recognition of the "special status" of the Klamath Tribes vis-à-vis lands now occupied by Crater Lake National Park, the park enacted a policy of free entrance for tribal members holding valid tribal identification cards. In addition, park managers are now moving toward a potentially momentous policy of regular "government-to-government relations" with the Klamath Tribes. For example, in 1997 the Park Service included tribal representatives in discussions about Crater Lake's Visitor

Annie Spring, flowing amid handsome rockwork, provides Crater Lake National Park with most of its water needs. (Courtesy National Park Service, Crater Lake National Park Museum and Archives Collection.)

Services Plan, and future consultations with native representatives will treat issues ranging from historical interpretation to natural-resource preservation.[5]

Joint work in archaeology offers one of the more promising areas of future government-to-government cooperation, although current Crater Lake superintendent Charles V. Lundy cautions that funding for such work will require a long-term effort to change the conventional perception within the Park Service that Crater Lake is not a rich archeological park. Ongoing discussions with regional Indians about archaeology and ethnography, begun in 1991, have yielded information that should help alter that perception. Current ethnographic work, conducted primarily by anthropologist Douglas Deur and supported by park historian Steve Mark, focuses on traditional native uses of park lands. Park officials hope that traditional-use studies will not only produce rich historical and cultural information but will contribute to a lasting dialogue between the NPS and local tribes.[6]

Just as contemporary Klamath Basin political disputes complicate the park's efforts to forge a constructive, mutually respectful relationship with the Klamath Tribes, Crater Lake's "Centennial Celebration Program," planned for the spring and summer of 2002, could hinder rapprochement with the Indians. For the descendants of native people who for thousands of years roamed the park area without constraint or prohibition, Crater Lake's one-hundredth anniversary is not a natural cause for celebration. In fact, for some Indians, the park's one-hundred-year history (and the preceding half-century of steady advance on the region by newcomers) represents an era of unparalleled cultural instability and trauma. Moreover, from the natives' perspective, establishment of the park in 1902 brought unfair prohibitions against traditional hunting and gathering practices, unjust limitations on travel, and degradation of religious sites.[7]

Granting the Indians' legitimate dissent, however, it is important to recognize that Park Service officials and others involved in planning the centennial celebration have been driven not by a sense of triumph in how Crater Lake and the surrounding region were wrested from those who had occupied it for millennia, but by personal and professional attachment to the place, as well as by pride in the role the NPS has played in making Crater Lake accessible and enjoyable to hundreds of thousands of people over the past century. Nonetheless, while the Park Service and the Friends of Crater Lake National Park (a support organization founded in 1993) promote and carry out the

Early assessments of Crater Lake National Park as an area with limited archaeological resources were based on inadequate information. Current archaeological work, planned and carried out in cooperation with the Klamath Tribes, is changing that picture. (Courtesy NPS, CLNP Museum and Archives Collection.)

Centennial Celebration events—an Artists-in-the-Park exhibition planned for Southern Oregon University's Schneider Museum of Art in 2002, performances of a one-act play re-creating the character of Will Steel, among other programs—the park's efforts to strengthen relations with the Klamath Tribes might well stall temporarily.[8]

The Park Service and National Politics

NEARLY ALL MAJOR NATIONAL PARKS and monuments in the West include Indian sacred areas within their boundaries. But not until the late 1980s did the Park Service begin to investigate these sites seriously and, in some cases, take steps to preserve them for traditional uses. For much of its history, as we have seen, the Park Service favored development and tourist enjoyment over preservation of either cultural or natural resources. But as ecological science and environmental politics gained ground in the later twentieth century, conventional NPS natural-resource practices were challenged repeatedly. After 1970, scientific and legal challenges regularly demonstrated that many of the oldest and most revered nature-based national parks were ecologically compromised and environmentally mismanaged.[9]

Even as a new constituency advocating preservationist principles took shape, the traditional constituency supporting maximum tourist enjoyment remained strong. Beginning with the Carter administration, which presided over an unprecedented expansion of the national park system in the late 1970s, the National Park Service became frequently enmeshed in broad ideological debates about the scope of federal government and the status of public lands. The succeeding Reagan administration (especially during James Watt's tenure as interior secretary) challenged several Carter administration public-lands policies in the 1980s, and American politicians of radically different stripes took opposite positions on Park Service policy and philosophy—all in the name of "fighting for the National Park Service" and all claiming to be rooted in the ever-mutable NPS Organic Act.[10]

Having survived the adverse political winds of the 1980s, the rhetoric of science-based preservationism continued to advance in the 1990s. In the later 1990s, preservationist deeds surged to catch up with preservationist rhetoric, partly as a result of Clinton administration interior secretary Bruce Babbitt's exceptional interest and initiative. For example, in April 2000, citing the need to protect public lands from excessive noise and air pollution, the government banned recreational snowmobile use on most Park Service land. Opponents

Snowmobile tracks and a snowmobile in Crater Lake National Park reflect use of the park's north-entrance road for this type of recreation. (Courtesy NPS, CLNP Museum and Archives Collection.)

immediately characterized the action as "nothing short of an attack on motorized recreation," part of a broad-based "campaign by [the Clinton] administration to limit public access to public lands." Then, in the waning days of the Clinton presidency, the NPS issued key administrative directives "designed to cement the agency's role as the nation's leading protector of natural and historic places." Some of the same voices attacked these new administrative rules as the culmination of a Park Service effort, accelerated during the Clinton administration, "to restrict and otherwise limit public access to our national parks."[11]

Such reactions to Park Service policies voiced *after* the presidential election of 2000 were aimed, at least in part, at the incoming George W. Bush administration, which had earlier signaled its intent to appoint new Park Service leadership and to concentrate the agency's budget on "a $4.9 billion backlog of park maintenance and repairs." When Bush representatives declared the new administration's determination to "restore" public enjoyment of the national parks, many understood this to mean that the new political regime would, in time, back away from the government's fresh commitment to preservation and reinstate the traditional Park Service emphasis on facilities development and public use. Preservationism may yet survive as the identified top priority of the NPS, but probably not without severe criticism and stiff political challenge.[12]

Changed Priorities at Crater Lake

STARTING IN THE LATE 1990s, Crater Lake National Park's fifty or so employees (around 125 during the busy season) began spending at least part of their time gearing up for the centennial year. The park's more than one hundred buildings, nine picnic areas, two campgrounds, eighty-five miles of trails, and seventy-five miles of roadway were groomed, and various other improvements were planned and paced with the centennial celebration in mind.[13]

During the summers of 1999 and 2000, for example, the Park Service began rehabilitation of the historic Watchman Lookout and Trailside Museum, at the top of Watchman Peak (also known as the Watchman), where public exhibits have been closed since 1975. In addition, Congress appropriated $1.7 million to begin rehabilitation and redevelopment of the Rim Village historic district during the summers of 2000 and 2001, with completion scheduled in time for the centennial events of 2002. Through these efforts, the restored Community House will return to its traditional use as a comfortable indoor spot for summer evening programs. The refashioned Sinnott Memorial will continue in its role as an incomparable site for talks on Mount Mazama geology and the Crater Lake ecosystem, but an enclosed portion of the structure, in recent years underused as a storage area, will come to life again as an

Current plans for Rim Village include downsizing the cafeteria and gift shop building to approximate its original appearance, as shown here circa 1930. (Courtesy NPS, CLNP Museum and Archives Collection.)

exhibition space. In conjunction with construction of a new, year-round visitor-contact station, the rehabilitated Exhibit Building (the former Kiser Studio) will offer exhibits on Rim Village history. And the historic cafeteria building will revert to its original 1928 appearance after additions from the 1950s and 1970s are removed.[14]

Crater Lake's 1999 Visitor Services Plan, a scaled-back version of a grandiose proposal launched during Bob Benton's years as superintendent, reflects the Park Service's current emphasis on preservation and reduced development. Though referred to as a *visitor services* plan, and though it specifies some construction and rehabilitation in the park's four main developed areas (Rim Village, Mazama Village, Cleetwood Cove, and Munson Valley), the overall document subtly affirms the goals of resource protection and economy over the priorities of visitor satisfaction and convenience. For example, one of the plan's central aims is to reduce the volume of Rim Village traffic associated with the pursuit of food and souvenirs. (The Visitor Services Plan delicately states the intent: "Services that will otherwise detain visitors in Rim Village will be provided elsewhere.") A large parking area that for decades occupied the pivotal area between the cafeteria and the caldera rim will be removed and replaced with natural landscaping and walking paths, and a smaller parking lot will be built behind the cafeteria. The controversial Rim Dormitory will be removed and the site restored to natural vegetation. These and other measures are calculated to produce a less cluttered and hectic pedestrian atmosphere for visitors willing to invest more than just a few minutes in viewing and learning about the lake, rim, and Rim Village.[15]

Along with plans for physical changes in Rim Village, the Park Service intends to bulk up its own presence in this key region of the park. Organized educational programs will be offered at several Rim Village sites, and NPS employees will be on hand in other locations to provide general information and orientation. In tailoring their guidance and suggestions to the types of visitors they encounter, staff will further affect the flow of traffic and activity throughout the park. Concession company employees, who for decades were more visible in the Rim Village area than Park Service staff, will follow the shift of commercial-oriented activities to Mazama Village. There, near the park's southern entrance, a new full-service restaurant, gift shop, and enlarged parking area will cater to the more than five hundred overnight guests (during the busy season) at the Mazama Village Motor Inn cabins and Mazama Campground.[16]

❧

The National Park Service intends to encourage a more dispersed pattern of visitation in twenty-first-century Crater Lake National Park, relieving pressure on the lake and Rim Village environments. (Courtesy NPS, CLNP Museum and Archives Collection.)

CRATER LAKE LODGE, INC., the park's concessionaire since 1976, announced in September 2001 that it would not bid for the next fifteen-year concession agreement, which will require the contract partner to team with the Park Service in carrying out the 1999 Visitor Services Plan. In an August 2000 interview, the company's president and general manager, Richard Gordon, seemed eager to take on the presumably brisk business of the centennial year, but he also found fault with the Visitor Services Plan on several counts. While welcoming the promised greater visibility of Park Service staff in Rim Village and other commercial areas (from the concession company's point of view, Park Service employees are, in essence, "free" support staff), Gordon insisted that the plan, as a whole, "underestimates the need for commercial services in the park."[17]

The 1999 plan's language reveals its priorities in mostly subtle and diplomatic ways. For example, the age-old Park Service goals of "visitor satisfaction" and "visitor fulfillment" are, in this plan, frequently replaced by "visitor appreciation." Subtlety and diplomacy aside, though, businessman Gordon foresaw diminished profits for his company in many of the plan's measures. And while he affirmed that Crater Lake Lodge, Inc., shared the Park Service's commitment to "preserving and protecting the park's natural resources," Gordon argued that in his role as general manager he must also be attuned to predictable "visitor expectations."[18]

Gordon maintained that the 1999 Visitor Services Plan falls considerably short in anticipating and serving visitor expectations. For example, he contended that the park's typical visitor unquestionably favors maximum availability of boat tours on the lake, but the Visitor Services Plan proposes to reduce their number. He also argued that the plan's proposed reduction in the size of the cafeteria building and its shift of food service and retail gift sales from Rim Village to Mazama Village will leave thousands of lake visitors frustrated and dissatisfied. (In this and other respects, Gordon believed the earlier, more elaborate Benton-era proposal was more apt to satisfy the public.) And he pointed out that the Park Service's planned removal of the Rim Dormitory promises to make the task of providing housing and transportation for seasonal concession workers more difficult. Meanwhile, the Park Service maintains that the 1999 plan meets basic visitor needs affordably while advancing the primary goals of protecting the park's natural features and minimizing the impact of commercial services and visitors.[19]

Though the decision of Crater Lake Lodge, Inc., and the parent Estey Corporation to sever their twenty-five-year relationship with Crater Lake National Park on the eve of the park's centennial year came as a surprise to Park Service officials, they now seem determined to make the best of a new arrangement with a new company. Management assistant John Miele was confident that financial terms in the contract prospectus issued by the Park Service offer the next concession company a good opportunity for profit, even in the changed, less-commercial environment prescribed by Crater Lake's ruling Visitor Services Plan. Miele revealed that four companies submitted bids for the new contract, and that three of the four operate concessions in at least one other national park. He expected the new Crater Lake concession operator to be in place sometime during the winter of 2001-2002.[20]

The Recreation Fee Program and Self-Direction

AS THOSE WHO LIVE AND WORK in the park looked ahead to the centennial celebration, their anticipation of the year's special events sometimes shaded into apprehension. Park Service observers expected two hundred thousand or more additional visitors, and some park employees wondered whether Crater Lake would be prepared for the demands of these additional tourists. Some questioned, too, how well the park would stand up to the inevitable wear and tear of the additional traffic. And others asked what, if anything, would be gained by a temporary increase in attendance associated with the park's anniversary.

These questions were particularly apt at a time when many NPS employees were recommitting themselves to the Park Service's recently affirmed identity as a preservation organization. In earlier decades, a significant jump in any national park's annual visitation was likely to prompt a strong bid for more dollars to finance more development and more infrastructure, since development was traditionally seen as the only way to accommodate larger audiences and to attract even larger ones. However, at Crater Lake, where a significant increase in visitation was anticipated for the centennial year, many park professionals no longer subscribed to the old formula of more visitors leading to more money leading to more development. Although park managers believed strongly that Crater Lake deserves a larger budget, they doubted whether the expected increase in centennial-related visitation could be parlayed into greater NPS support for the park's now-paramount goal of preserving natural and cultural resources.[21]

In light of superintendent Chuck Lundy's expectation of a "flat budget" in the years ahead, continuance of the Recreation Fee Demonstration Program—introduced by Congress in 1996 and subsequently extended through September 2001—appears critical. On the basis of this experimental program, which seeks to shift a greater percentage of the costs of managing national parks and other public lands to those who use them, Crater Lake doubled its basic entrance fee from five dollars to ten dollars per vehicle in 1997. The program allows participating parks to keep 80 percent of the additional revenue they collect (at Crater Lake, four dollars of the five added to the entrance fee) to fund projects according to their own priorities. The Recreation Fee Program—if Congress installs it permanently—should continue to allow Crater Lake and other national parks a measure of autonomy at a time when philosophies espoused by the Bush administration appear at odds with newly championed preservationist values. (The NPS reorganization of 1995, in which regional offices were abolished and replaced by smaller central offices, also granted greater independence to individual parks.[22])

Since the Recreation Fee Program's beginning in 1997, Crater Lake National Park has added more than $2 million to its operating revenue, of which around $1 million has been spent on a variety of projects, including the Watchman Lookout and Trailside Museum rehabilitation. The proposed Crater Lake Science and Learning Center promises to be one of the more ambitious applications of the program's funds. With ground breaking planned for 2002, in conjunction with centennial events, and completion expected by 2005, the project exemplifies the kind of in-park development that many current Crater Lake managers view as consistent with the park's overarching preservationist goals. The proposed Science and Learning Center will be housed in a restored historic structure—the impressive Superintendent's Residence in Munson Valley, built in 1933 but ramshackle and mostly unoccupied for decades—rather than occupy a new site with new construction. And the center's two primary missions—to support serious scientific research in the park and to promote basic education about the Mount Mazama ecosystem and Crater Lake history—are calculated both to advance the cause of the park's preservation *and* to share its wonders with the public.[23]

A New Formula for Popularity

THOUGH ITS BUREAUCRACY IS WEAK and its budget small, the National Park Service remained immensely popular with the public throughout the twentieth century. Even in the decades after 1970, when it became tangled in political debates reaching beyond its immediate scope, the

The Superintendent's Residence (top), built in its Munson Valley location in 1933 and designated as a national historic landmark in 1987, has been selected as the future quarters for the Crater Lake Science and Learning Center. The structure includes a variety of interior spaces, including the original living-room area, shown here. (Courtesy NPS, CLNP Museum and Archives Collection.)

Park Service continued to claim the "highest approval ratings of all government agencies." Ironically, though, this popularity, in combination with the elusive character of the NPS legislative mandate, has left the twenty-first-century Park Service more vulnerable to political vicissitudes than many richer, but less conspicuous, agencies of the federal government. Consequently, even those parks with a degree of autonomy can ill afford to ignore the Organic Act's ever-demanding dual mandate to promote both preservation *and* recreation. In short, national parks, in pursuing their commitment to science-based preservation, must also take care to offer engaging opportunities for public fulfillment. If they fail in this, they will surely leave themselves open to charges of elitism and environmental extremism.[24]

As a result of the recently changed emphasis in its mission, the National Park Service must find a new formula for attracting public support, and for translating popular support into political support. As commercial and recreational attractions recede, more of the burden of visitor satisfaction will fall to the interpretive/educational branch. Can national park interpretive programs broaden their approach and develop new forms of visitor fulfillment rooted in historical appreciation and science-based preservation? And can these new programs attract strong enough popular and political support to sustain the emphasis on preservation? In the NPS quest for a new formula for education and public outreach, Crater Lake National Park, with its unique physical and historical profile, appears well positioned to lead the way.

WHAT MAKES CRATER LAKE so well suited to this leading role? First, compared to many of the best-known western national parks, with their larger budgets and teeming crowds, Crater Lake has much less damage to undo on its way to becoming a preservation-oriented, ecosystem-based natural area. The most popular national parks, after decades of development, are saddled with elaborate, recreation-based commercial infrastructures and enormous vacation-oriented constituencies. The physical and political obstacles to taking a new course are consequently huge for these big-name parks. Crater Lake faces fewer such obstacles.[25]

Second, Crater Lake, as a largely intact ecosystem (the Mount Mazama ecosystem), is large enough to be of true scientific value but compact enough to allow resource-preservation and interpretive staff to cooperate effectively. The park's out-of-the-way location— surrounded by other public lands and removed from population and commercial/industrial centers—has helped minimize external threats.

Ironically, this factor of isolation, so long seen as a liability in the recreation-oriented Park Service, now assumes a key role in reinforcing the park's identity as a wilderness-based, preserved refuge.[26]

Third, in searching for a way to build popular support for the park in its preservation-oriented guise, Crater Lake can draw upon its own exemplary educational and interpretive tradition, which touted science-based ecological principles much earlier than the park's management or the Park Service as a whole. In doing so, educators at Crater Lake may find themselves returning to old methods of conveying information and awareness—interpreters in the field, leading walks, encountering visitors, taking advantage of nature as the teacher and the outdoors as the classroom—more than inventing new ones.[27]

Whatever teaching methods are used, park professionals must draw upon ecological science to show that preservationism is not so much a choice as an imperative for survival. And in the course of demonstrating this preservationist imperative, the concept of vulnerability should play a vital role. Whether the resources are natural (such as Crater Lake itself or the Castle Crest wildflower landscape) or cultural (such as the historic architecture of Munson Valley or prehistoric archaeological sites), the park is vulnerable to human-caused assaults of all kinds: from ill-advised construction projects to air pollution to simply too many people. In conveying this central notion of vulnerability to park visitors, history can be an effective ally. Examples of environmental and cultural-resource degradation, including explanations of how and why institutions and people made choices that caused such damage, can provide compelling illustrations, not in order to indict or embarrass but to show how preservationism is the only viable course for maintaining America's national parks in the next century.[28]

If park professionals can become active, successful practitioners and teachers of preservationist principles, more visitors will understand that Crater Lake National Park consists of far more than the lake and its spectacular scenery. More visitors will learn, too, that one must usually look beyond the spectacular to determine the real condition of natural areas. More will appreciate the character of the natural landscape confronted by their pre-industrial forebears. More will accept that extreme care must be taken to protect and maintain natural areas within developed, industrialized societies. And more will see the public value in preserving these last intact ecosystems in the United States—as instructive remnants of the past and as "laboratories" for studying natural systems in process.[29]

Thus, Crater Lake National Park's success in cultivating popular support for preservationist policies will probably rest in the foreseeable future on the effectiveness of its educational efforts. And since measuring success is sure to be one of the most difficult aspects of the whole undertaking, Crater Lake's current Strategic Plan proposes use of a visitor survey that will "assess the percentage of visitors who understand and appreciate the significance of the park," in addition to its providing the more conventional measurements of visitor "satisfaction."[30]

Assessments of visitors' understanding and appreciation will be difficult enough; measurement of other important aspects of park visitors' experiences will remain nearly impossible. Some who urge national parks to reshape their popular image point to certain desirable but hard-to-describe outcomes of the human encounter with wild nature: engagement of the "contemplative faculty," enhancement of inner peace, affirmation of spiritual values, to name a few. Certainly Crater Lake National Park, whose main feature has always been widely regarded as "a thing of the spirit," and whose total area consists mostly of "wilderness," is well equipped to provide plenty of such nature-based inspiration. Perhaps the Park Service and individual parks can develop methods for chronicling such personal experiences, as well as strategies for using personal testaments to political advantage.[31]

Enhancing the *quality* of national park visits will, in most instances, reinforce the broader preservationist objectives of national parks. Likewise, in acting to protect the natural and cultural resources of parks,

Crater Lake, powerful and enduring in so many ways, is nonetheless vulnerable to human assault and requires active protection. (OHS neg. OrHi 42076.)

NPS officials will reinforce the emphasis on the quality of visits by minimizing distractions and intrusions that "impede an independent and personal response to experience." In this dual emphasis on preservation and quality of visitor experiences, the Park Service is, in effect, choosing a different course for the national parks—one that seeks to stimulate demand for "reflective recreation," in the terminology of legal scholar Joseph L. Sax, and one that promotes "intensiveness of experience" rather than "intensiveness of consumption."[32]

The Challenge Ahead

WE HAVE ENTERED AN ERA in which the enticement of ever-larger crowds into America's national parks can no longer be reconciled with the government's commitment to protect and preserve the parks for future generations. The Park Service's acceptance and even encouragement of smaller crowds, far from signaling a lessened commitment to public service, should be seen—through the new emphasis on *quality* of visitor experiences, for example—as a renewed dedication to that task. Nonetheless, as Crater Lake and other great nature-based national parks move in the direction of preservationist policies and quality-based educational and recreational programs, some potential national park visitors will be confronted with the message: "Although you are welcome in this national park, it may not be the right place for the kind of experience you seek." Some Park Service professionals, still identifying with an institutional tradition that for so long stressed numbers of visitors, will be uncomfortable delivering this message, no matter how subtly or indirectly it is couched. And some would-be visitors who hear this message will probably not receive it without protest.[33]

To some extent, science-based preservationist policies and more challenging educational and recreational programs clash with the dominant American values of materialism, consumerism, and unrestrained commercialism. Discouraging these values in the national parks after more than a half-century of accommodating them is bound to be politically treacherous, and the tension between opposing national park philosophies is not likely ever to disappear entirely. But the preservationist point of view carries with it a simple, readily understandable, and indisputable rationale: without conscientious preservation of these great parcels of nature, which include such spectacular features as Mount Mazama's Crater Lake, we will degrade and lose them.[34]

Notes

Chapter 1

1. Elizabeth L. Orr, William W. Orr, and Ewart M. Baldwin, *Geology of Oregon*, 4th ed. (Kendall/Hunt, 1976), 141; and Donald A. Swanson et al., eds., *Cenozoic Volcanism in the Cascade Range and Columbia Plateau, Southern Washington and Northernmost Oregon* (American Geophysical Union, 1989), excerpted on the USGS/Cascades Volcano Observatory Web site: http://vulcan.wr.usgs.gov/Volcanoes/CraterLake/description_crater_lake.html.

2. Howel Williams, *Crater Lake: The Story of Its Origin* (University of California Press, 1972), 11. Originally published in 1941.

3. David R. Sherrod, in Charles A. Wood and Jurgen Kienle, eds., *Volcanoes of North America: United States and Canada* (Cambridge University Press, 1990), 169, excerpted on USGS/Cascade Volcano Observatory Web site; and Orr, Orr, and Baldwin, *Geology of Oregon*, 141.

4. Williams, *Crater Lake*, 15.

5. Charles R. Bacon, in Wood and Kienle, eds., *Volcanoes of North America*, 193-95, excerpted on USGS/Cascade Volcano Observatory Web site.

6. Williams, *Crater Lake*, 16, 19; and Steve Mark, "Small Shards of Stone," *Nature Notes from Crater Lake* 31 (2000), 27-28.

7. Williams, *Crater Lake*, 21-22.

8. Ibid., 25.

9. Ibid., 27.

10. Howel Williams, *The Geology of Crater Lake National Park, Oregon: With a Reconnaissance of the Cascade Range Southward to Mount Shasta* (Carnegie Institution, 1942), 2; and Ron Mastrogiuseppe and Steve Mark, "A 'New' Date for Mount Mazama's Climactic Eruption," *Nature Notes from Crater Lake* 23 (1992), 9-11.

11. Williams, *Crater Lake*, 30.

12. Ibid., 32.

13. Ibid., 34-35; and Charles R. Bacon, "Eruptive History of Mount Mazama and Crater Lake Caldera, Cascade Range, U.S.A.," *Journal of Volcanology and Geothermal Research* 18 (1983), 57-115.

14. Williams, *Crater Lake*, 35.

15. C. Melvin Aikens, *Archaeology of Oregon* (U.S. Bureau of Land Management, 1993), 268-70; and Kathryn Winthrop, "Prehistory of the Southern Oregon Cascades," in John Mairs, Kathryn R. Winthrop, and Robert H. Winthrop, *Archaeological and Ethnological Studies of Southwest Oregon and Crater Lake National Park: An Assessment* (National Park Service, 1994), 131.

16. Aikens, *Archaeology of Oregon*, 270.

17. L. S. Cressman, *The Sandal and the Cave: The Indians of Oregon* (Beaver Books, 1962), 16; and Constance Bordwell, "Fort Rock Cave: Monument to the 'First Oregonians'," *Oregon Historical Quarterly* (summer 1987), 123-24, 145 (includes a speech given by pioneer Oregon archaeologist Luther S. Cressman at the dedication of Fort Rock Cave as a national historic landmark on June 22, 1963); L. S. Cressman, Howell Williams, and Alex Krieger, *Early Man in Oregon: Archaeological Studies in the Northern Great Basin* (University of Oregon, 1940), 70; and L. S. Cressman, *Prehistory of the Far West: Homes of Vanished People* (University of Utah Press, 1977), 52, 53.

18. Theodore Stern, "Klamath and Modoc," in Deward E. Walker, Jr., ed., *Handbook of North American Indians: Volume 12, Plateau* (Smithsonian Institution Press, 1998), 446; and L. S. Cressman, *Klamath Prehistory* (American Philosophical Society, 1956), 400.

19. John Mairs, "Environment," in Mairs, Winthrop, and Winthrop, *Archaeological and Ethnological Studies*, 10-11.

20. K. Winthrop, "Prehistory," 130.

21. Williams, *Geology of Crater Lake National Park*, 129; and Stephen R. Mark, *Crater Lake: The Continuing Story* (KC Publications, 1996), 28.

22. K. Winthrop, "Prehistory," 135; and Robert H. Winthrop, "Crater Lake in Indian Tradition: Sacred Landscapes and Cultural Survival," *Nature Notes from Crater Lake* 28 (1997), 6-12.

23. Robert Winthrop, "Cultural Significance of Crater Lake," in Mairs, Winthrop, and Winthrop, *Archaeological and Ethnological Studies*, 69.

24. Robert Winthrop, "Ethnology of the Southern Oregon Cascades," in Mairs, Winthrop, and Winthrop, *Archaeological and Ethnological Studies*, 40-42; Stern, "Klamath and Modoc," 454, 457, 458, 459; and R. H. Winthrop, "Crater Lake in Indian Tradition," 8-10.

25. R. Winthrop, "Ethnology," 43-44; and Stern, "Klamath and Modoc," 450.

26. Melville Jacobs, "Our Knowledge of Pacific Northwest Indian Folklores," *Northwest Folklore*, vol. 2 (1967), 14-21; quoted in Robert Winthrop, "Evaluation in Research: Ethnology," in Mairs, Winthrop, Winthrop, *Archaeological and Ethnological Studies*, 17; R. Winthrop, "Cultural Significance," 71-73; and R. H. Winthrop, "Crater Lake in Indian Tradition," 9-10.

27. R. Winthrop, "Ethnology," 67.

28. Ibid., 62, 67.

29. Ibid., 67; and Douglas Deur, "Traditional Land Use Study of Crater Lake National Park and Lava Beds National Monument." Response to RFQ # RQ 908600026, National Park Service, Columbia-Cascades Support Office, Seattle (Apr. 1, 2000), n.p.

30. Kathryn Winthrop, "Crater Lake Archaeology," in Mairs, Winthrop, and Winthrop, *Archaeological and Ethnological Studies*, 119-20, 122, 132; Deur, "Traditional Land Use Study," n.p.; R. H. Winthrop, "Crater Lake in Indian Tradition," 10; author's interview with Charles V. Lundy, superintendent of Crater Lake National Park (Sept. 22, 2000); and Charles V. Lundy, *Strategic Plan for Crater Lake National Park: Fiscal Year 2001-2005* (National Park Service, 2000), section Ib2A.

31. K. Winthrop, "Prehistory," 140; and Cressman, *Sandal and the Cave*, 18.

32. K. Winthrop, "Prehistory," 137-38; Jay Miller and William R. Seaburg, "Athapaskans of Southwestern Oregon," in Wayne Suttles, ed., *Handbook of North American Indians: Volume 7, Northwest Coast* (Smithsonian Institution, 1990), 580; Deur, "Traditional Land Use Study," n.p.; Steve Mark, "Huckleberries," *Nature Notes from Crater Lake* 29 (1998), 29-30; Stern, "Klamath and Modoc," 449; Cressman, *Sandal and the Cave*, 47; and Henry B. Zenk and Bruce Rigsby, "Molala," in Walker, ed., *Handbook of North American Indians*, 441.

33. Deur, "Traditional Land Use Study," n.p.; Zenk and Rigsby, "Molala," 439-40; Stern, "Klamath and Modoc," 454; and Miller and Seaburg, "Athapaskans," 580.

34. Kathryn Winthrop, "Evaluation of Past Research: Archaeology," in Mairs, Winthrop, and Winthrop, *Archaeological and Ethnological Studies*, 109-10.

35. Stern, "Klamath and Modoc," 450.

36. Ibid., 459; and R. Winthrop, "Ethnology of the Southern Oregon Cascades," 40-41.

37. Cressman, *Sandal and the Cave*, 64-65; Zenk and Rigsby, "Molala," 443-44; Daythal L. Kendall, "Takelma," in Suttles, ed., *Handbook of North American Indians*, 591; and R. Winthrop, "Ethnology, 41.

38. Deur, "Traditional Land Use Study," n.p.; R. Winthrop, "Ethnology," 25; Earl U. Homuth, "An Indian Legend," *Nature Notes from Crater Lake* 2, 3 (1929), 2-3; R. Winthrop, "Cultural Significance," 69, 70; and R. H. Winthrop, "Crater Lake in Indian Tradition," 8-11.

39. Deur, "Traditional Land Use Study," n.p.

Chapter 2

1. Dorothy O. Johansen, *Empire of the Columbia: A History of the Pacific Northwest*, 2d ed. (Harper & Row, 1967), 122-24.

2. Ibid., 124; Jeff LaLande, *First over the Siskiyous: Peter Skene Ogden's 1826-1827 Journey through Oregon-California Borderlands* (Oregon Historical Society Press, 1987), xvii; and Theodore Stern, "The Klamath Indians and the Treaty of 1864," *Oregon Historical Quarterly* 57, 3 (1956), 231.

3. Theodore Stern, "Klamath and Modoc," in Deward E. Walker, Jr., ed., *Handbook of North American Indians: Volume 12, Plateau* (Smithsonian Institution Press, 1998), 456, 460; Stern, "Klamath Indians," 240; Robert Winthrop, "Ethnology of the Southern Oregon Cascades," in John Mairs, Kathryn R. Winthrop, and Robert H. Winthrop, *Archaeological and Ethnological Studies of Southwest Oregon and Crater Lake National Park: An Assessment* (National Park Service, 1994), 36; L. S. Cressman, *The Sandal and the Cave: The Indians of Oregon* (Beaver Books, 1962), 64; Jay Miller and William R. Seaburg, "Athapaskans of Southwestern Oregon," in Wayne Suttles, ed., *Handbook of North American Indians: Volume 7, Northwest Coast* (Smithsonian Institution Press, 1990), 583; Henry B. Zenk and Bruce Rigsby, "Molala," in Walker, ed., *Handbook of North American Indians*, 443; and Theodore Stern, *The Klamath Tribe: A People and Their Reservation* (University of Washington Press, 1965), 22-23.

4. Stern, "Klamath and Modoc," 456, 460; Stern, "Klamath Indians," 241; and R. Winthrop, "Ethnology," 31-32, 36.

5. LaLande, *First over the Siskiyous*, xxi, 123-24; and Robert H. Ruby and John A. Brown, *A Guide to the Indian Tribes of the Pacific Northwest* (University of Oklahoma Press, 1986), 91.

6. Zenk and Rigsby, "Molala," 444.

7. Allan Nevins, *Fremont: Pathmarker of the West* (University of Nebraska Press, 1992), 250-51. Originally published in 1939.

8. Ibid.; and Stern, "Klamath Indians," 235-36.

9. Stephen Dow Beckham, *Requiem for a People: The Rogue Indians and the Frontiersmen* (Oregon State University Press, 1996), 39-40 (originally published in 1971); and Stern, "Klamath Indians," 247-48.

10. Stern, "Klamath Indians," 237-39; and Zenk and Rigsby, "Molala," 444.

11. Beckham, *Requiem for a People*, 47; Daythal L. Kendall, "Takelma," in Suttles, ed., *Handbook of North American Indians*, 592; and Miller and Seaburg, "Athapaskans," 586.

12. M. W. Gorman, "The Discovery and Early History of Crater Lake," *Mazama: A Record of Mountaineering in the Pacific Northwest* ("Crater Lake Number") 1, 2 (1897), 153-54; and Larry B. Smith and Lloyd C. Smith, *A Chronological History and Important Event Log of Crater Lake National Park, Including Significant Crater Lake Records and Area "Firsts,"* rev. ed. (privately published, 1997), n.p., entries for 1853.

13. Gorman, "Discovery and Early History," 153-54; Smith and Smith, *Chronological History*, n.p.; and Stanton C. Lapham, *The Enchanted Lake: Mount Mazama and Crater Lake in Story, History and Legend* (J. K. Gill Co., 1931), 109-11.

14. Kathryn Winthrop, "Prehistory of the Southern Oregon Cascades," in Mairs, Winthrop, and Winthrop, *Archaeological and Ethnological Studies*, 141; and Stern, "Klamath and Modoc," 460.

15. Gorman, "Discovery and Early History," 154-55; and Smith and Smith, *Chronological History*, n.p., entries for 1862.

16. Gorman, "Discovery and Early History," 155; and quoted in Smith and Smith, *Chronological History*, n.p.

17. Stern, "Klamath and Modoc," 460; Stern, "Klamath Indians," 240-52; and Lapham, *Enchanted Lake*, 113.

18. Stern, "Klamath Indians," 252-56; and Linda W. Greene, *Historic Resource Study: Crater Lake National Park, Oregon* (National Park Service, 1984), 19.

19. Lapham, *Enchanted Lake*, foreword, 113-14.

20. Ibid.; Stern, "Klamath and Modoc," 460; Ruby and Brown, *Guide to Indian Tribes*, 91; and Stern, "Klamath Indians," 258-62.
21. Gorman, "Discovery and Early History," 155-56; Steve Mark, "On an Old Road to Crater Lake," *Nature Notes from Crater Lake* 28 (1997), 16-19; Smith and Smith, *Chronological History*, n.p., entries for 1865; and O. A. Stearns, "How Crater Lake Was Discovered," *Ashland Tidings* (Feb. 24, 1888), quoted in Greene, *Historic Resource Study*, 20.
22. Gorman, "Discovery and Early History," 155-56; and Stearns, quoted in Greene, *Historic Resource Study*, 21-22.
23. Harlan D. Unrau, *Administrative History: Crater Lake National Park, Oregon*, vol. 1 (National Park Service, 1987), 22.
24. Gorman, "Discovery and Early History," 157; and *Oregon Sentinel* (Aug. 7, 1869), quoted in Smith and Smith, *Chronological History*, n.p., entries for 1869.
25. Gorman, "Discovery and Early History," 157; *Oregon Sentinel*, quoted in Smith and Smith, *Chronological History*, n.p.; Mark, "On an Old Road," 16-19; and Howard and Marian Place, *The Story of Crater Lake National Park* (Caxton Printers, 1974), 24-26.
26. Gorman, "Discovery and Early History," 157; Greene, *Historic Resource Study*, 24-25; and Smith and Smith, *Chronological History*, n.p.
27. Gorman, "Discovery and Early History," 157-58; and quoted in Smith and Smith, *Chronological History*, n.p.
28. Smith and Smith, *Chronological History*, n.p., entries for 1874; Greene, *Historic Resource Study*, 77; and Alan Clark Miller, "Peter Britt: Pioneer Photographer of the Siskiyous" (M.A. thesis, Trinity College, 1972), 63.
29. Smith and Smith, *Chronological History*, n.p.; Miller, "Peter Britt," 63; and Place and Place, *Story of Crater Lake*, 31-33.
30. Smith and Smith, *Chronological History*, n.p.; Miller, "Peter Britt," 63-64; and Place and Place, *Story of Crater Lake*, 34.
31. Miller, "Peter Britt," 62, 65.
32. Alfred Runte, *National Parks: The American Experience*, 3d ed. (University of Nebraska Press, 1997), 8-14.
33. Ibid., 16-34.
34. Ibid., 14, 50-51.
35. Robert D. Clark, *The Odyssey of Thomas Condon: Irish Immigrant, Frontier Missionary, Oregon Geologist* (Oregon Historical Society Press, 1989), 322.
36. Gorman, "Discovery and Early History," 158; J. S. Diller, "Crater Lake, Oregon," *National Geographic Magazine* 8, 2 (1897), 34; Unrau, *Administrative History*, vol. 1, 23; and Greene, *Historic Resource Study*, 77-78.
37. Stern, "Klamath and Modoc," 460-61, 464; and "Klamath Land," *Overland Monthly* 11, 6 (Dec. 1873), 548.
38. Ruby and Brown, *Guide to Indian Tribes*, 91; and Lapham, *Enchanted Lake*, 114.
39. Lapham, *Enchanted Lake*, 114-16; and Stern, "Klamath and Modoc," 460.
40. Stern, "Klamath and Modoc," 461-62; Stern, "Klamath Indians," 243; and "Klamath Land," 549.
41. Lapham, *Enchanted Lake*, 114-16; and Stern, "Klamath and Modoc," 461-62.
42. Stern, "Klamath and Modoc," 461-62; Albert Samuel Gatschet, *Ethnological Sketch of the Klamath Indians of Southwestern Oregon* (U.S. Department of the Interior, 1890), 39-40; and "Klamath Land," 553.
43. Unrau, *Administrative History*, 22-23; and Greene, *Historic Resource Study*, 74-75, 77.
44. Robert H. Keller and Michael F. Turek, *American Indians and National Parks* (University of Arizona Press, 1998), 236; Greene, *Historic Resource Study*, 29; and Stern, *Klamath Tribe*, 111-21.

Chapter 3

1. Stephen R. Mark, comp., "William Gladstone Steel, Mazamas Founder: A Chronology," on the Web site for Crater Lake National Park (www.nps.gov/crla/steel.htm), n.p.

2. Ibid., n.p.; and Erik Lawrence Weiselberg, "Ascendancy of the Mazamas: Environment, Identity, and Mountain Climbing in Oregon, 1870 to 1930" (Ph.D. diss., University of Oregon, 1999), 15-17, 67.

3. "Crater Lake," *Steel Points (Junior)* 1, 2 (Aug. 1925), n.p.; and Stanton C. Lapham, *The Enchanted Lake: Mount Mazama and Crater Lake in Story, History and Legend* (J. K. Gill Co., 1931), 112-13.

4. M. W. Gorman, "Discovery and Early History of Crater Lake," *Mazama: A Record of Mountaineering in the Pacific Northwest* ("Crater Lake Number") 1, 2 (1897), 160; and "Crater Lake," *Steel Points (Junior)*, n.p.

5. Dorothy O. Johansen, *Empire of the Columbia: A History of the Pacific Northwest*, 2d ed. (Harper & Row, 1967), 309; Mark, "Steel Chronology," n.p.; and Lapham, *Enchanted Lake*, 107.

6. Lapham, *Enchanted Lake*, 106-7; Howard and Marian Place, *The Story of Crater Lake National Park* (Caxton Printers, 1974), 36; Larry B. Smith and Lloyd C. Smith, *A Chronological History and Important Log of Crater Lake National Park, Including Significant Crater Lake Records and Area "Firsts,"* rev. ed. (privately printed, 1997), n.p., entries for 1885; "The Llaos," *Steel Points (Junior)* 1, 3 (June 1927), n.p.; and Earl U. Homuth, "An Indian Legend," *Nature Notes from Crater Lake* 2, 3 (1929), 2-3.

7. Smith and Smith, *Chronological History*, n.p.; and Lapham, *Enchanted Lake*, 107.

8. W. G. Steel, "Crater Lake and How To See It," *West Shore* 12, 3 (Mar. 1886), 104-6, quoted in Place and Place, *Story of Crater Lake*, 37; Lapham, *Enchanted Lake*, 107; and W. G. Steel, *The Mountains of Oregon* (David Steel, Successor to Himes the Printer, 1890), 17.

9. Steel, "Crater Lake and How To See It," quoted in Place and Place, *Story of Crater Lake*, 38-39; Steel, *Mountains of Oregon*, 14; and Smith and Smith, *Chronological History*, n.p.

10. Place and Place, *Story of Crater Lake*, 39-40; Lapham, *Enchanted Lake*, 107-8; "Crater Lake," *Steel Points* 1, 2 (Jan. 1907), 39; and Stephen R. Mark, "Seventeen Years to Success: John Muir, William Gladstone Steel, and the Creation of Yosemite and Crater Lake National Parks," on the Web site for Crater Lake National Park (www.nps.gov/crla/steel.htm), 4.

11. "Petition for a National Park," *Steel Points* 1, 2 (Jan. 1907), 68-72.

12. Harlan D. Unrau, *Administrative History: Crater Lake National Park, Oregon*, vol. 1 (National Park Service, 1987), 28-30; "Crater Lake," *Steel Points*, 37; and Lapham, *Enchanted Lake*, 108.

13. Unrau, *Administrative History*, vol. 1, 29-31.

14. Lary M. Dilsaver, ed., *America's National Park System: The Critical Documents* (Rowman and Littlefield, 1994), 8; and Linda W. Greene, *Historic Resource Study: Crater Lake National Park, Oregon* (National Park Service, 1984), 79.

15. Dilsaver, *America's National Park System*, 8; Alfred Runte, *National Parks: The American Experience*, 3d ed. (University of Nebraska Press, 1997), 29; and Unrau, *Administrative History*, vol. 1, 43-44.

16. Unrau, *Administrative History*, vol. 1, 44-45.

17. Runte, *National Parks*, 53-54.

18. Unrau, *Administrative History*, vol. 1, 31; and C. E. Dutton, "Crater Lake, Oregon: A Proposed National Reservation," *Science* 7, 160 (Feb. 26, 1886), 179.

19. Steel, *Mountains of Oregon*, 17; Place and Place, *Story of Crater Lake*, 41; Mark, "Seventeen Years to Success," 5; and Howel Williams, *The Geology of Crater Lake National Park, Oregon: With a Reconnaissance of the Cascade Range Southward to Mount Shasta* (Carnegie Institution, 1942), 7.

20. Place and Place, *Story of Crater Lake*, 41; "Crater Lake," *Steel Points*, 39-40; Steel, *Mountains of Oregon*, 18; and Greene, *Historic Resource Study*, 83, 85.

21. Steel, *Mountains of Oregon*, 18; and Place and Place, *Story of Crater Lake*, 41-42.
22. Steel, *Mountains of Oregon*, 18; Greene, *Historic Resource Study*, 85; and Dutton, quoted in Place and Place, *Story of Crater Lake*, 42.
23. Steel, *Mountains of Oregon*, 18-19; and Dutton, quoted in Place and Place, *Story of Crater Lake*, 42.
24. Dutton, quoted in Place and Place, *Story of Crater Lake*, 42; and Steel, *Mountains of Oregon*, 19-20.
25. Steel, *Mountains of Oregon*, 17-31; and Mark, "Seventeen Years to Success," 4.
26. Steel, *Mountains of Oregon*, 20-22; and Stephen R. Mark, *Administrative History, Chapter 17: Planning and Development at Rim Village, Crater Lake National Park* (National Park Service, 1991), 704.
27. Steel, *Mountains of Oregon*, 22-23; Place and Place, *Story of Crater Lake*, 42; and Smith and Smith, *Chronological History*, entries for 1886.
28. Steel, *Mountains of Oregon*, 23, 24.
29. Smith and Smith, *Chronological History*, n.p.; Steel, *Mountains of Oregon*, 26; and "Crater National Park Museum To Preserve Apparatus Used in First Sounding of Crater Lake in 1886," *Rogue River Valley Herald* (July 1931), in Steel Scrapbooks, vol. 9, no. 41 (microfiche).
30. "Crater Lake," *Steel Points (Junior)*, n.p.; Steel, *Mountains of Oregon*, 26; Place and Place, *Story of Crater Lake*, 42, 44; Greene, *Historic Resource Study*, 85; Lapham, *Enchanted Lake*, 71; and "Crater Lake," *Steel Points*, 40.
31. "Crater Lake," *Steel Points (Junior)*, n.p.; Greene, *Historic Resource Study*, 85; "Crater Lake," *Steel Points*, 40-41; Smith and Smith, *Chronological History*, n.p.; Steel, *Mountains of Oregon*, 26; and Place and Place, *Story of Crater Lake*, 44-45.
32. Place and Place, *Story of Crater Lake*, 44-46; Greene, *Historic Resource Study*, 85-86; and Smith and Smith, *Chronological History*, n.p.
33. Greene, *Historic Resource Study*, 86-88; Williams, *Geology of Crater Lake National Park*, 7; Place and Place, *Story of Crater Lake*, 46; and J. S. Diller, "Crater Lake, Oregon," *National Geographic Magazine* 8, 2 (Feb. 1897), 34.
34. "Crater Lake," *Steel Points*, 33.
35. Unrau, *Administrative History*, vol. 1, 33-36.
36. Ibid., 34-36.
37. Ibid., 35.
38. Ibid., 36-37; Lapham, *Enchanted Lake*, 105; and "Crater Lake," *Steel Points*, 37.
39. "Crater Lake," *Steel Points*, 37; Mark, "Seventeen Years to Success," 1, 3; Lapham, *Enchanted Lake*, 105; Unrau, *Administrative History*, vol. 1, 44; and Greene, *Historic Resource Study*, 88.
40. Unrau, *Administrative History*, vol. 1, 37-38; and John Ise, *Our National Park Policy: A Critical History* (Johns Hopkins Press, 1961), 130-31.
41. "Crater Lake," *Steel Points*, 42; Ruth Kirk, *Exploring Crater Lake Country* (University of Washington Press, 1975), 20-21; R. S. Robinson, "How Fish Came to Crater Lake," *Nature Notes from Crater Lake* 16 (1950), 15-17; and Douglas W. Larson, "Probing the Depths of Crater Lake: A Century of Scientific Research," *Oregon Historical Quarterly* 100, 3 (fall 1999), 298.
42. Mark, "Steel Chronology," n.p.; Weiselberg, "Ascendancy of the Mazamas," 4-9; and Lapham, *Enchanted Lake*, 112.
43. Weiselberg, "Ascendancy of the Mazamas," 4-9, 14.
44. Ibid., 28-40; and Mark, "Steel Chronology," n.p.
45. Weiselberg, "Ascendancy of the Mazamas," 31-61, 64-65, 77-92; Mark, "Seventeen Years to Success," 4; Lapham, *Enchanted Lake*, 106; and Mark, "Steel Chronology," n.p.
46. Weiselberg, "Ascendancy of the Mazamas," 7, 22-23, 75-76.
47. Ibid., 75-76; Mark, "Seventeen Years to Success," 2, 4; and Jeff LaLande, "A Wilderness Journey with Judge John B. Waldo, Oregon's First 'Preservationist'," *Oregon Historical Quarterly* 90, 2 (summer 1989), 119-20, 158-59.
48. Runte, *National Parks*, 29, 48-49, 65.

49. Mark, "Seventeen Years to Success," 4; and Unrau, *Administrative History*, vol. 1, 38.

50. Unrau, *Administrative History*, vol. 1, 45-49.

51. Gerald W. Williams and Stephen R. Mark, comps., *Establishing and Defending the Cascade Range Forest Reserve: As Found in the Letters of William G. Steel, John B. Waldo, and Others. Supplemented by Newspapers, Magazines, and Official Reports, 1885-1912* (U.S. Forest Service and National Park Service, 1995), iv; and Gerald W. Williams, "John B. Waldo and William G. Steel: Forest Reserve Advocates for the Cascade Range of Oregon," in Harold K. Steen, ed., *The Origins of the National Forests: A Centennial Symposium* (Forest History Society, 1992), 315.

52. LaLande, "Wilderness Journey," 118, 139-40.

53. Ibid., 155; and Williams, "Waldo and Steel," 316.

54. W. G. Steel to Hon. John B. Waldo (Mar. 30, 1891); Waldo to Steel (Apr. 4, 1891), in Williams and Mark, *Cascade Range Forest Reserve*, v, 27, 28; Williams, "Waldo and Steel," 318; Gerald W. Williams, ed., *Judge John Breckenridge Waldo: Diaries and Letters from the High Cascades of Oregon, 1880-1907* (U.S. Forest Service, 1989), vii; and Weiselberg, "Ascendancy of the Mazamas," 109-10.

55. Williams, "Waldo and Steel," 318; Unrau, *Administrative History*, vol. 1, 49-51; Williams, *Diaries and Letters*, vii; and Weiselberg, "Ascendancy of the Mazamas," 111.

56. Unrau, *Administrative History*, vol. 1, 52-53.

57. Weiselberg, "Ascendancy of the Mazamas," 222; Unrau, *Administrative History*, vol. 1, 53, 59; and Williams, "Waldo and Steel," 321.

58. Williams, "Waldo and Steel," 321; "The Cascade Range Forest Reserve," *Steel Points* 1, 1 (Oct. 1906), 14; Unrau, *Administrative History*, vol. 1, 59-61; and Lapham, *Enchanted Lake*, 105.

59. Unrau, *Administrative History*, vol. 1, 61-62; Weiselberg, "Ascendancy of the Mazamas," 125-26; Lapham, *Enchanted Lake*, 116-17; Place and Place, *Story of Crater Lake*, 48-50; Greene, *Historic Resource Study*, 91; Williams, "Waldo and Steel," 322-23; and C. H. Sholes, "President's Address for 1896," *Mazama* 1, 2 (1897), 278.

60. Williams, "Waldo and Steel," 322-24; LaLande, "Wilderness Journey," 156-57; and Williams and Mark, *Cascade Range Forest Reserve*, 196-410.

61. Williams and Mark, *Cascade Range Forest Reserve*, 551.

62. Ibid., 149-56, 196-410; and Williams, "Waldo and Steel," 322.

63. Williams and Mark, *Cascade Range Forest Reserve*, 252-53.

64. Ibid., v, 551.

65. Unrau, *Administrative History*, vol. 1, 62; Greene, *Historic Resource Study*, 92; T. Brook White, "Historian's Report for 1896," *Mazama* 1, 2 (1897), 273; Mark, "Seventeen Years to Success," 5; Fay Fuller, "Christened Mount Mazama," Tacoma *Ledger* (Sept. 6, 1896), excerpted in *Nature Notes from Crater Lake* 25 (1994), 4-5; and Lapham, *Enchanted Lake*, 119.

66. Unrau, *Administrative History*, vol. 1, 62; Greene, *Historic Resource Study*, 92; Diller, "Crater Lake," 40; C. H. Sholes, "The Mazamas' Outing of 1896," *Mazama* 1, 2 (1897), 239-42; Sholes, "President's Address," 279; Fuller, "Christened Mount Mazama," 4-5; and Lapham, *Enchanted Lake*, 119-20.

67. Unrau, *Administrative History*, vol. 1, 62; Greene, *Historic Resource Study*, 92; Lapham, *Enchanted Lake*, 120; Place and Place, *Story of Crater Lake*, 50, 52; Fuller, "Christened Mount Mazama," 4-5; and Smith and Smith, *Chronological History*, n.p., entries for 1896.

68. Unrau, *Administrative History*, vol. 1, 62-63; *Mazama: A Record of Mountaineering in the Pacific Northwest* ("Crater Lake Number") 1, 2 (1897); and conversation with Stephen R. Mark, Crater Lake National Park historian.

69. Mark, "Seventeen Years to Success," 5, 10-11; Williams, "Waldo and Steel," 327; Place and Place, *Story of Crater Lake*, 54-55; and Greene, *Historic Resource Study*, 93-95.

70. Mark, "Seventeen Years to Success," 6-7; Unrau, *Administrative History*, vol. 1, 54; and Williams, "Waldo and Steel," 327-28.

71. Mark, "Seventeen Years to Success," 11; Place and Place, *Story of Crater Lake*, 56; Unrau, *Administrative History*, vol. 1, 54-57; Greene, *Historic Resource Study*, 95-96; and Williams, "Waldo and Steel," 327-28.

72. "Crater Lake," *Steel Points*, 35-36; "The Llaos," n.p.; Homuth, "Indian Legend," 2-3; and F. F. Victor, "The Gem of the Cascades," *West Shore* 2, 3 (Nov. 1876), quoted in Greene, *Historic Resource Study*, 31.

73. Greene, *Historic Resource Study*, 27-29; Lapham, *Enchanted Lake*, 109; "Crater Lake," *Steel Points*, 35-36; "The Llaos," n.p.

74. Smith and Smith, *Chronological History*, n.p.; and Lapham, *Enchanted Lake*, 119.

75. Lapham, *Enchanted Lake*, 119.

Chapter 4

1. Earl Morse Wilbur, "Description of Crater Lake," *Mazama: A Record of Mountaineering in the Pacific Northwest* ("Crater Lake Number") 1, 2 (1897), 139-40, 149-50; Stephen R. Mark, *Administrative History, Chapter 17: Planning and Development at Rim Village, Crater Lake National Park* (National Park Service, 1991), 704-5; "The Discovery and Rediscovery of Crater Lake," *Table Rock Sentinel* 4, 7 (July 1984), 5; Caspar W. Hodgson, "Crater Lake by Night and Day," *Sunset* 9 (May 1902), 68-73; Nora Batchelor, "Crater Lake National Park," *Overland Monthly* 41 (May 1903), 334-38; and Joaquin Miller, "The Sea of Silence," *Sunset* 11 (Sept. 1904).

2. Wilbur, "Description," 139-50; Mark, *Planning and Development at Rim Village*, 704-5; "Discovery and Rediscovery," 5; Harlan D. Unrau, *Administrative History: Crater Lake National Park, Oregon*, vol. 1 (National Park Service, 1987), 62-63; Linda W. Greene, *Historic Resource Study: Crater Lake National Park, Oregon* (National Park Service, 1982), 121-24; and J. S. Diller, "Crater Lake, Oregon," *National Geographic Magazine* 8, 2 (Feb. 1897), 34.

3. Wilbur, "Description," 141-42; Joseph Silas Diller and Horace Bushnell Patton, *The Geology and Petrography of Crater Lake National Park* (U.S. Geological Survey, 1902), 7-8; and Diller, "Crater Lake," 36-37.

4. Ibid.

5. Wilbur, "Description," 142-43; Diller and Bushnell, *Geology and Petrography*, 6-7; and Diller, "Crater Lake," 36.

6. Ibid.

7. Wilbur, "Description," 143; and Diller and Bushnell, *Geology and Petrography*, 7.

8. Ibid.

9. "The Fletcher Linn Diary: Crater Lake Trip, August 1889," *Table Rock Sentinel* 4, 7 (July 1984), 11; and George W. Kirkman, "Crater Lake," *Harper's Weekly* 40 (Sept. 19, 1896), 932.

10. Wilbur, "Description," 141, 143-44; and "Linn Diary," 12.

11. Diller and Bushnell, *Geology and Petrography*, 7-8.

12. Wilbur, "Description," 147-49; Diller and Bushnell, *Geology and Petrography*, 7-9; and Mark, *Planning and Development at Rim Village*, 704-5.

13. Wilbur, "Description," 148-49; and Diller and Bushnell, *Geology and Petrography*, 9.

14. Stephen R. Mark, "Seventeen Years to Success: John Muir, William Gladstone Steel, and the Creation of Yosemite and Crater Lake National Parks," Web site for Crater Lake National Park (www.nps.gov/crla/steel.htm), 5; John Ise, *Our National Park Policy: A Critical History* (Johns Hopkins Press, 1961), 131; and Unrau, *Administrative History*, vol. 1, 95-97.

15. J. S. Diller, "The Geology of Crater Lake," *Mazama* 1, 2 (1897), 161-70; J. S. Diller, "Crater Lake, Oregon," *American Journal of Science* 3, 165 (Mar. 1897); Diller, "Crater Lake," 48; Howel Williams, *The Geology of Crater Lake National Park, Oregon: With a Reconnaissance of the Cascade Range Southward to Mount Shasta* (Carnegie Institution, 1942), 8; and Unrau, *Administrative History*, vol. 1, 64.

16. Frederick V. Coville, "The August Vegetation of Mount Mazama, Oregon," *Mazama* 1, 2 (1897), 170-203; C. Hart Merriam, "The Mammals of Mount Mazama, Oregon," *Mazama* 1, 2 (1897), 204-30; and Unrau, *Administrative History*, vol. 1, 64-67.

17. Barton Warren Evermann, "U.S. Fish Commission Investigations at Crater Lake," *Mazama* 1, 2 (1897), 230-38; "Crater Lake," *Steel Points* 1, 2 (Jan. 1907), 42-43; R. S. Robinson, "How Fish Came to Crater Lake," *Nature Notes from Crater Lake* 16 (1950), 15-17; and Unrau, *Administrative History*, vol. 1, 63-64.

18. Ise, *National Park Policy*, 131; and Unrau, *Administrative History*, vol. 1, 94-98.

19. Gerald W. Williams and Stephen R. Mark, comps., *Establishing and Defending the Cascade Range Forest Reserve: As Found in the Letters of William G. Steel, John B. Waldo, and Others. Supplemented by Newspapers, Magazines, and Official Reports, 1885-1912*, v-vi; and Gerald W. Williams, "John B. Waldo and William G. Steel: Forest Reserve Advocates for the Cascade Range of Oregon," in Harold K. Steen, ed., *The Origins of the National Forests: A Centennial Symposium* (Forest History Society, 1992), 329.

20. Unrau, *Administrative History*, vol. 1, 98-100; "Crater Lake," 37; and news clipping from a Portland newspaper (1902), in Scrapbook 38, p. 163, Oregon Historical Society Research Library.

21. Alfred Runte, *National Parks: The American Experience*, 3d ed. (University of Nebraska Press, 1997), 65-67; and Unrau, *Administrative History*, vol. 1, 100.

22. Unrau, *Administrative History*, vol. 1, 100; and conversation with Stephen R. Mark, Crater Lake National Park historian.

23. Unrau, *Administrative History*, vol. 1, 100; Mark, "Seventeen Years to Success," 6-7; and Williams and Mark, *Cascade Range Forest Reserve*, vi.

24. Unrau, *Administrative History*, vol. 1, 101-9; Greene, *Historic Resource Study*, 97-100; Ise, *National Park Policy*, 132; and Runte, *National Parks*, 67.

25. Unrau, *Administrative History*, vol. 1, 107-9; and Mark, "Seventeen Years to Success," 7.

26. Howard and Marian Place, *The Story of Crater Lake National Park* (Caxton Printers, 1974), 58-59; Greene, *Historic Resource Study*, 100; Stephen R. Mark, comp., "William Gladstone Steel, Mazamas Founder: A Chronology," Web site for Crater Lake National Park (www.nps.gov/crla/steel.htm), n.p.; and Unrau, *Administrative History*, vol. 1, 127-28.

27. Unrau, *Administrative History*, vol. 1, 127, 143; Larry B. Smith and Lloyd C. Smith, *A Chronological History and Important Log of Crater Lake National Park, Including Significant Crater Lake Records and Area "Firsts,"* rev. ed. (privately printed, 1997), n.p., entries for 1902; and Ise, *National Park Policy*, 132.

28. Unrau, *Administrative History*, vol. 1, 143; Greene, *Historic Resource Study*, 125-26, 128-29; Mark, *Planning and Development at Rim Village*, 705; and Ise, *National Park Policy*, 132.

29. Unrau, *Administrative History*, vol. 1, 144, 151-52, 164-65; Greene, *Historic Resource Study*, 129; Ise, *National Park Policy*, 132; and "Improve the Park: New Roads and Trails Needed at Crater Lake," *Oregonian* (Nov. 1906), vertical files, OHS Research Library.

30. Unrau, *Administrative History*, vol. 1, 125, 144-46, 150, 157; and Greene, *Historic Resource Study*, 179-80.

31. Unrau, *Administrative History*, vol. 1, 156, 157, 168; and M. A. Loosley, "Visited in Midwinter: A Trip to Crater Lake in 1897," *Nature Notes from Crater Lake* 28 (1997), 13-15.

32. Unrau, *Administrative History*, vol. 1, 121, 143, 144, 147-48, 149, 155, 157-58, 163-64; and Ise, *National Park Policy*, 132.

33. Unrau, *Administrative History*, vol. 1, 151-52, 154, 164-65, 168; Mark, *Planning and Development at Rim Village*, 705; and Greene, *Historic Resource Study*, 155-56, 163.

34. Unrau, *Administrative History*, vol. 1, 149, 168; Richard West Sellars, *Preserving Nature in the National Parks* (Yale University Press, 1997), 24, 80-88; Robinson, "How Fish Came to Crater Lake," 15-17; and Mark, "William Gladstone Steel," n.p.

35. Ise, *National Park Policy*, 133; and Unrau, *Administrative History*, vol. 1, 158, 166-68.

36. Lee Juillerat, *Lodge of the Imagination: The Crater Lake Lodge Story* (Crater Lake Natural History Association, 1995), 3; "Crater Lake National Park," *Steel Points* 1, 3 (Apr. 1907), 136-37; and Greene, *Historic Resource Study*, 101, 111.

37. "Crater Lake National Park," 136-37; Unrau, *Administrative History*, vol. 1, 152-54; Mark, *Planning and Development at Rim Village*, 705; Ise, *National Park Policy*, 133-34; Mark, "William Gladstone Steel," n.p.; *Steel Points* 1, 4 (July 1907); Juillerat, *Crater Lake Lodge*, 3-4; and Greene, *Historic Resource Study*, 111, 170-71.

38. Unrau, *Administrative History*, vol. 1, 156; Mark, *Planning and Development at Rim Village*, 705; Mark, "William Gladstone Steel," n.p.; *Steel Points* 1, 4 (July 1907); Juillerat, *Crater Lake Lodge*, 5; "Gold Hill Man Recalls Early Trip to Crater Lake," Medford *Mail Tribune* (Mar. 2, 1930), in Steel Scrapbooks, vol. 9, no. 41 (microfiche); and Greene, *Historic Resource Study*, 111-12.

39. Unrau, *Administrative History*, vol. 1, 159-63; and Ise, *National Park Policy*, 134.

40. Unrau, *Administrative History*, vol. 1, 169, 171-72.

41. Ibid., 165-66; Greene, *Historic Resource Study*, 101, 132-38; Mark, *Planning and Development at Rim Village*, 706; and Cathy Gilbert and Marsha Tolon, *Cultural Landscape Recommendations: Park Headquarters at Munson Valley, Crater Lake National Park* (1991), National Park Service, 3.

42. Unrau, *Administrative History*, vol. 1, 157, 165-66; "Crater Lake," *Steel Points* 1, 2 (Aug. 1925), n.p.; and Mark, *Planning and Development at Rim Village*, 706.

43. Unrau, *Administrative History*, vol. 1, 161-62, 170, 181-83; Greene, *Historic Resource Study*, 101, 103, 105; and Erik Lawrence Weiselberg, "Ascendancy of the Mazamas: Environment, Identity, and Mountain Climbing in Oregon, 1870 to 1930" (Ph.D. diss., University of Oregon, 1999), 7, 22, 375-76.

44. Unrau, *Administrative History*, vol. 1, 181-83.

45. Ibid., 184-88.

46. Ibid., 188-91; and interview with Howard Arant (Nov. 30, 1988), 5, Crater Lake National Park Oral History Series.

47. Unrau, *Administrative History*, vol. 1, 183-84, 193-201.

48. Ibid., 203-4, 210-11; Greene, *Historic Resource Study*, 180, 182; and Smith and Smith, *Chronological History*, n.p., entries for 1912.

49. Unrau, *Administrative History*, vol. 1, 204-5, 207-9, 219-20; "Crater Lake," *Ladd and Bush Quarterly* 2, 4 (Dec. 1914), 11; and "Improvements at Crater Lake" (May 4, 1909), news clipping in Scrapbook 48, p. 34, OHS Research Library.

50. Unrau, *Administrative History*, vol. 1, 216-18

51. Ibid., 203, 206-7, 214-15; and Greene, *Historic Resource Study*, 106.

52. Christine Barnes, *Great Lodges of the West* (W. W. West, 1997), 60; Juillerat, *Crater Lake Lodge*, 1, 5-6; Greene, *Historic Resource Study*, 113; and Unrau, *Administrative History*, vol. 1, 220.

53. Barnes, *Great Lodges*, 57-60; Juillerat, *Crater Lake Lodge*, 5-6; and Greene, *Historic Resource Study*, 112.

54. Weiselberg, "Ascendancy of the Mazamas," 67; Ise, *National Park Policy*, 132-33; Unrau, *Administrative History*, vol. 1, 204-5, 207-9, 212-13; and Smith and Smith, *Chronological History*, n.p., entries for 1915.

55. Barnes, *Great Lodges*, 57; Unrau, *Administrative History*, vol. 1, 212; Greene, *Historic Resource Study*, 103, 105; and Smith and Smith, *Chronological History*, n.p.

56. Barry Mackintosh, *The National Parks: Shaping the System* (National Park Service, 1991), 18-19.

57. Mark, *Planning and Development at Rim Village*, 706-7; and Sellars, *Preserving Nature*, 21.

58. Mackintosh, *National Parks System*, 18-19; Horace M. Albright, as told to Robert Cahn, *The Birth of the National Park Service: The Founding Years, 1913-33* (Howe Brothers, 1985), 26; and Robert Shankland, *Steve Mather of the National Parks* (Knopf, 1951), 75.

59. Runte, *National Parks*, 70, 74, 89, 91, 100, 102, 105; and Mackintosh, *National Parks System*, 19.

60. "Park Chief Heard: S. T. Mather Declares Crater Lake Must Be Developed," *Oregonian* (Sept. 2, 1916).

61. Ise, *National Park Policy*, 134-35; Unrau, *Administrative History*, vol. 1, 306; and Greene, *Historic Resource Study*, 101.

62. Theodore Stern, "Klamath and Modoc," in Deward E. Walker, Jr., *Handbook of North American Indians: Volume 12, Plateau* (Smithsonian Institution, 1998), 462; Mark David Spence, *Dispossessing the Wilderness: Indian Removal and the Making of the National Parks* (Oxford University Press, 1999), 3-6; and Unrau, *Administrative History*, vol. 1, 112.

63. Robert H. Ruby and John A. Brown, *A Guide to the Indian Tribes of the Pacific Northwest* (University of Oklahoma Press, 1986), 91-93; and Stern, "Klamath and Modoc," 460-62.

64. Alexander Blackburn, "A Trip to Crater Lake" (Aug. 28, 1901), news clipping in Scrapbook 48, p. 157, OHS Research Library; and Kirkman, "Crater Lake," 932.

65. Ruby and Brown, *Indian Tribes of the Pacific Northwest*, 92-93; and "Linn Diary," 11-12.

Chapter 5

1. Barry Mackintosh, *The National Parks: Shaping the System* (U.S. Department of the Interior, 1991), 19-20; William Swift, "Stephen T. Mather," in *National Park Service: The First 75 Years* (Eastern National Park and Monument Association, 1990), 15; and Newton B. Drury, "The National Park Service—The First Thirty Years," in *American Planning and Civic Annual* (American Planning and Civic Association, 1945), 29-30.

2. Lary M. Dilsaver, ed., *America's National Park System: The Critical Documents* (Rowman and Littlefield, 1994), 53-54.

3. Horace M. Albright, as told to Robert Cahn, *The Birth of the National Park Service: The Founding Years, 1913-33* (Howe Brothers, 1985), 28; Linda Flint McClelland, *Building the National Parks: Historic Landscape Design and Construction* (Johns Hopkins University Press, 1998), 131; "Park Chief Head Declares Crater Lake Must Be Developed," *Oregonian* (Sept. 2, 1916); Drury, "First Thirty Years," 30; and Harlan D. Unrau, *Administrative History: Crater Lake National Park, Oregon*, vol. 2 (National Park Service, 1987), 553.

4. John Albright, "Robert Sterling Yard," in *National Park Service*, 17; Alfred Runte, *National Parks: The American Experience*, 3d ed. (University of Nebraska Press, 1997), 110; McClelland, *Building the National Parks*, 131; Unrau, *Administrative History*, vol. 1, 232-35; and Drury, "First Thirty Years," 30.

5. Albright, *Birth of the National Park Service*, 26; and Unrau, *Administrative History*, vol. 1, 232, 297; vol. 2, 553.

6. Dilsaver, *National Park System*, 53; Unrau, *Administrative History*, vol. 1, 298; vol. 2, 460-61; *Report of the Director of the National Park Service to the Secretary of the Interior for the Fiscal Year Ended June 30, 1918* (U.S. Department of the Interior, 1918), 61; Donald C. Swain, *Wilderness Defender: Horace M. Albright and Conservation* (University of Chicago Press, 1970), 92; Robert Shankland, *Steve Mather and the National Parks* (Knopf, 1951), 106; Richard West Sellars, *Preserving Nature in the National Parks* (Yale University Press, 1997); and Ethan Carr, *Wilderness by Design: Landscape Architecture and the National Park Service* (University of Nebraska Press, 1998), 149-50.

7. *Report of the Director, 1918*, 62-63; Unrau, *Administrative History*, vol. 1, 273-78; and Linda W. Greene, *Historic Resource Study: Crater Lake National Park, Oregon* (National Park Service, 1982), 106-9.

8. *Report of the Director, 1918*, 62, 63; Unrau, *Administrative History*, vol. 1, 276; and Greene, *Historic Resource Study*, 106.

9. Unrau, *Administrative History*, vol. 1, 277-80; Hal K. Rothman, "'A Regular Ding-Dong Fight': Agency Culture and Evolution in the NPS-USFS Dispute, 1916-1937,"

Western Historical Quarterly 20, 2 (May 1989), 141-61; and Greene, *Historic Resource Study*, 106-9.

10. Runte, *National Parks*, 138-54; and Ronald A. Foresta, *America's National Parks and Their Keepers* (Resources for the Future, Inc., 1984), 30-33.

11. *Report of the Director, 1918*, 60, 61; and Unrau, *Administrative History*, vol. 2, 553-61.

12. Unrau, *Administrative History*, vol. 2, 561-65; Greene, *Historic Resource Study*, 171-72; Christine Barnes, *Great Lodges of the West* (W. W. West, 1997), 61; and Lee Juillerat, *Lodge of the Imagination: The Crater Lake Lodge Story* (Crater Lake Natural History Association, 1995), 7-8.

13. Unrau, *Administrative History*, vol. 2, 565-67; Greene, *Historic Resource Study*, 113-14; and Juillerat, *Crater Lake Lodge*, 8.

14. Unrau, *Administrative History*, vol. 2, 567-72; Greene, *Historic Resource Study*, 113-14; and Juillerat, *Crater Lake Lodge*, 8-9.

15. Unrau, *Administrative History*, vol. 2, 572-76; Juillerat, *Crater Lake Lodge*, 9; Stephen R. Mark, *Administrative History, Chapter 17: Planning and Development at Rim Village* (National Park Service, 1991), 708; and Greene, *Historic Resource Study*, 114-15.

16. Runte, *National Parks*, 102-10; Joseph L. Sax, *Mountains without Handrails: Reflections on the National Parks* (University of Michigan Press, 1980), 9-12; Sellars, *Preserving Nature*, 4, 57; and Polly Welts Kaufman, *National Parks and the Woman's Voice* (University of New Mexico Press, 1996), xii.

17. Sellars, *Preserving Nature*, 21.

18. Unrau, *Administrative History*, vol. 1, 299, 311-16; vol. 2, 574, 580.

19. Ibid., vol. 1, 314-15; vol. 2, 543; and interview with Albert Hackert and Otto Heckert (Oct. 31, 1991), 4-5, Crater Lake National Park Oral History Series.

20. Unrau, *Administrative History*, vol. 2, 385-87; and interview with Emmett Blanchfield (Mar. 7, 1995), 4, CLNP Oral History Series.

21. Unrau, *Administrative History*, vol. 2, 413-14.

22. Ibid., 411-19; and Sellars, *Preserving Nature*, 80-81, 84, 130.

23. Drury, "First Thirty Years," 30; Unrau, *Administrative History*, vol. 2, 455-56, 459-60, 531-32; McClelland, *Building the National Parks*, 230; Sellars, *Preserving Nature*, 4; Greene, *Historic Resource Study*, 139-40, 157, 163; Mark, *Planning and Development at Rim Village*, 707; Cathy A. Gilbert, *The Rustic Landscape of Rim Village, 1927-1941, Crater Lake National Park* (National Park Service, 1990), 4; and Lillian Gilstrap Diary (1927), Webster Jones Collection, Mss 2927, Oregon Historical Society Research Library.

24. Drury, "First Thirty Years," 31-32; Unrau, *Administrative History*, vol. 2, 456-57, 459, 461-62, 463-64, 465-66, 467-68, 531-32, 534-35, 536-41, 543; Greene, *Historic Resource Study*, 139-40; and Runte, *National Parks*, 156-58.

25. Unrau, *Administrative History*, vol. 2, 457-58, 460, 463, 575; McClelland, *Building the National Parks*, 153-55; Mark, *Planning and Development at Rim Village*, 708; Gilbert, *Rim Village*, 4; and Greene, *Historic Resource Study*, 185-87.

26. Juillerat, *Crater Lake Lodge*, 9; Barnes, *Great Lodges*, 61; Mark, *Planning and Development at Rim Village*, 708; D. S. Libbey, "The Community House," *Nature Notes from Crater Lake* 5, 3 (1932), 2-4; Unrau, *Administrative History*, vol. 2, 575, 578-81; and Greene, *Historic Resource Study*, 115, 188, 193.

27. Unrau, *Administrative History*, vol. 1, 314; vol. 2, 469-73; Greene, *Historic Resource Study*, 195; McClelland, *Building the National Parks*, 292; Mark, *Planning and Development at Rim Village*, 709-10; Drury, "First Thirty Years," 33; and Gilbert, *Rim Village*, 4.

28. Unrau, *Administrative History*, vol. 2, 473-74, 582, 584; McClelland, *Building the National Parks*, 154-55, 212, 219, 237, 264-65; letter from Matilda Hall to John Morrison (Feb. 29, 1988), Mss 1500, OHS Research Library; Mark, *Planning and Development at Rim Village*, 709-10, 711-12; Larry B. Smith and Lloyd C. Smith, *A Chronological History and Important Log of Crater Lake National Park, Including*

Significant Crater Lake Records and Area "Firsts," rev. ed. (privately printed, 1997), n.p., entries for 1922; Greene, *Historic Resource Study*, 206, 223, 225; Blanchfield interview, 4-5; and interview with Francis G. Lange (Aug. 8, 1987), 3-5, CLNP Oral History Series.

29. Cathy Gilbert and Marsha Tolon, *Cultural Landscape Recommendations: Park Headquarters at Munson Valley, Crater Lake National Park* (National Park Service, 1991), 4; Greene, *Historic Resource Study*, 187-88, 195; Unrau, *Administrative History*, vol. 1, 314; vol. 2, 470-71; and Lange interview (1987), 7.

30. Gilbert and Tolon, *Park Headquarters*, 4; Greene, *Historic Resource Study*, 195, 198; and Steve Mark, *Park Headquarters Historic Walking Tour: Crater Lake National Park* (Crater Lake Natural History Association, 1999).

31. Unrau, *Administrative History*, vol. 2, 474-79, 540-41; and Mark, *Planning and Development at Rim Village*, 711-12.

32. Swain, *Horace M. Albright*, 92; and Unrau, *Administrative History*, vol. 1, 300-1.

33. Mark, *Planning and Development at Rim Village*, 711-12; Unrau, *Administrative History*, vol. 2, 478-81; Greene, *Historic Resource Study*, 158, 204, 209, 225-26; McClelland, *Building the National Parks*, 264-65; Steve Mark, "Victor Rock and Victor View," *Nature Notes from Crater Lake* 29 (1998), 13-15; and Medford *Mail Tribune* (July 1, 1930), in Steel Scrapbooks, vol. 9, no. 41 (microfiche).

34. Mark, *Planning and Development at Rim Village*, 711; Unrau, *Administrative History*, vol. 2, 481, 641-42; Gilbert, *Rim Village*, 14-15; McClelland, *Building the National Parks*, 247, 249; Greene, *Historic Resource Study*, 205-6; and Lange interview (1987), 8-10.

35. Mark, *Planning and Development at Rim Village*, 712; Unrau, *Administrative History*, vol. 2, 479-83; McClelland, *Building the National Parks*, 22, 255, 265, 472; Gilbert and Tolon, *Park Headquarters*, 4; Greene, *Historic Resource Study*, 204-5, 211, 212, 215, 218-19, 226-27; Lange interview (1987), 10-14; interview with Francis G. Lange (Sept. 13, 1988), 9, 15-16, CLNP Oral History Series; Mark, *Walking Tour*; and Carr, *Wilderness by Design*, 255.

36. Gilbert, *Rim Village*, 4; Blanchfield interview, 5; McClelland, *Building the National Parks*, 219; Mark, *Walking Tour*; and interview with Mabel Hedgpeth (Aug. 23, 1986, and June 18, 1987), 15, CLNP Oral History Series.

37. Barnes, *Great Lodges*, 61; Juillerat, *Crater Lake Lodge*, 10; and Unrau, *Administrative History*, vol. 2, 583.

38. Marian Albright Schenck, "Horace Marden Albright," in *National Park Service*, 28; Unrau, *Administrative History*, vol. 1, 301, 317-18; interview with Howard Arant (Nov. 30, 1988), 3-4, CLNP Oral History Series; interview with Doug and Sadie Roach (Aug. 25, 1987), 3, CLNP Oral History Series; and conversation with Stephen R. Mark, Crater Lake National Park historian.

39. Unrau, *Administrative History*, vol. 1, 301-2, 317-20; vol. 2, 483, 541, 543, 584-85; Dilsaver, *National Park System*, 111-12; Mark, *Planning and Development at Rim Village*, 712-13; Greene, *Historic Resource Study*, 221-23; and Drury, "First Thirty Years," 33-35.

40. Mark, *Planning and Development at Rim Village*, 713; Unrau, *Administrative History*, vol. 2, 496; Lange interview (1987), 5-6; and Lange interview (1988), 2, 4, 11-12.

41. Unrau, *Administrative History*, vol. 2, 484-96; Greene, *Historic Resource Study*, 227, 230-31, 233; Mark, *Planning and Development at Rim Village*, 713; Gilbert, *Rim Village*, 4; Roach and Roach interview, 11-12; Lange interview (1987), 14-21; Lange interview (1988), 5-7; Hedgpeth interview, 42-43; conversation with Mark; and interview with Vivienne Meola (Aug. 29, 1987), 1-2, 4, 7-9, CLNP Oral History Series.

42. Gilbert and Tolon, *Park Headquarters*, 4-5; Unrau, *Administrative History*, vol. 2, 487; Mark, *Walking Tour*; Lange interview (1987), 6-7; and Meola interview, 2.

43. Gilbert and Tolon, *Park Headquarters*, 4; Unrau, *Administrative History*, vol. 1, 319; vol. 2, 489; Greene, *Historic Resource Study*, 216, 218; and Mark, *Walking Tour*.

44. Gilbert and Tolon, *Park Headquarters*, 5; and Unrau, *Administrative History*, vol. 1, 320-22.

45. Unrau, *Administrative History*, vol. 2, 544, 585-92; Joe Cowley, "After Crater Lake Winter, Frost Fight Is Nothing to Orchard Boss Roach," Medford *Mail Tribune* (Mar. 19, 1972), 7; Roach and Roach interview, 3; Hedgpeth interview, 53-54; and interview with Hazel Frost (Aug. 4, 1987), 3, CLNP Oral History Series.

46. Unrau, *Administrative History*, vol. 1, 281; and Rothman, "NPS-USFS Dispute," 141-61.

47. Unrau, *Administrative History*, vol. 1, 242-45; and Steve Mark and Ron Mastrogiuseppe, "A Pause in the Panhandle," *Nature Notes from Crater Lake* 27 (1996), 26-28.

48. Unrau, *Administrative History*, vol. 1, 281-83; and Foresta, *America's National Parks*, 30-33.

49. Unrau, *Administrative History*, vol. 1, 318; vol. 2, 387-90; and Roach and Roach interview, 5-6.

50. Max G. Johl, *The United States Commemorative Stamps of the Twentieth Century: Volume 1, 1901-1935* (H. L. Lindquist, 1947), 305-8; Stanley A. Sprecher, "Stamps and Parks," *National Parks Magazine* 28, 119 (Oct.-Dec. 1954), 170-71; and conversation with Mark.

51. Unrau, *Administrative History*, vol. 2, 387, 390-93; and interview with Herbert Armentrout (Aug. 4, 1987), 6, CLNP Oral History Series.

52. Unrau, *Administrative History*, vol. 2, 392-93, 419-21; and James H. McCool, "Wild Life Lines," Medford *Mail Tribune* (Jan. 12, 1930), in Steel Scrapbooks, vol. 9, no. 41 (microfiche).

53. Unrau, *Administrative History*, vol. 2, 420; Hackert and Heckert interview, 10-11, 18; Hedgpeth interview, 32-33; Earl U. Homuth, "Our Bears," *Nature Notes from Crater Lake* 1, 1 (1928), 6; 2, 1 (1929), 6; F. Lyle Wynd, "Triplets," *Nature Notes from Crater Lake* 3, 1 (1930), 2-6; and David H. Canfield, "A Bear Story," *Nature Notes from Crater Lake* 6, 1 (1933), 8-9.

54. A. Cooper Allen, "The Guardian of Crater Lake," *Sunset Magazine* 56 (May 1926), 51-52.

55. Quoted in Erik Lawrence Weiselberg, "Ascendancy of the Mazamas: Environment, Identity, and Mountain Climbing in Oregon, 1870 to 1930" (Ph.D. diss., University of Oregon, 1999), 369.

56. Unrau, *Administrative History*, vol. 1, 306-7.

57. "Citizens of Oregon Honor John Hillman" (Sept. 21, 1925), news clipping in vertical file, OHS Research Library; Stanton C. Lapham, *The Enchanted Lake: Mount Mazama and Crater Lake in Story, History and Legend* (J. K. Gill Co., 1931); and Unrau, *Administrative History*, vol. 2, 642.

58. Unrau, *Administrative History*, vol. 1, 311-13.

59. "Passing of Parkhurst Recalls Pioneering Struggle at Crater Lake," Medford *Mail Tribune* (Apr. 13, 1930); and William Gladstone Steel, *The Crater Lake Scandal* (privately published, 1924), 2-4.

60. Steel, *Crater Lake Scandal*, 6-8.

61. Ibid.; Carl Smith, "Crater Lake Scandal Discussed in Congress," *Oregon Journal* (Feb. 10, 1924); and "Tell the Public" (editorial), *Oregon Journal* (Sept. 11, 1920).

62. Unrau, *Administrative History*, vol. 1, 280-81.

63. Will G. Steel, "Crater Is Place for Road," *Oregonian* (Sept. 1, 1926), in *Steel Points (Junior)* 1, 3 (May 1927), n.p.; and "Petitioning Letter of Will G. Steel," Central Point *American* (May 26, 1932), in Steel Scrapbooks, vol. 9, no. 41 (microfiche).

64. Editorial in *Pacific Northwest Hotel News*; letter of opposition from Medford Chamber of Commerce to Steel, published in Medford *News* (June 2, 1932); letter of opposition from Robert W. Sawyer to Steel (May 24, 1932); letter of opposition from Bend Chamber of Commerce to Steel, in Steel Scrapbooks, vol. 9, no. 41 (microfiche); and Thomas R. Cox, *The Park Builders: A History of State Parks in the Pacific Northwest* (University of Washington Press, 1988), 33.

65. Unrau, *Administrative History*, vol. 2, 574; and Blanchfield interview, 8.

66. Blanchfield interview, 7.

67. Mark, "Steel Chronology," n.p.; and "Obituary," Medford *Mail Tribune* (Oct. 22, 1934), in Steel Scrapbooks, vol. 9, no. 41 (microfiche).

68. *Mazama: A Record of Mountaineering in the Pacific Northwest* ("Crater Lake Number") 1, 2 (Oct. 1897).

69. Pocket journal of John William Meldrum, including account of a trip to Crater Lake in 1911, Mss 1293B, OHS Research Library; W. Kuykendall collection, including an account of historical discussions at Crater Lake in 1896, Mss 2130, OHS Research Library; "Citizens of Oregon Honor John Hillman"; and letter from Will G. Steel to Fletcher Linn (Nov. 26, 1929), Mss 847, OHS Research Library.

70. Unrau, *Administrative History*, vol. 2, 635-37; and Libbey, "Community House," 2-4.

71. Unrau, *Administrative History*, vol. 2, 637-40; and *Nature Notes from Crater Lake* 1, 1 (July 1, 1928).

72. Phil F. Brogan, "Oregon Geology: The Century-Old Story," *Oregon Historical Quarterly* 67, 1 (Mar. 1966), 25-26; conversation with Mark; and Unrau, *Administrative History*, vol. 2, 641-42.

73. Unrau, *Administrative History*, vol. 2, 637, 641; John C. Merriam, "Memorandum Regarding Relation of Aesthetic to Scientific Elements in Study of Crater Lake" (unpublished), biographical files, historian's office, CLNP; John C. Merriam, "Crater Lake: A Study in Appreciation of Nature," *American Magazine of Art* 26, 8 (Aug. 1933), 357-61; and Sax, *Mountains without Handrails*, 20-22.

74. Unrau, *Administrative History*, vol. 2, 641-43; and D. S. Libbey, "The Sinnott Memorial Orientation Station and Museum," *Nature Notes from Crater Lake* 5, 2 (1932), 2-3.

75. Unrau, *Administrative History*, vol. 2, 643-45; W. Drew Chick, Jr., "Adventure and Discovery, 1931: A Personal Account," *Nature Notes from Crater Lake* 27 (1996), 6-8; Libbey, "Community House," 2-4; Barry Mackintosh, *Interpretation in the National Park Service: A Historical Perspective* (National Park Service, 1986), 83-84; and Freeman Tilden, *Interpreting Our Heritage*, rev. ed (University of North Carolina Press, 1977), 32-39.

76. Unrau, *Administrative History*, vol. 2, 645-47; Luther S. Cressman, *A Golden Journey: Memoirs of an Archaeologist* (University of Utah Press, 1988), 378-79; Howel Williams, *The Geology of Crater Lake National Park: With a Reconnaissance of the Cascade Range Southward to Mount Shasta* (Carnegie Institution, 1942), 9; Blanchfield interview, 6; and interview with John Eliot Allen (Sept. 24, 1991), 1, 22-23, CLNP Oral History Series.

77. Unrau, *Administrative History*, vol. 2, 647-50; Drury, "First Thirty Years," 32; and Armentrout interview, 1-2.

78. Theodore Stern, *The Klamath Tribe: A People and Their Reservation* (University of Washington Press, 1965), 259; Patrick Haynal, "Termination and Tribal Survival: The Klamath Tribes of Oregon," *Oregon Historical Quarterly* 101, 3 (fall 2000), 272; and "Klamath Tribes: History," Klamath Tribes Web site (www.klamathtribes.org/history.html), 2.

79. Ibid.; Theodore Stern, "Klamath and Modoc," in Deward E. Walker, Jr., *Handbook of North American Indians: Volume 12, Plateau* (Smithsonian Institution, 1998), 462; and Robert H. Ruby and John A. Brown, *A Guide to the Indian Tribes of the Pacific Northwest* (University of Oklahoma Press, 1986), 92-93.

80. Haynal, "Termination," 272, 275-76; Stern, "Klamath and Modoc," 462; and Stern, *Klamath Tribe*, 260-66.

81. R. P. Andrews, "An Indian Giver," *Nature Notes from Crater Lake National Park* 6, 3 (Aug. 1933), 2; and Robert H. Keller and Michael F. Turek, *American Indians and National Parks* (University of Arizona Press, 1998), 232-33.

Chapter 6

1. Newton B. Drury, "The National Parks in Wartime," *American Forests* (Aug. 1943), offprint, n.p.; Lary M. Dilsaver, ed., *America's National Park System: The Critical Documents* (Rowman and Littlefield, 1994), 165; and Freeman Tilden, *The National Parks*, rev. ed. (Knopf, 1968), 38.

2. Harlan D. Unrau, *Administrative History: Crater Lake National Park, Oregon* (National Park Service, 1988), vol. 1, 324; vol. 2, 592, 594.

3. Drury, "National Parks in Wartime," n.p.; and Unrau, *Administrative History*, vol. 1, 322-24.

4. Unrau, *Administrative History*, vol. 1, 302, 322-24; vol. 2, 496-97; and Stephen R. Mark, *Administrative History, Chapter 17: Planning and Development at Rim Village, Crater Lake National Park* (National Park Service, 1991), 714.

5. Unrau, *Administrative History*, vol. 1, 324-26; and Cathy A. Gilbert, *The Rustic Landscape of Rim Village, 1927-1941: Crater Lake National Park* (National Park Service, 1990), 4-5.

6. Unrau, *Administrative History*, vol. 1, 307-8; and conversation with Stephen R. Mark, Crater Lake National Park historian.

7. Unrau, *Administrative History*, vol. 1, 326-27; vol. 2, 594-95; *Crater Lake National Park and Oregon Caves National Monument Vacation Travel Study* (U.S. Department of the Interior, 1950), 11; and interview with Wayne R. Howe (Sept. 1, 1988), 4-5, 52, 62, CLNP Oral History Series.

8. Interview with Doug and Sadie Roach (Aug. 25, 1987), 4, 7-8, CLNP Oral History Series; and Howe interview, 31, 33, 34-35, 36-38.

9. Unrau, *Administrative History*, vol. 1, 302, 328; Howe interview, 33, 35, 42; and interview with Ruth Hopson Keen (June 8, 1994), tape 10 (side 2), tape 11 (side 1), Oregon Historical Society Research Library.

10. Interview with Hazel Frost (Aug. 4, 1987), 4, 6, CLNP Oral History Series; interview with James Kezer (Nov. 26, 1997), 7, CLNP Oral History Series; interview with Bruce W. Black (Sept. 27, 1988), 17, CLNP Oral History Series; and interview with Ted Arthur (Sept. 1, 1992), 20, CLNP Oral History Series.

11. Howe interview, 11, 26, 41-42, 45, 52; and interview with O. W. "Pete" Foiles (Aug. 4, 1987), 1, 4, CLNP Oral History Series.

12. Unrau, *Administrative History*, vol. 2, 498; and Mark, *Planning and Development at Rim Village*, 714.

13. Unrau, *Administrative History*, vol. 2, 498-500; and Cathy Gilbert and Marsha Tolon, *Cultural Landscape Recommendations: Park Headquarters at Munson Valley, Crater Lake National Park* (National Park Service, 1991), 5.

14. Erik Lawrence Weiselberg, "Ascendancy of the Mazamas: Environment, Identity, and Mountain Climbing in Oregon, 1870 to 1930" (Ph.D. diss., University of Oregon, 1999), 375-76.

15. Ibid.; *Vacation Travel Study*, 11; Alfred Runte, *National Parks: The American Experience*, 3d ed. (University of Nebraska Press, 1997), 165; Dilsaver, ed., *National Park System*, 112; Unrau, *Administrative History*, vol. 2, 500-4; Mark, *Planning and Development at Rim Village*, 714-19; and Linda W. Greene, *Historic Resource Study: Crater Lake National Park, Oregon* (National Park Service, 1982), 236-37.

16. Mark, *Planning and Development at Rim Village*, 716; Unrau, *Administrative History*, vol. 2, 575-92; and Greene, *Historic Resource Study*, 117.

17. Lee Juillerat, *Lodge of the Imagination: The Crater Lake Lodge Story* (Crater Lake Natural History Association, 1995), 10; Unrau, *Administrative History*, vol. 2, 502, 594; and Mark, *Planning and Development at Rim Village*, 716-17.

18. Juillerat, *Crater Lake Lodge*, 10; Unrau, *Administrative History*, vol. 2, 593, 596-97, 601-2; Mark, *Planning and Development at Rim Village*, 716-18; Howe interview, 70-71; and Greene, *Historic Resource Study*, 117.

19. Unrau, *Administrative History*, vol. 2, 393-98.

20. Ibid., 398-404, 428, 430; and Howe interview, 10-11.
21. Howe interview, 6-7, 12-18, 26, 31; Unrau, *Administrative History*, vol. 2, 404, 597; Foiles interview, 1-2, 4-6; interview with Larry Smith (Feb. 10, 1989), 2-3, CLNP Oral History Series; and L. Howard Crawford, "Crater Lake in Winter," *Nature Notes from Crater Lake* 8, 1 (1935), 2-4.
22. Unrau, *Administrative History*, vol. 1, 308-11.
23. Ibid., vol. 2, 399, 426; and Howe interview, 10.
24. Unrau, *Administrative History*, vol. 2, 426-27; Donald Van Tassel, "Bears Are Wild Animals," *Nature Notes from Crater Lake* 20 (1954), 3-5; and Howe interview, 20-24.
25. Douglas W. Larson, "Probing the Depths of Crater Lake: A Century of Scientific Research," *Oregon Historical Quarterly* 100, 3 (fall 1999), 297-98; and Unrau, *Administrative History*, vol. 2, 428.
26. Unrau, *Administrative History*, vol. 2, 431-32; O. L. Wallis, "The 1947 Catch in Crater Lake," *Nature Notes from Crater Lake* 13 (1947), 17-18; and Richard West Sellars, *Preserving Nature in the National Parks: A History* (Yale University Press, 1997), 123-26.
27. Larson, "Scientific Research," 301.
28. Dilsaver, ed., *National Park System*, 166; and Sellars, *Preserving Nature*, 182.
29. Sellars, *Preserving Nature*, 182-83; Douglas Caldwell, "Conrad Wirth," in *National Park Service: The First 75 Years* (Eastern National Park and Monument Association, 1990), 45; Runte, *National Parks*, 173; Barry Mackintosh, *The National Parks: Shaping the System* (U.S. Department of the Interior, 1991), 62; Black interview, 30-31; and Unrau, *Administrative History*, vol. 2, 504-5.
30. Sellars, *Preserving Nature*, 183; and Dilsaver, ed., *National Park System*, 197.
31. Mark, *Planning and Development at Rim Village*, 719; Unrau, *Administrative History*, vol. 1, 303; Smith interview, 13; and Arthur interview, 19.
32. Mark, *Planning and Development at Rim Village*, 719-24; Unrau, *Administrative History*, vol. 2, 506-10; and Smith interview, 30-32.
33. Unrau, *Administrative History*, vol. 2, 602-6.
34. Mark, *Planning and Development at Rim Village*, 721.
35. Ibid., 722-24; Gilbert and Tolon, *Park Headquarters*, 5; and Unrau, *Administrative History*, vol. 1, 334.
36. Mark, *Planning and Development at Rim Village*, 725-26; Unrau, *Administrative History*, vol. 1, 335, 337; Howe interview, 73-74; interview with Dick Brown (Sept. 15, 1988), 27-28, CLNP Oral History Series; interview with Donald M. Spalding (Apr. 2, 1991), 24-27, CLNP Oral History Series; Smith interview, 32-33, 36; and interview with Marvin L. Nelson (Jan. 12, 2000), 5, CLNP Oral History Series.
37. Mark, *Planning and Development at Rim Village*, 718; Unrau, *Administrative History*, vol. 2, 601-2; Juillerat, *Crater Lake Lodge*, 10-11; and Arthur interview, 23.
38. Mark, *Planning and Development at Rim Village*, 720, 722, 723, 724; Unrau, *Administrative History*, vol. 2, 602, 609; Christine Barnes, *Great Lodges of the West* (W. W. West, 1997), 62; and Juillerat, *Crater Lake Lodge*, 11.
39. Unrau, *Administrative History*, vol. 2, 608-9; Mark, *Planning and Development at Rim Village*, 725; Howe interview, 69-71; and Black interview, 23-24.
40. Juillerat, *Crater Lake Lodge*, 11; Mark, *Planning and Development at Rim Village*, 725; Unrau, *Administrative History*, vol. 2, 609; Spalding interview, 14-16; Arthur interview, 23; and Howe interview, 69-71.
41. Sellars, *Preserving Nature*, 53-56; and Polly Welts Kaufman, *National Parks and the Woman's Voice* (University of New Mexico Press, 1996), xi-xii.
42. Sellars, *Preserving Nature*, 53-56.
43. Howe interview, 36; and Unrau, *Administrative History*, vol. 1, 390-405.
44. Sellars, *Preserving Nature*, 1-2, 26, 54, 55; Kaufman, *Woman's Voice*, xii-xiii; Smith interview, 11; Black interview, 22, 33; and Howe interview, 8, 34.
45. Kaufman, *Woman's Voice*, xi-xiii; Sellars, *Preserving Nature*, 171-72, 221-24; Howe interview, 29; Arthur interview, 18; and Unrau, *Administrative History*, vol. 2, 650.

46. Sellars, *Preserving Nature*, 91-148, 214-17, 254, 255; Runte, *National Parks*, 182-84, 198-201, 207-9; and Dilsaver, ed., *National Park System*, 197-99.

47. Unrau, *Administrative History*, vol. 2, 432-33; Sellars, *Preserving Nature*, 79-80, 160-62; Van Tassel, "Bears Are Wild Animals," 3-5; and Brown interview, 51-52.

48. Unrau, *Administrative History*, vol. 2, 433-35; Sellars, *Preserving Nature*, 123-26; Wallis, "1947 Catch,"17-18; and C. Warren Fairbanks, "Crater Lake Fishing, 1952," *Nature Notes from Crater Lake* 18 (1952), 19-22.

49. Larson, "Scientific Research," 301-5; Unrau, *Administrative History*, vol. 2, 658; Black interview, 19-20; and Brown interview, 49-50.

50. Larson, "Scientific Research," 305, 307-8; interview with Douglas W. Larson (Feb. 14, 2000), 3-6, CLNP Oral History Series; and interview with F. Owen Hoffman (Aug. 25, 1998), 6-7, CLNP Oral History Series.

51. Unrau, *Administrative History*, vol. 2, 435-36; Sellars, *Preserving Nature*, 126-31, 253-54; Runte, *National Parks*, 203; Dilsaver, ed., *National Park System*, 271; Norman D. Wild, "Crater Lake Fires for 1955," *Nature Notes from Crater Lake* 21 (1955), 3-5; Brown interview, 4-5, 50-51; and Howe interview, 19-20.

52. Sellars, *Preserving Nature*, 187-92.

53. Runte, *National Parks*, 241; Unrau, *Administrative History*, vol. 1, 260; Sellars, *Preserving Nature*, 187, 191-94; and Howe interview, 25.

54. Sellars, *Preserving Nature*, 193; Unrau, *Administrative History*, vol. 1, 260-63; Howe interview, 63; and Brown interview, 33.

55. Sellars, *Preserving Nature*, 240-41; and Dilsaver, ed., *National Park System*, 271.

56. Unrau, *Administrative History*, vol. 2, 650-51.

57. Ibid., 653-54.

58. Ibid., 656; and Keen interview, tape 10 (side 2), tape 11 (side 1).

59. Kezer interview, 2, 9, 12; Brown interview, 21; and Unrau, *Administrative History*, vol. 2, 656-57.

60. Unrau, *Administrative History*, vol. 2, 652-53.

61. Ibid., 654, 657, 658, 662.

62. Ibid., 654-56, 657-58; and Kezer interview, 5.

63. Unrau, *Administrative History*, vol. 2, 606, 608-9, 654; Steve Mark, "Victor Rock and Victor View," *Nature Notes from Crater Lake* 29 (1998), 13-15; news clipping (1953), CLNP public information, vertical files, OHS Research Library; and Arthur interview, 6-11.

64. Unrau, *Administrative History*, vol. 2, 654-55.

65. Ibid., 657; Sellars, *Preserving Nature*, 4-5, 267, 274, 285-87; Barry Mackintosh, *Interpretation in the National Park Service: A Historical Perspective* (U.S. Department of the Interior, 1986), 12-17; Larson, "Scientific Research," 305; and Brown interview, 3-4, 5, 20, 49-50, 52, 56.

66. Sellars, *Preserving Nature*, 221-23; and Brown interview, 5, 8, 19.

67. Mackintosh, *Interpretation*, 83-88; Freeman Tilden, *Interpreting Our Heritage*, rev. ed. (University of North Carolina Press, 1977), 3-9, 32-39; Hoffman interview, 6-7; and Brown interview, 21

68. Kezer interview, 13; Brown interview, 2, 9; and Black interview, 11.

69. Arthur interview, 2; and Hoffman interview, 2.

70. Brown interview, 54-55.

71. Arthur interview, 2-3.

72. Patrick Haynal, "Termination and Tribal Survival: The Klamath Tribes of Oregon," *Oregon Historical Quarterly* 101, 3 (fall 2000), 272, 276.

73. Ibid., 275-77, 282; and Theodore Stern, *The Klamath Tribe: A People and Their Reservation* (University of Washington Press, 1965), 248-51.

74. Haynal, "Termination and Tribal Survival," 272-74, 277-79; and Stern, *Klamath Tribe*, 248-51.

75. Haynal, "Termination and Tribal Survival," 279-81; Robert H. Ruby and John A. Brown, *A Guide to the Indian Tribes of the Pacific Northwest* (University of Oklahoma Press, 1986), 92, 94; and Theodore Stern, "Klamath and Modoc," in Deward E. Walker, Jr., *Handbook of North American Indians: Volume 12, Plateau* (Smithsonian Institution, 1998), 462.

76. Haynal, "Termination and Tribal Survival," 282-85, 287-93; and Stern, *Klamath Tribe,* 266.

Chapter 7

1. Robert Cahn, "George B. Hartzog, Jr.," in *National Park Service: The First 75 Years* (Eastern National Park and Monument Association, 1990), 53; and George B. Hartzog, Jr., *Battling for the National Parks* (Moyer Bell, 1988), 259.

2. Cahn, "Hartzog," 53; interview with Wayne R. Howe (Sept. 1, 1988), 58-59, CLNP Oral History Series; interview with Donald M. Spalding (Apr. 2, 1991), 12-13, CLNP Oral History Series; and interview with Robert E. Benton (Mar. 1994), 4, CLNP Oral History Series,

3. Spalding interview, 12-13, 28-29.

4. Ibid., 13-14, 17-18, 21.

5. Harlan D. Unrau, *Administrative History: Crater Lake National Park, Oregon* (National Park Service, 1988), vol. 1, 303-4, 337; and interview with Larry Smith (Feb. 10, 1989), 16-17, 32-33, 36, CLNP Oral History Series.

6. Unrau, *Administrative History*, vol. 1, 338-39; vol. 2, 610; Stephen R. Mark, *Administrative History, Chapter 17: Planning and Development at Rim Village* (National Park Service, 1991), 727-28; Lee Juillerat, *Lodge of the Imagination: The Crater Lake Lodge Story* (Crater Lake Natural History Association, 1995), 11-12; Smith interview, 17-18; and Howe interview, 75-77.

7. Unrau, *Administrative History*, vol. 1, 339-41; Smith interview, 17-18; and Howe interview, 75-77.

8. Unrau, *Administrative History*, vol. 1, 341; vol. 2, 611-12; Juillerat, *Crater Lake Lodge*, 12; Smith interview, 17-18; and Howe interview, 75-77.

9. Unrau, *Administrative History*, vol. 1, 340-41; vol. 2, 508-9; and Richard West Sellars, *Preserving Nature in the National Parks: A History* (Yale University Press, 1997), 186-87, 202-3.

10. Unrau, *Administrative History*, vol. 2, 510; Michael Frome, *Regreening the National Parks* (University of Arizona Press, 1992), 189; and Juillerat, *Crater Lake Lodge*, 12.

11. Mark, *Planning and Development at Rim Village*, 726-28; and Unrau, *Administrative History*, vol. 2, 511.

12. Mark, *Planning and Development at Rim Village*, 727-29; and Juillerat, *Crater Lake Lodge*, 11.

13. Mark, *Planning and Development at Rim Village*, 728-31; Unrau, *Administrative History*, vol. 2, 511-13; and Juillerat, *Crater Lake Lodge*, 12.

14. Mark, *Planning and Development at Rim Village*, 731-35; Unrau, *Administrative History*, vol. 2, 514-15 517; Christine Barnes, *Great Lodges of the West* (W. W. West, 1997), 62; and Juillerat, *Crater Lake Lodge*, 12-13.

15. Interview with James S. Rouse (Sept. 18, 1997), 29, CLNP Oral History Series; and Benton interview, 50.

16. Unrau, *Administrative History*, vol. 2, 512-17, 609; Rouse interview, 15-16, 29; Smith interview, 27-28; and Benton interview, 22.

17. Unrau, *Administrative History*, vol. 2, 610-11.

18. Ibid., vol. 1, 342-43; vol. 2, 512-17.

19. Sellars, *Preserving Nature*, 187-94, 211-12.

20. Benton interview, 7.

21. Howe interview, 25, 63.

22. Benton interview, 8; and Rouse interview, 11.

23. Benton interview, 8; and Rouse interview, 8-9, 11.

24. Unrau, *Administrative History*, vol. 1, 253, 263-65; and Rouse interview, 8-11.

25. Unrau, *Administrative History*, vol. 1, 251-55; Rouse interview, 21-22; and Frome, *Regreening the National Parks*, 189.

26. Unrau, *Administrative History*, vol. 1, 251-55; Rouse interview, 21-22, 29; and Paul W. Hirt, *A Conspiracy of Optimism: Management of the National Forests since World War II* (University of Nebraska Press, 1994), xxxix, 272.

27. Sellars, *Preserving Nature*, 233-34.

28. Ibid., 234, 240-41, 270, 278-79; and Lary M. Dilsaver, ed., *America's National Park System: The Critical Documents* (Rowman and Littlefield, 1994), 371.

29. Sellars, *Preserving Nature*, 235-36; Unrau, *Administrative History*, vol. 2, 667; Lincoln Constance, "Crater Lake National Park As a Field for Scientific Research," *Nature Notes from Crater Lake* 23 (1992), 2-6; interview with John Salinas (Apr. 7, 1998), 14-15, CLNP Oral History Series; and interview with Douglas W. Larson (Feb. 14, 2000), 56, CLNP Oral History Series.

30. Sellars, *Preserving Nature*, 241; and Unrau, *Administrative History*, vol. 2, 437-39.

31. Unrau, *Administrative History*, vol. 2, 439-40; and Sellars, *Preserving Nature*, 162-63, 256-58.

32. Sellars, *Preserving Nature*, 275-76; and Unrau, *Administrative History*, vol. 2, 441-44.

33. Douglas W. Larson, "Probing the Depths of Crater Lake: A Century of Scientific Research," *Oregon Historical Quarterly* 100, 3 (fall 1999), 309-10; interview with Douglas W. Larson (Feb. 10, 1996), 3, Oregon Historical Society Oral History Collection; Larson interview (2000), 20-22, 23, 25; interview with F. Owen Hoffman (Aug. 25, 1998), 13-14, CLNP Oral History Series; and Salinas interview, 12.

34. Larson, "Scientific Research," 308, 310-12; C. Warren Fairbanks and John R. Rowley, "A Tribute to the Clarity of Crater Lake," *Nature Notes from Crater Lake* 20 (1954), 34-36; Larson interview (2000), 22, 31-33, 47-49; Hoffman interview, 13-14; Salinas interview, 12-14; and Douglas W. Larson, "Waldo Lake, Oregon: Eutrophication of a Rare Ultraoligotrophic, High-Mountain Lake," *Lake and Reservoir Management* 16, 1-2 (June 2000), 2-16.

35. Larson, "Scientific Research," 316; Larson interview (2000), 33-34; and Salinas interview, 14.

36. Larson, "Scientific Research," 311; Hoffman interview, 13; and Larson interview (2000), 34-35.

37. Wes Ruble, "Experts Say Crater Lake May Be Losing Its Clarity," *Oregonian* (Dec. 20, 1981); Larson, "Scientific Research," 312; Rouse interview, 26; Salinas interview, 14; and Mark, *Planning and Development at Rim Village*, 728.

38. Larson, "Scientific Research," 312; Unrau, *Administrative History*, vol. 1, 257-58; Salinas interview, 14; and Larson interview (2000), 25, 27, 35-36.

39. Unrau, *Administrative History*, vol. 1, 258; and Larson interview (2000), 37-38.

40. Larson interview (2000), 38-40; conversation with Doug Larson; and Larson, "Scientific Research," 313.

41. Larson, "Scientific Research," 312-13; Hoffman interview, 14; and Larson interview (2000), 39-40.

42. Unrau, *Administrative History*, vol. 1, 258; Larson interview (1996), 1-3; and Larson interview (2000), 40-41.

43. Larson interview (2000), 36-37, 40; Rouse interview, 26; and Salinas interview, 14, 18.

44. Unrau, *Administrative History*, vol. 1, 258; Salinas interview, 15; Larson, "Scientific Research," 312-13; and Larson interview (2000), 41-42.

45. *Interpretive Prospectus: Crater Lake National Park, Oregon* (National Park Service, 1973), 1, 2, 7; and Unrau, *Administrative History*, vol. 2, 662-66.

46. Hoffman interview, 8-9.

47. Barry Mackintosh, *Interpretation in the National Park Service: A Historical Perspective* (National Park Service, 1986), 91-93.

48. Ibid., 94.

49. Unrau, *Administrative History*, vol. 2, 610; Howe interview, 77; and Smith interview, 18-19.

50. Salinas interview, 1-7; Smith interview, 17, 21-22, 29; Hoffman interview, 9; and Ted Haeger, "Heresies of an Interpreter," *Nature Notes from Crater Lake* 23 (1992), 19-20.

51. Salinas interview, 3-5, 11.

52. Mackintosh, *Interpretation*, 18-37, 54-67; and Salinas interview, 4-7.

53. Salinas interview, 4-7; and Mackintosh, *Interpretation*, 54-67.

54. Interview with Dick Brown (Sept. 15, 1988), 39-40, 42, 54, CLNP Oral History Series; and Unrau, *Administrative History*, vol. 2, 667.

55. Unrau, *Administrative History*, vol. 2, 668; Michael Kammen, *Mystic Chords of Memory: The Transformation of Tradition in American Culture* (Vintage Books, 1993), 610, 613-14; and Mackintosh, *Interpretation*, 25, 35-37.

56. Benton interview, 6, 20, 27-28, 30-31.

57. Patrick Haynal, "Termination and Tribal Survival: The Klamath Tribes of Oregon," *Oregon Historical Quarterly* 101, 3 (fall 2000), 279-81, 282-85, 287-92, 297; Doug Foster, "Returning Ancestral Land," *Oregonian* (Apr. 3, 1994), B1, B4; and Klamath Tribes Web site (www.klamathtribes.org), "History."

58. Haynal, "Termination and Tribal Survival," 284, 286, 290-91; Robert H. Ruby and John A. Brown, *A Guide to the Indian Tribes of the Pacific Northwest* (University of Oklahoma Press, 1986), 94; and Benton interview, 19.

59. Haynal, "Termination and Tribal Survival," 294-96; Ruby and Brown, *Indian Tribes of the Pacific Northwest*, 94; and Joe Mosley, "Klamath Legacy: A Family at War," Eugene *Register-Guard* (July 27, 1987), 1B, 12B.

60. Haynal, "Termination and Tribal Survival," 289, 293; Ruby and Brown, *Indian Tribes of the Pacific Northwest*, 95; and Joe Mosley, "Indian Pride," Eugene *Register-Guard* (July 27, 1987), 1B, 12B.

61. Haynal, "Termination and Tribal Survival," 294-96.

62. Ibid., 296-98.

63. Ibid., 297-98; Klamath Tribes Web site, "History"; Mosley, "Indian Pride"; and Mosley, "Klamath Legacy."

64. Haynal, "Termination and Tribal Survival," 298; "Tribes Reach $500,000 Goal To Buy Back Artifacts," *Columbian*, n.d.; and Theodore Stern, "Klamath and Modoc," in Deward Walker, Jr., *Handbook of North American Indians: Volume 12, Plateau* (Smithsonian Institution, 1998), 462.

Chapter 8

1. Stephen R. Mark, *Administrative History: Planning and Development at Rim Village* (National Park Service, 1991), 735-37; Lee Juillerat, *Lodge of the Imagination: The Crater Lake Lodge Story* (Crater Lake Natural History Association, 1995), 13; Christine Barnes, *Great Lodges of the West* (W. W. West, 1997), 62; and Harlan D. Unrau, *Administrative History: Crater Lake National Park, Oregon* (National Park Service, 1988), vol. 2, 517, 614.

2. Mark, *Planning and Development at Rim Village*, 738-41; and Juillerat, *Crater Lake Lodge*, 15.

3. Juillerat, *Crater Lake Lodge*, 15-16; and Barnes, *Great Lodges*, 62-63.

4. Juillerat, *Crater Lake Lodge*, 15-16; and Barnes, *Great Lodges*, 63-64.

5. Interview with Robert E. Benton (Mar. 1994), 22-23, CLNP Oral History Series; and Superintendent's Annual Report for 1987, 1988, 1989, and 1990, CLNP, park historian's files.

6. Superintendent's Annual Report for 1989, 1991, 1992, 1993, and 1995; and author's interview with Richard Gordon (Aug. 31, 2000).

7. Gordon interview; Michael Milstein, "Crater Lake Facility Operator Will Let Contract End," *Oregonian* (Sept. 28, 2001), C4; and conversation with John Miele, CLNP management assistant.

8. Author's interview with John Miele (Aug. 31, 2000); Superintendent's Annual Report for 1995, 1996, and 1998; and Gordon interview.

9. Benton interview, 13-16, 18, 28, 52.

10. Superintendent's Annual Report for 1987.

11. Benton interview, 11-12, 16, 29.

12. "Crater Lake National Park: 1984-1990," 2-3, park historian's files; Superintendent's Annual Report for 1987, 1988, 1989, and 1990, n.p.; Benton interview, 38, 40; author's interview with Kent Taylor (Aug. 29, 2000); and Unrau, *Administrative History*, vol. 2, 446, 514.

13. Benton interview, 11-12, 14, 21; and Jeff Barnard, "Crater Lake Residents Cope with Winter Stress," news clipping, park historian's files.

14. Benton interview, 4, 12-13, 41, 53.

15. Ibid., 4, 10, 13, 14, 15, 21, 51, 53.

16. Benton interview, 33-35; Unrau, *Administrative History*, vol. 1, 259; Lary M. Dilsaver, ed., *America's National Park System: The Critical Documents* (Rowman and Littlefield, 1994), 409; Timothy Egan, *The Good Rain: Across Time and Terrain in the Pacific Northwest* (Vintage, 1991), 157; and Alfred Runte, *National Parks: The American Experience*, 3rd ed. (University of Nebraska Press, 1997), 260-62.

17. Benton interview, 33-34.

18. Egan, *Time and Terrain*, 157; "Bill Adds Crater Lake to Regions Containing Geothermal Features," *Oregonian* (Sept. 29, 1988); "Crater Lake National Park, 1984-1990," 5; Superintendent's Annual Report for 1987, n.p.; and Charles E. Beggs, "A Voyage to Bottom of Crater Lake," Albany *Democrat-Herald*, n.d., vertical files, OHS Research Library.

19. Interview with John Salinas (Apr. 7, 1998), 19-20, CLNP Oral History Series; "Bottom of Crater Lake Subject of Study," Salem *Statesman-Journal* (Aug. 5, 1987); Richard L. Hill, "Researchers Will Dive to Crater Lake's Bottom," *Oregonian* (July 28, 1988), E1, E3; Beggs, "Voyage to Bottom"; Egan, *Time and Terrain*, 157; Unrau, *Administrative History*, vol. 2, 446; and Superintendent's Annual Report for 1987, n.d.

20. Lisa Strycker, "What's Clouding Crater?" Eugene *Register-Guard* (Sept. 27, 1987), 1C, 2C; Beggs, "Voyage to Bottom"; Salinas interview, 19-22; Mark Buktenica, "Why Enter a Sleeping Volcano in a Submarine?" *Nature Notes from Crater Lake* 27 (1996), 12-18; "Bill Adds Crater Lake"; Superintendent's Annual Report for 1988, 1989, n.d.; and "Crater Lake National Park, 1984 to 1990," 6.

21. Douglas W. Larson to Director, National Park Service (Mar. 12, 1987), (copies furnished to Sen. Mark Hatfield; Sen. Robert Packwood; Cong. Denny Smith; Donald Hodel, secretary of the interior; Gail Achterman, assistant to the governor of Oregon for natural resources), author's collection; and conversation with Doug Larson.

22. "Save Crater Lake's Clarity," *Register-Guard* (Sept. 9, 1987); Strycker, "What's Clouding Crater?"; Douglas Larson, "Decades of Stalling Muddied Crater Lake," *Oregonian* (May 24, 1992), B1, B4; and *Crater Lake National Park, Mazama Campground/Rim Village Corridor, Supplement to the 1984 EA/DCP* (National Park Service, 1987), 18.

23. "Save Crater Lake's Clarity"; Strycker, "What's Clouding Crater?"; Jim Stiak, "Unwelcome Visitors Sully Crater Lake," *Sierra* (Jan./Feb. 1988); Richard L. Hill, "A Question of Clarity," *Oregonian* (July 28, 1988), E1, E3; and letter from F. Owen Hoffman to Eugene *Register-Guard* (Oct. 21, 1987), author's collection.

24. Letter from Robert E. Benton to Gary Lord (Oct. 1, 1987), author's collection; interview with Douglas W. Larson (Feb. 14, 2000), 40, CLNP Oral History Series; conversation with Doug Larson; letter from Gary R. Lord to Robert E. Benton (Oct.

30, 1987), author's collection; Alston Chase, "Politics Adds to Murky Crater Lake Issue," *Oregonian* (Oct. 17, 1989); and Robert Sterling, "Letter to Corps Angers Scientist," Medford *Mail Tribune* (Dec. 11, 1987).

25. Strycker, "What's Clouding Crater?"; "Save Crater Lake's Clarity"; and conversation with Doug Larson.

26. Larson interview (2000), 42, 54; Ellen T. Drake, Gary L. Larson, Jack Dymond, and Robert Collier, *Crater Lake: An Ecosystem Study* (American Association for the Advancement of Science, 1990), 5; Larson, "Decades of Stalling"; and Chase, "Politics Adds to Murky Crater Lake Issue."

27. "Crater Lake National Park, 1984 to 1990," 5-6; Superintendent's Annual Report for 1991, 1992, and 1993, n.p.; "BLM Halts Testing Near Crater Lake," *Oregonian* (Feb. 17, 1991), C1, C6; and Elizabeth L. Orr, William N. Orr, and Ewart M. Baldwin, *Geology of Oregon*, 4th ed. (Kendall/Hunt, 1976), 159.

28. Larson, "Scientific Research," 313-14; Larson interview (2000), 40; Larson, "Decades of Stalling"; Burton, "Lake's Depths Crowded"; and Superintendent's Annual Report for 1991, n.p.

29. Larson, "Decades of Stalling"; "Park Chief Denies Sewage Entering Crater Lake," *Oregonian* (May 29, 1992); Paul R. Huard, "Crater Lake Still Pristine, Superintendent Says," Roseburg *News-Review* (June 8, 1993); and Betty Brickson, "A Clear Bill of Health," *Oregonian* (May 5, 1993), B1, B3.

30. Hill, "Question of Clarity"; William Burton, "Lake's Depths Crowded," *Oregonian* (July 28, 1988), E1, E2; and letter from Douglas W. Larson to Cong. George Miller (June 25, 1993), author's collection.

31. Larson, "Scientific Research"; Douglas W. Larson, "Crater Lake's Renewed Clarity Not Explained by Park Service," *Oregonian* (Sept. 20, 1994); Douglas W. Larson, "Sewage Dumping Blamed for Decline of Crater Lake Clarity Measurement," *Oregonian* (July 10, 1997); Douglas W. Larson, "Science and Shoestring Technology," *National Forum* 80, 4 (fall 2000), 6-7; author's interview with William M. "Mac" Brock (Aug. 31, 2000); Brickson, "Clear Bill of Health"; Hill, "Question of Clarity"; Burton, "Lake's Depths Crowded"; and Tom McDonough, "Not So Static a Scene," *Nature Notes from Crater Lake* 31 (2000), 5-8.

32. Huard, "Crater Lake Pristine."

33. Hoffman interview, 13; and Salinas interview, 12, 18.

34. Larson, "Scientific Research," 313-16; Larson, "Sewage Dumping Blamed"; Larson, "Science"; conversation with Doug Larson; Larson interview (2000), 49-55; and Douglas W. Larson, Clifford N. Dahm, and N. Stan Geiger, "Limnological Response of Crater Lake to Possible Long-Term Sewage Influx," in Drake et al., *Crater Lake*, 197-212.

35. Scott Sonner, "Park Service To Study Crater Lake Water," *Oregonian* (July 28, 1993); Superintendent's Annual Report for 1992, n.p.; and Larson interview (2000), 51.

36. Sonner, "Crater Lake Water"; Hill, "Question of Clarity"; Burton, "Lake's Depths Crowded"; Hill, "Crater Lake Bottom"; McDonough, "Not So Static," 5-8; Salinas interview, 15-16; and Superintendent's Annual Reports for 1994 (p. 2), 1995 (2-3), 1996 (2), and 1998 (3-4).

37. Superintendent's Annual Reports for 1995 (p. 3) and 1998 (3); Brock interview; Tom McDonough, "Getting to the Bottom of Crater Lake," *Crater Lake Reflections* (summer 2001), 7; and U.S. Geological Survey Web site, Crater Lake Data Clearinghouse, Western Geographic Science Center (http://tahoe.usgs.gov/craterlake/bathymetry.html).

38. Brock interview; and Jeff DeLong, "Crater Lake Gets Tahoe Treatment," Reno *Gazette-Journal* (Aug. 31, 2000).

39. DeLong, "Tahoe Treatment"; U.S.G.S. Web site; and Brock interview.

40. Larson, "Scientific Research," 314-16; and Richard West Sellars, *Preserving Nature in the National Parks: A History* (Yale University Press, 1997), 267.

41. Brock interview; and Unrau, *Administrative History*, vol. 1, 343-46; vol. 2, 444-45.

42. Jeff Barnard, "Crater Lake Behind on Ecology, Chief Agrees," *Oregonian* (Nov. 17, 1992); Sellars, *Preserving Nature*, 4, 267-68; and Brock interview.

43. Brock interview; Sellars, *Preserving Nature*, 233, 270; and Victoria Bruce, "Lake's Forest Bestows Bounty of Ecological Treasures," *Oregonian* (July 23, 1997), B11.

44. Mark Buktenica, "Saving Bull Trout in Sun Creek," *Nature Notes from Crater Lake* 23 (1992), 15-16; Mark Buktenica, "Native Species Protection and Exotic Species Control: A Bull Trout Restoration Project in Sun Creek," *Nature Notes from Crater Lake* 24 (1993), 3-5; Barnard, "Crater Lake Behind on Ecology"; and Superintendent's Annual Reports for 1991, 1992, 1993, n.p.; 1994 (p. 2), 1995 (2), 1996 (2-3), and 1998 (4).

45. "Crater Lake National Park, 1984 to 1990," 4, 9; Superintendent's Annual Reports for 1988, 1990, n.p.; 1995 (p. 4), 1996 (3), and 1998 (5); conversation with Stephen R. Mark, CLNP historian; and Benton interview, 37, 54.

46. Superintendent's Annual Reports for 1987, 1988, 1989, 1990, 1991, 1992, n.p.; and 1998 (p. 10); and Barnard, "Crater Lake Behind on Ecology."

47. Superintendent's Annual Reports for 1992, 1993, n.p.; 1994 (pp. 2-3), 1995 (2-3, 4), and 1998 (6, 7-8); Barnard, "Crater Lake Behind on Ecology"; Brock interview; and Bruce, "Lake's Forest."

48. Superintendent's Annual Report for 1993, n.p.; and Annual Statement for Interpretation, Fiscal Year 1991, 7.

49. Superintendent's Annual Report for 1991, n.p.; and 1998 (p. 9); Unrau, *Administrative History*, vol. 2, 445; Ted Haeger, "Heresies of an Interpreter," *Nature Notes from Crater Lake* 23 (1992), 19-20; and Annual Statement for Interpretation, 1991, 3-4.

50. *Visitor Services Plan: Crater Lake National Park, Oregon* (National Park Service, 1999), 13, 21; and Superintendent's Annual Report for 1993, n.p.; 1994 (p. 4), 1995 (5), 1996 (5), and 1998 (5).

51. Superintendent's Annual Report for 1994 (pp. 4-5), 1995 (5), 1996 (5, 6), and 1998 (4); and conversation with Mark.

52. Benton interview, 6, 20, 27-28; conversation with Mark; and Taylor interview.

53. Robert H. Keller and Michael F. Turek, *American Indians and National Parks* (University of Arizona Press, 1998), 233-34.

Chapter 9

1. Patrick Haynal, "Termination and Tribal Survival: The Klamath Tribes of Oregon," *Oregon Historical Quarterly* 101, 3 (fall 2000), 294-98; Doug Foster, "Returning Ancestral Land," *Oregonian* (Apr. 3, 1994); and "The Klamath Tribes Economic Self-Sufficiency Plan" (Oct. 31, 2000), 12-13, 26, 31, 32, on the Web site for the Klamath Tribes (www.klamathtribes.org/ESSP).

2. Beth Quinn, "Klamath Tribe Seeks To Regain Control of Land," *Oregonian* (Nov. 1, 2000), D1, D8; Beth Quinn, "Klamaths Head to U.S. Capital in Quest for Restoring Tribal Lands," *Oregonian* (Oct. 28, 2000), D7; Foster, "Returning Ancestral Land"; Mark David Spence, *Dispossessing the Wilderness: Indian Removal and the Making of the National Parks* (Oxford University Press, 1999), 7, 136-39; and "Economic Self-Sufficiency Plan," 14-15, 27, 31, 33.

3. Author's interview with CLNP superintendent Charles V. Lundy (Sept. 22, 2000); and William K. Reilly, *National Parks for a New Generation: Visions, Realities, Prospects* (Conservation Foundation, 1985), xxii.

4. William Kittredge, *Balancing Water: Restoring the Klamath Basin* (University of California Press, 2000); Beth Quinn, "Water Fight May Go to the Top for Klamath Basin Farmers, Fish," *Oregonian* (Mar. 15, 2001); Michael Milstein, "State Seeks Give-Take on Water," *Oregonian* (July 19, 2001), A1, A14; Mark Buktenica, "Annie Spring Responds to Long-Term Drought and Municipal Water Use," *Nature Notes from*

Crater Lake 24 (1993), 16-17; "Crater Lake National Park, 1984 to 1990," 9, CLNP historian's files; and Superintendent's Annual Report for 1995 (pp. 1, 2, 5), 1996 (4), and 1998 (8), CLNP historian's files.

5. "Klamath Basin Farmers Vent Anger over Irrigation Plan," *Oregonian* (Apr. 8, 2001), B10; "Farmers Force Open Canal in Fight with U.S. over Water," *New York Times* (July 6, 2001); Lundy interview; conversation with CLNP historian Stephen R. Mark; Douglas Deur, "Response to RFQ# RQ908600026: Traditional Land-Use Study of Crater Lake National Park and Lava Beds National Monument" (Apr. 1, 2000), n.p., CLNP historian's files; Robert H. Keller and Michael F. Turek, *American Indians and National Parks* (University of Arizona Press, 1998), 234-38; Spence, *Dispossessing the Wilderness*, 136-39; author's interview with CLNP management assistant John Miele (Aug. 31, 2000); Visitor Services Plan, Crater Lake National Park, Oregon (Nov. 1999), 23; and Superintendent's Annual Report for 1998 (p. 10).

6. Lundy interview; conversation with Mark; Superintendent's Annual Reports for 1994 (p. 11) and 1998 (2, 4-5); Douglas Deur and Steve Mark, "Traditional Land Use As Starting Point: Opening Cross-Cultural Dialogue at Crater Lake and Lava Beds," *CRM* 23, 3 (2000), 16-17; Strategic Plan for Crater Lake National Park: Fiscal Year 2001-2005, 17, on the Crater Lake National Park Web site (http://www.nps.gov/crla/gpra.htm); and Spence, *Dispossessing the Wilderness*, 136-39.

7. Deur, "Traditional Land-Use Study," n.p.; and Keller and Turek, *Indians and National Parks*, 232-40.

8. Miele interview; Superintendent's Annual Report for 1993 (n.p.) and 1998 (p. 16); and Beth Quinn, "Crater Lake Filling Camera or Lens for Artists Worldwide," *Oregonian* (Nov. 24, 2000), B1, B3.

9. Richard West Sellars, *Preserving Nature in the National Parks: A History* (Yale University Press, 1997), 267, 280, 285; Keller and Turek, *Indians and National Parks*, xiii-xiv, 234; Lary M. Dilsaver, ed., *America's National Park System: The Critical Documents* (Rowman and Littlefield, 1994), 1, 371-73, 409-10; and Alfred Runte, *National Parks: The American Experience*, 3d ed. (University of Nebraska Press, 1997), xi-xii.

10. Sellars, *Preserving Nature*, 2, 285; and Runte, *National Parks*, 213, 233-35.

11. Douglas Fehl, "National Parks Will Ban Recreation Snowmobiling," *New York Times* (Apr. 26, 2000); Beth Quinn, "National Parks Ban Snowmobiles," *Oregonian* (Apr. 27, 2000), B1; and Michael Milstein, "Park Service Directives Put Nature First," *Oregonian* (Jan. 6, 2001), A1, A11.

12. Milstein, "Park Service Directives"; Scott Lindlaw, "Bush Announces Plan To Help National Parks," Associated Press/America Online (May 30, 2001); Sellars, *Preserving Nature*, 2; and Dennis McCann, "Repairing the Nation's Parks," *Oregonian* (Aug. 9, 2001), A14.

13. Beth Quinn, "Popular Sites Get New Tours, Looks in Upcoming Season," *Oregonian* (Mar. 11, 2001), A19, A20; and Strategic Plan, 5-6.

14. Kent Taylor, "Rehabilitating the Watchman Fire Lookout and Trailside Museum," *Crater Lake Reflections* (summer 1999), 3; Superintendent's Annual Report for 1998, 2; Kent Taylor, "Rehabilitation of the Rim Village Historic District Continues," *Crater Lake Reflections* (summer 2000), 3; Visitor Services Plan, 4-6, 9; Taylor interview; and Miele interview.

15. Taylor interview; "Crater Lake National Park," 4; Visitor Services Plan, 1, 9-10; and Miele interview.

16. Taylor interview; Miele interview; Visitor Services Plan, 10; author's interview with Richard Gordon (Aug. 31, 2000).

17. Visitor Services Plan, 1; Gordon interview; and Michael Milstein, "Crater Lake Facility Operator Will Let Contract End," *Oregonian* (Sept. 28, 2001), C4.

18. Visitor Services Plan, 1; and Gordon interview.

19. Visitor Services Plan, 7, 10; and Gordon interview.

20. Conversation with John Miele; and Milstein, "Crater Lake Facility Operator."

21. Strategic Plan, 6, 7, 9; William M. Brock, "Looking toward the New Millennium," *Crater Lake Reflections* (summer 2000), 4; and Reilly, *National Parks for a New Generation*, xxi.

22. Strategic Plan, 6; Kevin L. Bacher, "New Fee Program Contributes Directly to Vital Park Programs," *Crater Lake Reflections* (summer 1999), 4; Lundy interview; Beth Quinn, "Recreation Fees Fund Fix-up Spree," *Oregonian*, n.d., D1, D4; Sellars, *Preserving Nature*, 289; and Brock interview

23. Taylor, "Rehabilitating the Watchman," 3; Brock interview; Miele interview; Lundy interview; Strategic Plan, 17; Steve Mark, "A National Historic Landmark," *Nature Notes from Crater Lake* 28 (1997), 34-36; and Steve Mark, *Park Headquarters Historic Walking Tour: Crater Lake National Park* (Crater Lake Natural History Association, 1999), n.p.

24. Lundy interview; Keller and Turek, *Indians and National Parks*, xii; and Sellars, *Preserving Nature*, 287.

25. Freeman Tilden, *The National Parks*, rev. and enlarged ed. (Knopf, 1968), 26.

26. Ibid., 8; Ted Haeger, "Heresies of an Interpreter," *Nature Notes from Crater Lake* 23 (1992), 19-20; interview with Bruce Black (Sept. 27, 1988), 31, CLNP Oral History Series; Lundy interview; and conversation with Mark.

27. Sellars, *Preserving Nature*, 280; interview with Robert E. Benton (Mar. 1994), 55, CLNP Oral History Series; Freeman Tilden, *Interpreting Our Heritage*, rev. ed. (University of North Carolina Press, 1977), 8-9, 32-39; Haeger, "Heresies," 19-20; and Tilden, *National Parks*, 32.

28. Joseph L. Sax, *Mountains without Handrails: Reflections on the National Parks* (University of Michigan Press, 1980), 105; interview with Lundy; interview with Taylor; interview with Brock; and Strategic Plan, 8, 11-18, 21-22, 26.

29. Strategic Plan, 21-22, 26; Sellars, *Preserving Nature*, 287; Sax, *Reflections on National Parks*, 42; Tilden, *National Parks*, 22; John C. Miles, *Guardians of the Parks: A History of the National Parks and Conservation Association* (Taylor and Francis, 1995), xiv; Visitor Services Plan, 9; and Brock interview.

30. Strategic Plan, 26.

31. Sax, *Reflections on National Parks*, 20, 42; Kathryn Winthrop and Robert Winthrop, "Modeling the Cultural Landscape of Crater Lake," in John Mairs, Kathryn R. Winthrop, and Robert H. Winthrop, *Archaeological and Ethnological Studies of Southwest Oregon and Crater Lake National Park: An Overview and Assessment* (National Park Service, 1994), 155-59; and Tilden, *National Parks*, 115.

32. Sax, *Reflections on National Parks*, 22, 48, 61, 77, 82, 83; Runte, *National Parks*, 264; and *Rethinking the National Parks for the 21st Century: A Report of the National Park System Advisory Board* (July 2001), on the National Park Service Web site (www.nps.gov/policy/report.htm).

33. Reilly, *National Parks for a New Generation*, xx; Sax, *Reflections on National Parks*, 81; and *Rethinking the National Parks*.

34. Runte, *National Parks*, xiii, 264; Sax, *Reflections on National Parks*, 66; and *Rethinking the National Parks*.

Additional Reading

Books

Albright, Horace M., as told to Robert Cahn. *The Birth of the National Park Service: The Founding Years, 1913-33*. Salt Lake City, UT: Howe Brothers, 1985.

Cranson, K. R. *Crater Lake—Gem of the Cascades*. Lansing, MI: KRC Press, 1982.

Cressman, L. S. *Klamath Prehistory*. Philadelphia: American Philosophical Society, 1956.

———. *The Sandal and the Cave: The Indians of Oregon*. Portland, OR: Beaver Books, 1962.

Diller, Joseph Silas. *The Geology and Petrography of Crater Lake National Park*. Washington, DC: U.S. Geological Survey, 1902.

Farner, Donald S. *The Birds of Crater Lake National Park*. Lawrence: University of Kansas Press, 1952.

Follett, Dick. *Birds of Crater Lake National Park*. Crater Lake, OR: Crater Lake Natural History Association, 1979.

Foresta, Ronald A. *America's National Parks and Their Keepers*. Washington, DC: Resources for the Future, Inc., 1984.

Greene, Linda W. *Historic Resource Study: Crater Lake National Park, Oregon*. Denver, CO: National Park Service, 1984.

Heacox, Kim. *An American Idea: The Making of the National Parks*. Washington, DC: National Geographic, 2001.

Howe, Carrol B. *Ancient Tribes of the Klamath Country*. Portland, OR: Binford and Mort, 1968.

Ise, John. *Our National Park Policy: A Critical History*. Baltimore: Johns Hopkins Press, 1961.

Juillerat, Lee. *Lodge of the Imagination: The Crater Lake Lodge Story*. Crater Lake, OR: Crater Lake Natural History Association, 1995.

Keller, Robert H., and Michael F. Turek. *American Indians and National Parks*. Tucson: University of Arizona Press, 1998.

Kirk, Ruth. *Exploring Crater Lake Country*. Seattle: University of Washington Press, 1975.

Lapham, Stanton C. *The Enchanted Lake: Mount Mazama and Crater Lake in Story, History and Legend*. Portland, OR: J. K. Gill Co., 1931.

Mairs, John, Kathryn R. Winthrop, and Robert H. Winthrop. *Archaeological and Ethnological Studies of Southwest Oregon and Crater Lake National Park: An Assessment*. Seattle, WA: National Park Service, 1994.

Mark, Stephen R. *Administrative History, Chapter 17: Planning and Development at Rim Village, Crater Lake National Park*. Seattle, WA: National Park Service, 1991.

———. *Crater Lake: The Continuing Story*. Las Vegas, NV: KC Publications, 1996.

———. *Park Headquarters Historic Walking Tour: Crater Lake National Park*. Crater Lake, OR: Crater Lake Natural History Association, 1999.

Place, Howard, and Marian Place. *The Story of Crater Lake National Park*. Caldwell, ID: Caxton Printers, 1974.

Ruhle, George R. *Along Crater Lake Roads: A Road Guide to Crater Lake National Park, Oregon*. Crater Lake, OR: Crater Lake Natural History Association, 1964. Revised edition.

Runte, Alfred. *National Parks: The American Experience*. Lincoln: University of Nebraska Press, 1997. Third edition.

Sax, Joseph L. *Mountains without Handrails: Reflections on the National Parks*. Ann Arbor: University of Michigan Press, 1980.

Schaffer, Jeffrey P. *Crater Lake National Park and Vicinity*. Berkeley, CA: Wilderness Press, 1983.

Schullery, Paul D. *America's National Parks*. New York: Dorling Kindersley Publishing, 2001.

Sellars, Richard West. *Preserving Nature in the National Parks*. New Haven, CT: Yale University Press, 1997.

Shankland, Robert. *Steve Mather of the National Parks*. New York: Knopf, 1951.

Sharpe, Grant, and Wenonah Sharpe. *101 Wildflowers of Crater Lake National Park*. Seattle: University of Washington Press, 1959.

Smith, Larry B., and Lloyd C. Smith. *A Chronological History and Important Event Log of Crater Lake National Park, Including Significant Crater Lake Records and Area "Firsts."* Privately published, 1997. Revised edition.

Spence, Mark David. *Dispossessing the Wilderness: Indian Removal and the Making of the National Parks*. New York: Oxford University Press, 1999.

Steel, W. G. *The Mountains of Oregon*. Portland, OR: David Steel, Successor to Himes the Printer, 1890.

Stern, Theodore. *The Klamath Tribe: A People and Their Reservation*. Seattle: University of Washington Press, 1965.

Swain, Donald C. *Wilderness Defender: Horace M. Albright and Conservation*. Chicago: University of Chicago Press, 1970.

Tilden, Freeman. *The National Parks*. New York: Knopf, 1968. Revised edition.

Toops, Constance. *Crater Lake National Park Trails*. Crater Lake, OR: Crater Lake Natural History Association, 1983. Revised edition by Ron and Beckie Warfield.

Unrau, Harlan D. *Administrative History: Crater Lake National Park, Oregon*. Volumes 1 and 2. Denver, CO: National Park Service, 1988.

Warfield, Ron. *A Guide to Crater Lake: The Mountain That Used To Be*. Crater Lake, OR: Crater Lake Natural History Association, 1997. Revised edition.

Warfield, Ronald G., Lee Juillerat, and Larry Smith. *Crater Lake: The Story behind the Scenery*. Las Vegas, NV: KC Publications, 1982.

Williams, Gerald W., and Stephen R. Mark, comps. *Establishing and Defending the Cascade Range Forest Reserve: As Found in the Letters of William G. Steel, John B. Waldo, and Others. Supplemented by Newspapers, Magazines, and Official Reports, 1885-1912*. Portland, OR: U.S. Forest Service and National Park Service, 1995.

Williams, Howel. *Crater Lake: The Story of Its Origins.* Berkeley: University of California Press, 1972. Originally published in 1941.

———. *The Geology of Crater Lake National Park, Oregon: With a Reconnaissance of the Cascade Range Southward to Mount Shasta.* Washington, DC: Carnegie Institution, 1942.

Yard, Robert Sterling. *The Book of the National Parks.* New York: Scribner's, 1919.

———. *National Parks Portfolio.* New York: Scribner's, 1916.

Yocum, Charles F. *Shrubs of Crater Lake.* Crater Lake, OR: Crater Lake Natural History Association, 1964.

Articles

Allen, A. Cooper. "The Guardian of Crater Lake." *Sunset Magazine* 56 (May 1926): 51-52.

Cook, Truman B. "Crater Lake, 1915." *Oregon Historical Quarterly* 81, 1 (1980): 43-56.

Deur, Douglas, and Steve Mark. "Traditional Land Use As Starting Point: Opening Cross-Cultural Dialogue at Crater Lake and Lava Beds." *CRM* 23, 3 (2000): 16-17.

Diller, J. S. "Crater Lake, Oregon." *National Geographic Magazine* 8, 2 (1897): 32-48.

———. "The Wreck of Mt. Mazama." *Science* (Feb. 7, 1902): 203-11.

Dutton, C. E. "Crater Lake, Oregon: A Proposed National Reservation." *Science* 7, 160 (1886): 179-82.

Evans, Samuel M. "Forty Gallons of Gasoline to Forty Miles of Water: Recipe for a Motor Trip to Crater Lake, Oregon." *Sunset Magazine* 27 (Oct. 1911): 393-99.

"The Fletcher Linn Diary: Crater Lake Trip, August, 1889." *Table Rock Sentinel* 4 (July 1984): 6-14.

Haynal, Patrick. "Termination and Tribal Survival: The Klamath Tribes of Oregon." *Oregon Historical Quarterly* 101, 3 (2000): 270-301.

Kirkman, George W. "Crater Lake." *Harper's Weekly* 40 (Sept. 19, 1896): 932.

Larson, Douglas W. "Probing the Depths of Crater Lake: A Century of Scientific Research." *Oregon Historical Quarterly* 100, 3 (1999): 288-319.

Mather, Stephen T. "The National Parks on a Business Basis." *American Review of Reviews* 51 (Apr. 1915): 429-30.

Merriam, John C. "Crater Lake: A Study in Appreciation of Nature." *American Magazine of Art* 26, 8 (1933): 357-61.

Miller, Joaquin. "The Sea of Silence." *Sunset* 11 (Sept. 1904): 394-401.

Steel, W. G. "Crater Lake and How To See It." *West Shore* 12, 3 (1886): 104-6.

Stern, Theodore. "The Klamath Indians and the Treaty of 1864." *Oregon Historical Quarterly* 57, 3 (1956): 229-73.

———. "Klamath and Modoc." In *Handbook of North American Indians: Volume 12, Plateau,* edited by Deward E. Walker, Jr., 446-65. Washington, DC: Smithsonian Institution Press, 1998.

Williams, Gerald W. "John B. Waldo and William G. Steel: Forest Reserve Advocates for the Cascade Range of Oregon." In *The Origins of the National Forests: A Centennial Symposium*, edited by Harold K. Steen, 314-32. Durham, NC: Forest History Society, 1992.

Others

Crater Lake National Park Oral History Series.

Crater Lake Reflections. Biannual, 1975 to present.

Journal of the Shaw Historical Library 15 (2001). "The Mountain with a Hole in the Top: Reflections on Crater Lake."

Lundy, Charles V. *Strategic Plan for Crater Lake National Park: Fiscal Year 2001-2005*. Crater Lake, OR: National Park Service, 2000.

Mark, Stephen R. "Seventeen Years to Success: John Muir, William Gladstone Steel, and the Creation of Yosemite and Crater Lake National Parks." Crater Lake National Park Web site (www.nps.gov/crla/steel.htm).

———. "William Gladstone Steel, Mazamas Founder: A Chronology." Crater Lake National Park Web site (www.nps.gov/crla/steel.htm).

Mazama: A Record of Mountaineering in the Pacific Northwest. Vol. 1, no. 2 (1897). "Crater Lake Number."

Nature Notes from Crater Lake. Vol. 1 (1928)-Vol. 11 (1938); Vol. 12 (1946)-Vol. 22 (1956); Vol. 23 (1992)-Vol. 31 (2000).

Oregon Historical Quarterly, Vol. 103, no. 1 (2002), "Crater Lake Issue."

Steel Points 1 (Oct. 1906, Jan. 1907, Apr. 1907, July 1907).

Steel Points (Junior) 1 (July 1925, Aug. 1925, May 1927).

Index

979.5915
Harrison 11/03

Independence Public Library